IMAGES of America

HOPKINTON

IMAGES
of America

HOPKINTON

Kirk W. House

ARCADIA
PUBLISHING

ISBN 978-0-7385-3638-5

Published by Arcadia Publishing
Charleston, South Carolina

Printed in the United States of America

Library of Congress Catalog Card Number: 2004106381

For all general information, contact Arcadia Publishing:
Telephone 843-853-2070
Fax 843-853-0044
E-mail sales@arcadiapublishing.com
For customer service and orders:
Toll-free 1-888-313-2665

Visit us on the Internet at www.arcadiapublishing.com

*To the memory of my mother, Carolyn Dow House,
who lived in Hopkinton for the last 45 of her 69 years.*

Contents

Acknowledgments

Every book I have ever written has been a true pleasure, but this one strikes an even deeper chord.

I had the privilege of growing up in Hopkinton, benefiting from its schools, its Scout troops, its ponds and brooks and woods. I never really wanted to live anyplace else, and though my work has taken me elsewhere, I still think of Hopkinton as home.

Growing up literally next door to the Langworthy Public Library helped set the course for my life, and it was to the library that I turned, as I had so many times before, when first I dreamed of creating this book. Dave Panciera and Josie Langworthy generously gave me complete access to the local history files, even outside regular business hours. With only a few exceptions (noted in the captions), all of the images in this book come from the Langworthy collection and are used with the library's kind permission.

I especially want to thank Josie for taking extra time to set me on my way and for making my wife and me welcome as we scoured the local history holdings. We should note that at the heart of those holdings lie materials donated or assembled by Gladys Segar. It is hard to imagine that anyone will ever match her contribution to the local history collection and to the library, not to mention all she did for the town itself.

Hope Andrews took time to write me with information on several images and to send me several helpful books, particularly her own history of Hopkinton City. Hope's family members and their colleagues were helpful long before this project was even dreamed of. Annie Greene, Kay Burdick, and Ellen Rathbun taught me to read nigh on 50 years ago, and look what comes of it now.

Anybody working in the history of Hopkinton cannot get along without the work of Betty Salomon (who photographed several of the included images from the 1970s) and Lucy Rawlings Tootel. Those interested in local heritage should take out a membership in the Hopkinton Historical Association, which deserves a special vote of thanks for republishing Rev. S. S. Griswold's 1876 history. Although Gladys Segar, whenever that work came up, would quietly say, "Of course, we now know he was not always accurate," it is nevertheless a vital resource.

Doug and Peggy Yattaw, along with Georgia Ure, have been encouraging since I broached the project to them, and that is always a help! My wife, Joyce, spent two long days helping me scour hundreds of photographs, and my father, Harold B. House, made us welcome while we did the job. My mother always claimed that we moved a mile down the road from Richmond to Hopkinton so that I could attend kindergarten. Be that as it may, they bought the house her uncle had built, which has had two owners, both from the same family, in its 80 years or so of life. That is not unusual in Hopkinton, except that many homes are far, far older.

Thanks to each and every person who helped get this book ready. Deep thanks to the people of my hometown: the teachers at Hope Valley and at Chariho; Scout leaders such as Al Gunther and Bill Breckinridge; Bob and Alice Bitgood and Bobby and Georgie Wilcox, with whom I worked for nine years at Western Auto; pastors such as Edgar Wheeler and Clifford Bond; family friends such as Kyran and Barbara Quinn; wildlife mentor John Cronin; librarians such as Lilly Stone and Jean Nichols; "Pat" Celestino; Frank Cregan; Ted Smith; Barbara Cataldo; Lou Cimolore; Bill Novak; Joe Capalbo; hundreds of schoolmates; and thousands of customers at the store. I hope that they and their families enjoy this book, because I certainly enjoyed them.

INTRODUCTION

The story of Hopkinton starts out with a bit of political one-upsmanship. The Chariho towns (Charlestown, Richmond, and Hopkinton) were in Colonial days parts of Westerly, which itself was founded by two lovers eloping from Newport in an open boat. As the population grew, folks in the outlying districts petitioned for separate incorporations, citing hardships (which were truly considerable back then) in getting to town meeting.

The northwestern district's turn for incorporation came in 1757, when the Rhode Island General Assembly acceded to the citizens' request, naming the new town for Gov. Stephen Hopkins. This was certainly an honor for the governor, but presumably it was also a thumb of the nose to Hopkins's lifelong political rival, Samuel Ward of Westerly.

Hopkins became a leading theorist of independence. He joined Ward to represent Rhode Island in the First Continental Congress and was a signer of the Declaration of Independence. For its official seal, Hopkinton adopted the governor's coat of arms, adorned with a quill pen for that courageous signature.

In some ways, Hopkinton is a line on a map. Unincorporated villages dot the rural landscape, and residents often identify themselves with their village rather than with the official town. Farming and lumbering were vital businesses in the early days, but one factor above all others drove the economy and population growth: waterpower.

Brooks and rivers tumble down the Hopkinton hills on their way to Block Island Sound, and Hopkinton settlers exploited them to the hilt. Wood River, which forms the eastern and southern boundary of the town, is not a particularly large stream, but it boasts 12 dams in that stretch. Another 18 or so arose on smaller tributaries across the town.

The dams are still in place, though most of the mills have played out. Carriage manufactories have disappeared, along with the stagecoach lines that once made Hopkinton City a boom town. Farming and lumbering are not what they used to be, either. To some extent, the town is a bedroom community for people pursuing careers in Westerly, Warwick, or Providence.

But Hopkinton, despite ongoing population growth, remains a distinctly rural town. Between the settlements, forest reigns again, and on some back roads miles will pass between houses. Hunters, fishers, and campers love the place. Boaters enjoy millponds so huge that they are often mistaken for natural lakes. Hikers work their way through hemlocks, up and down gorges along the Connecticut line. Camp Yawgoog thrills thousands of Scouts every summer.

Mobility and change are hallmarks of the 21st century, and Hopkinton is experiencing them along with other towns. But still, there is a certain stability here. Many of the dams (and their ponds) are over 200 years old. Narragansett Indian names are still part of the town, along with numerous Narragansetts themselves. The phone books are filled with the same Burdicks, Babcocks, Barbers, Kenyons, and Crandalls that filled the first voters' roll.

Change is all well and good, and Hopkinton has certainly evolved along with the rest of the nation. But we should also remember that Hopkinton was incorporated in 1757, during the French and Indian War. And by the time this book was published 247 years later, voters had elected exactly 16 town clerks. These are people who know something good when they see it. That is why they live in Hopkinton.

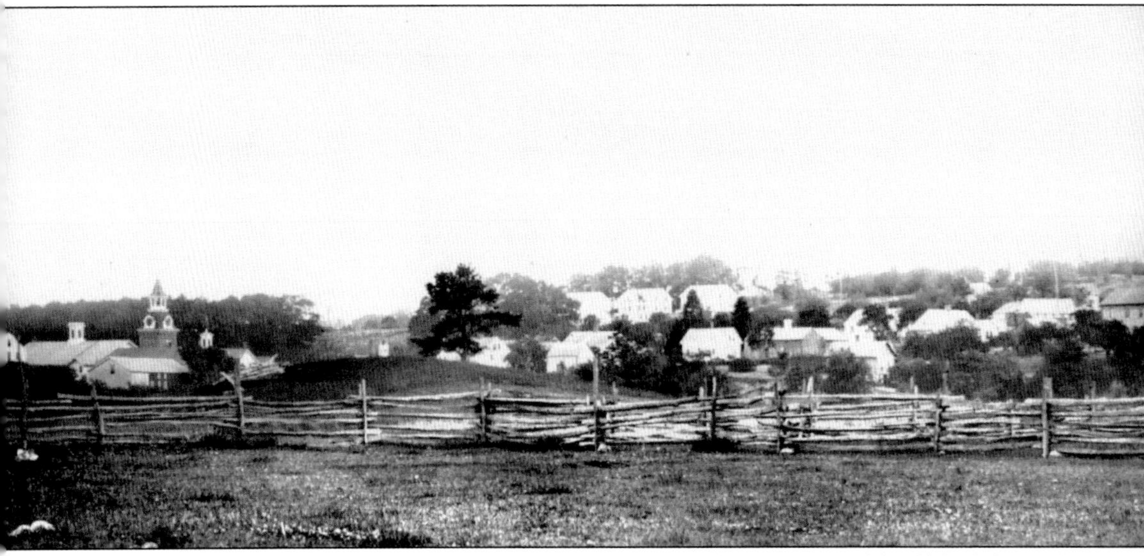

Mills, hills, and a riverside pasture—townsfolk from the 19th century would still find themselves at home in Hopkinton.

One

BELOVED FACES

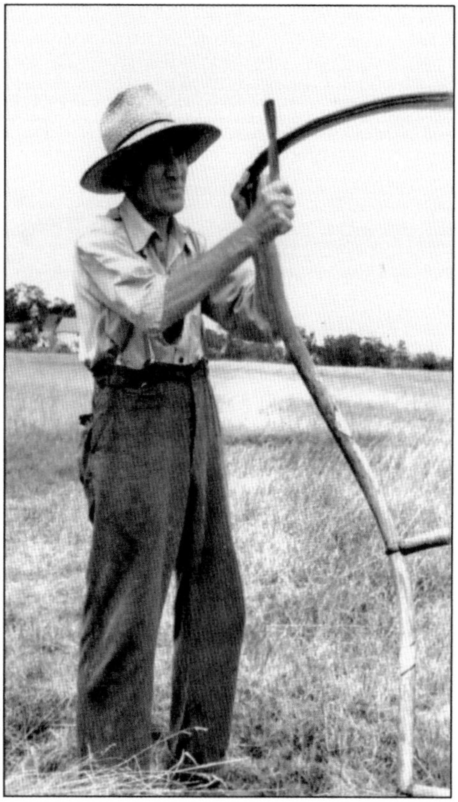

People bring a town to life, and Hopkinton has had its share of unique characters. Granny Mott lived here in the 1700s and was feared to be a witch. She died mysteriously when her neighbor shot a troublesome bird with a silver button. Les Kenyon, the unofficial "mayor of Hope Valley," was known for wearing a dime-store Indian headdress. Lawrence Kenyon was town clerk for 25 years. Schoolmistress Prudence Crandall enrolled black and white young ladies together in her Connecticut schoolhouse, going to jail for her vision. Annie Greene inspired generations of children, becoming one of the rare kindergarten teachers with an honorary doctorate. Baby boomer Don Bosquet took up his pen and turned "the New England experience" into a professional cartooning career. Narragansett Indian Tarzan Brown twice won the Boston Marathon barefoot. Grade-schooler Billy Gilman became a country-western superstar. What Hopkinton residents will make their marks in the new century?

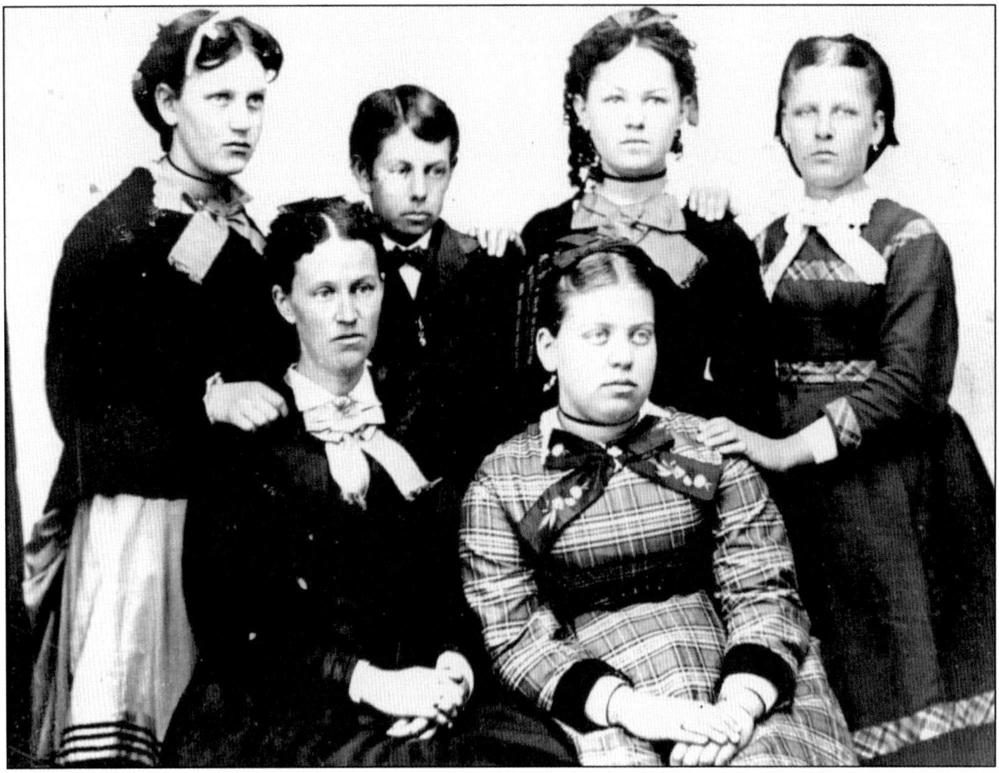

Sarah Griffith (seated on the left), the wife of Nathan Griffith, taught this Ashaway Sunday school class in 1868. From left to right are the following: (front row) Sarah Griffith and Annie May Babcock; (back row) Emma (Lawton) Hart, George D. Griffith, Ruth (White) Briggs, and Lucretia Tucker.

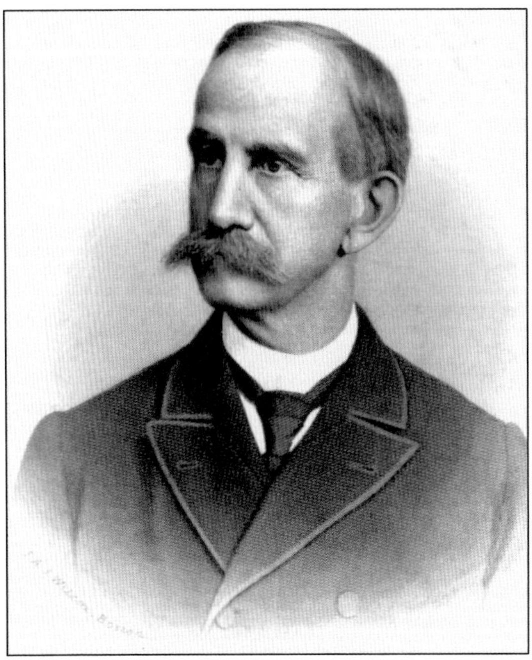

Edwin Allen, besides being town clerk of Hopkinton for 50 years, was also lieutenant governor of Rhode Island. At least three townsfolk have had that state job—and they all lived in Hopkinton City. Since the town's incorporation in 1757, just 16 people have served as town clerk of Hopkinton.

Henry H. Godfrey was one of the many area men who joined the 7th Rhode Island Regiment. Like thousands of Civil War soldiers, he had himself photographed.

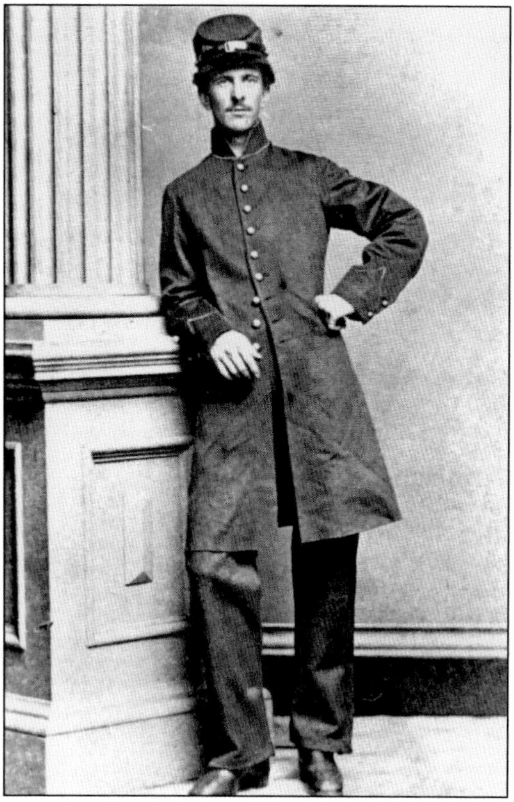

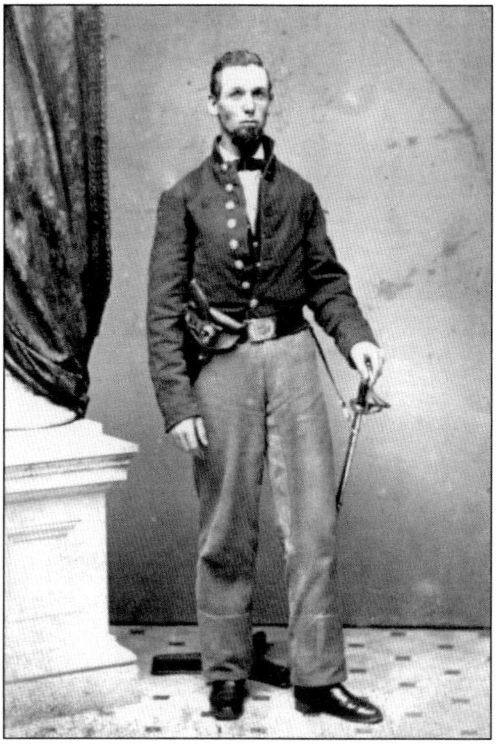

G. A. Franklin of the Rhode Island Artillery also had his portrait taken.

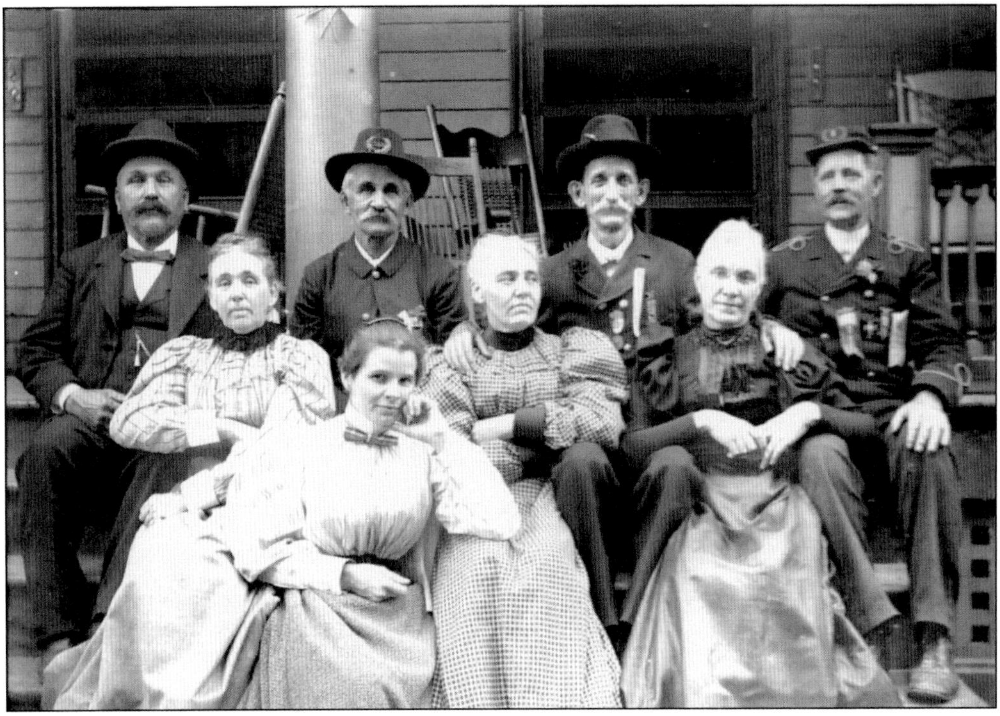

In the decades following the Civil War, veterans proudly marched as members of the Grand Army of the Republic (GAR). The veteran seated second from the left is George Nichols.

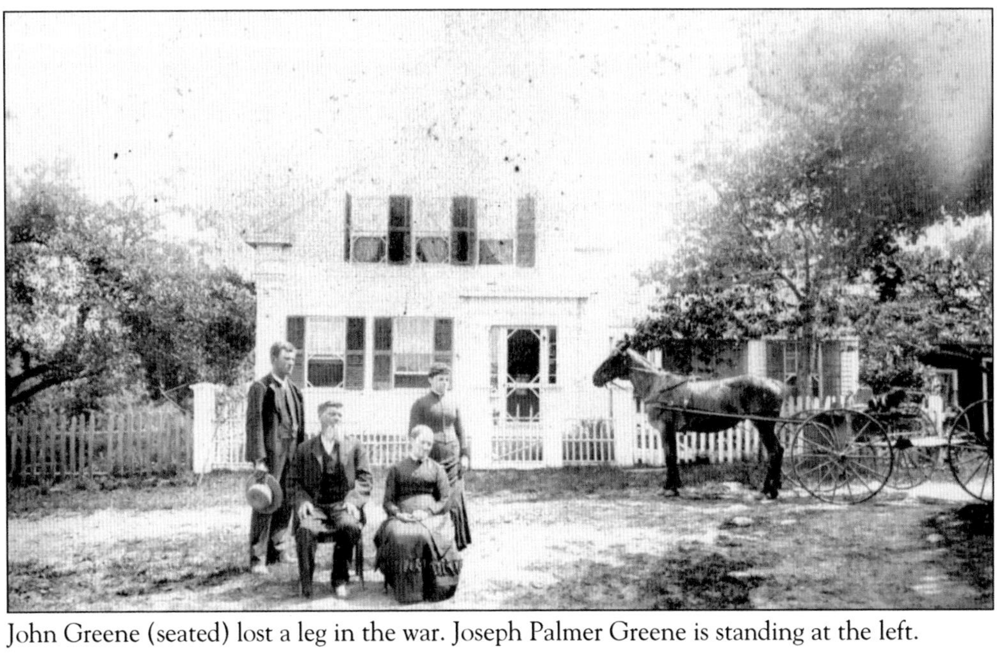

John Greene (seated) lost a leg in the war. Joseph Palmer Greene is standing at the left.

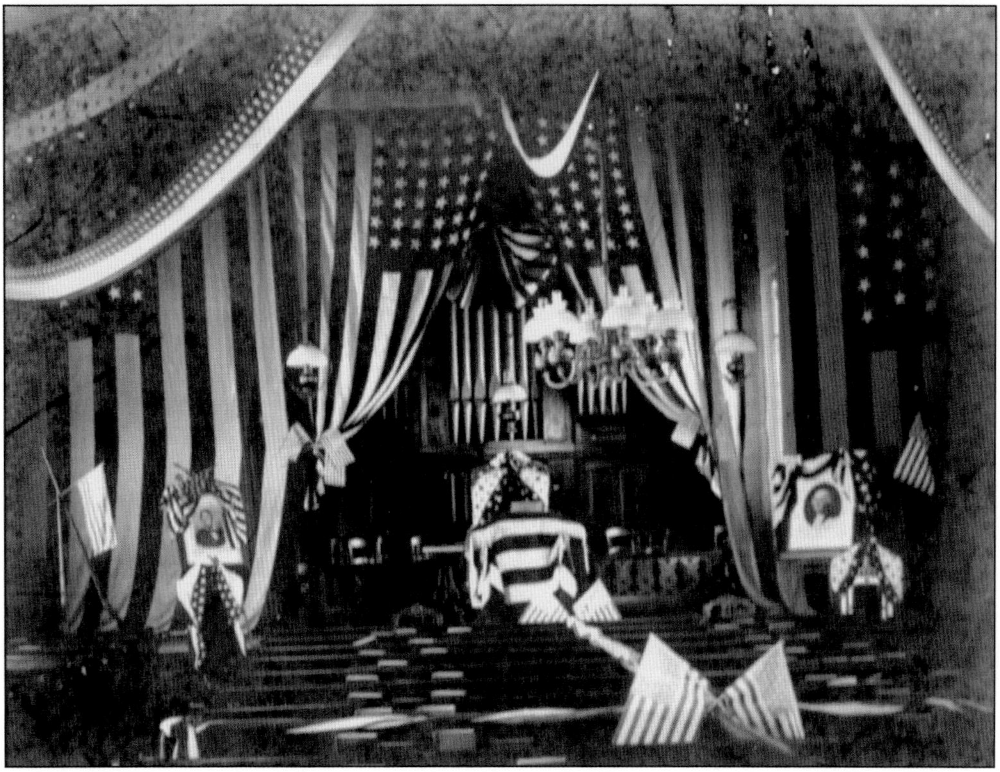

Communities enthusiastically supported their veterans. The Hope Valley Baptist Church held a GAR Sunday in their honor.

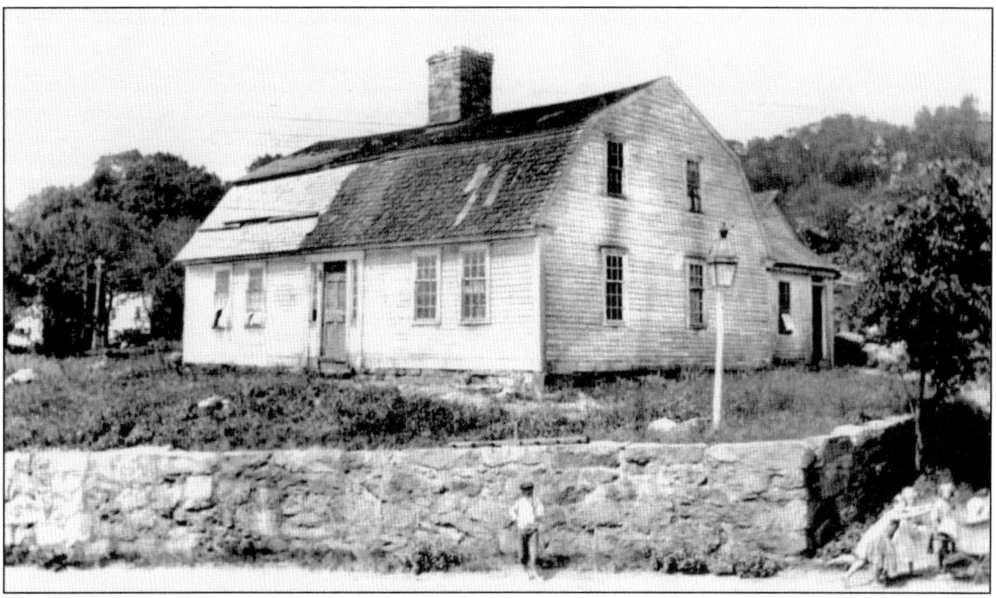

Photography was very cumbersome in its early days, and photographs of children being children are rare. This photographer seems to have inadvertently captured such an image while shooting the Brand-Arnold house in Hope Valley.

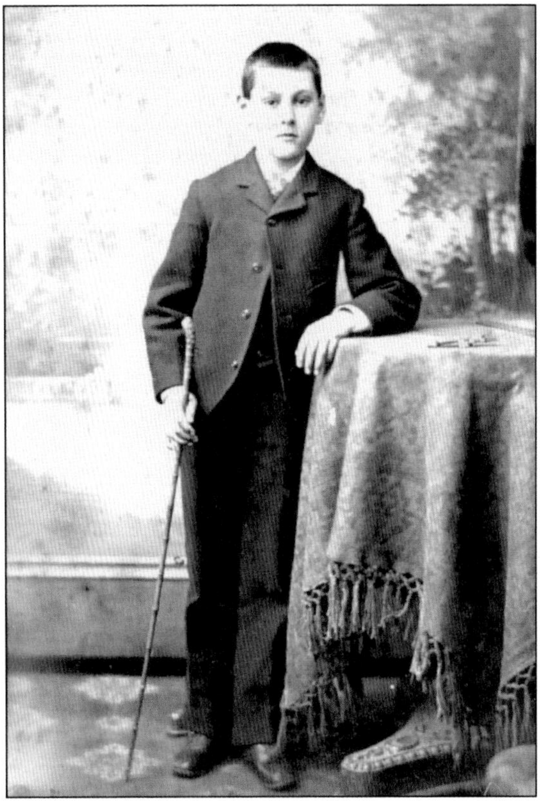

Since Elmer Burdick had endured being braced into place for his photograph (look behind his right foot), why did the photographer let him list so far to port? Elmer later married Grace Tefft. His father and grandfather were Albert and Tyler Burdick. On the table there appears to be either a drafting compass or calipers, which may have been used by the photographer.

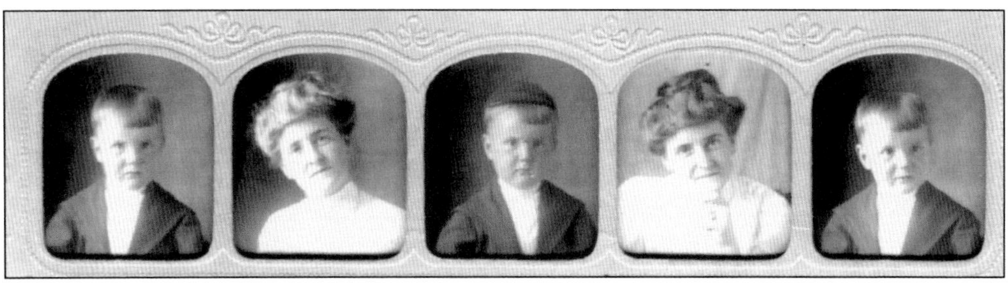

This lovely montage of a mother (or possibly a grandmother) and a small boy is tentatively identified as being from the Woodmansee family c. 1910.

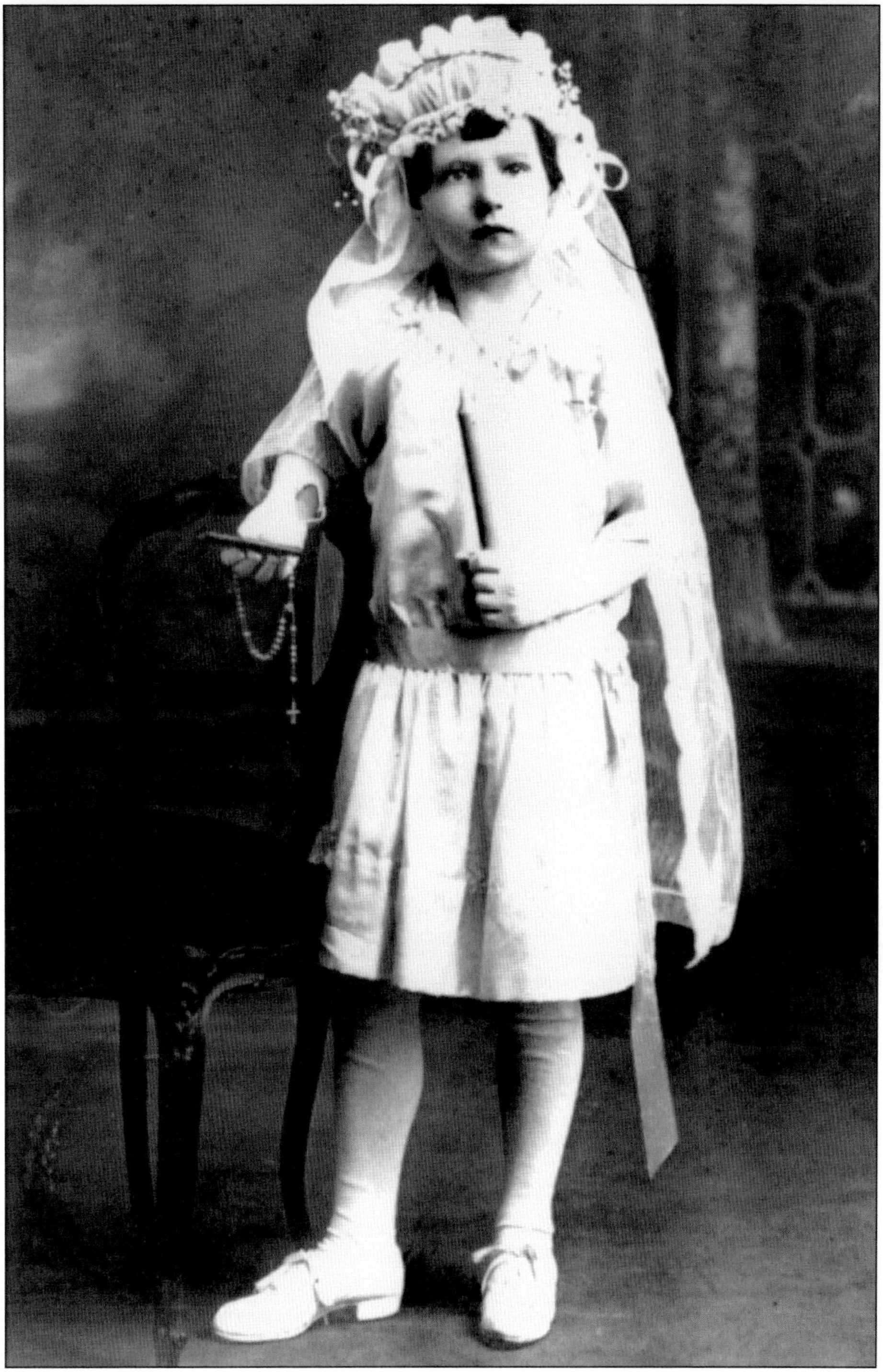

Polish immigrants, along with the Irish, Italians, French Canadians, Portuguese, and others, made Catholic parishes vital parts of the town. St. Joseph's Church in Hope Valley opened in 1922; Our Lady of Victory Church in Ashaway opened in 1946. This girl is identified as Mary Popiolek.

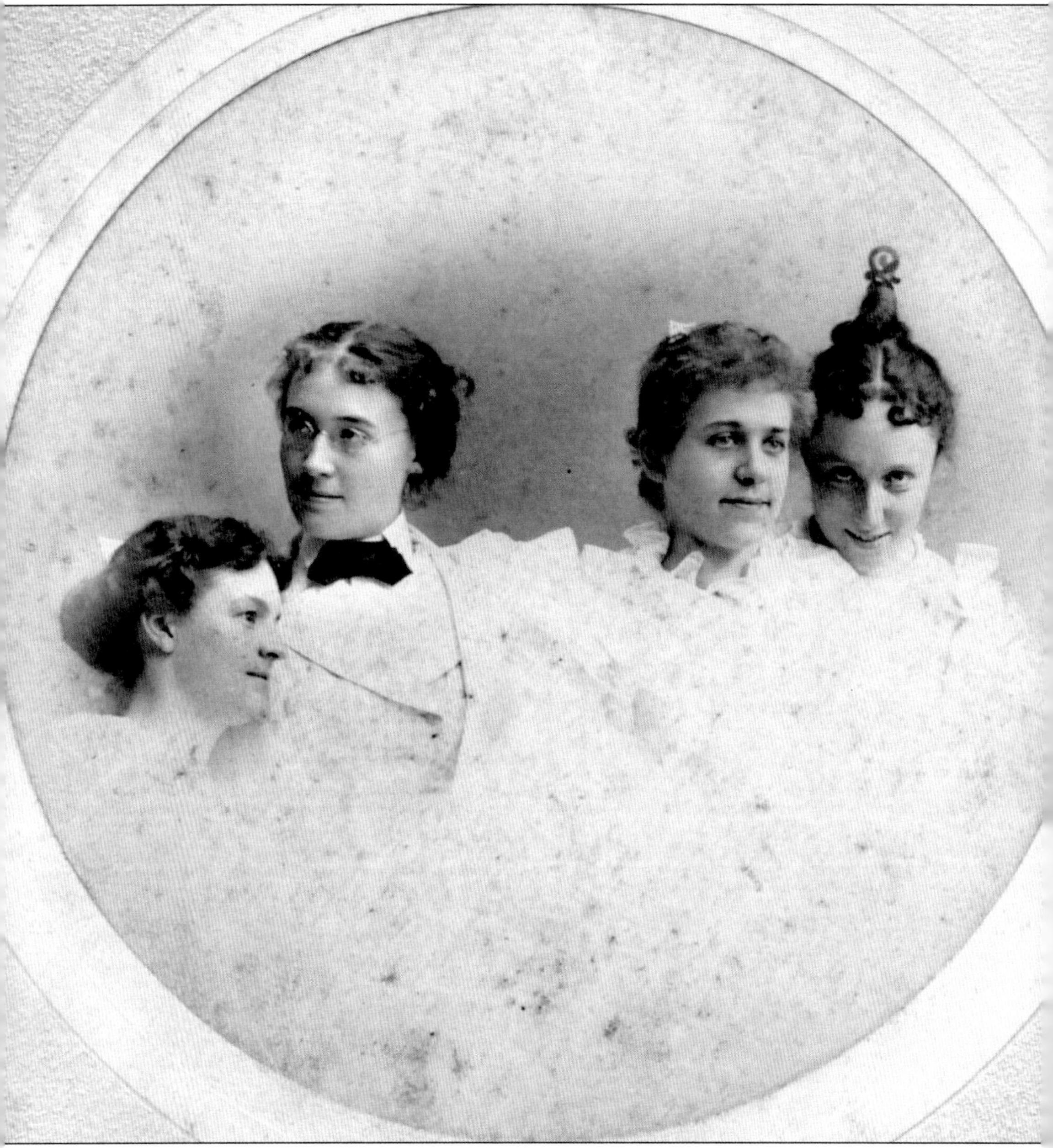

In the past, young ladies were photographed often, just as they are today. Lyda McGean and her friends enjoyed this unusual circular photographic display. They seem like a high-spirited crowd.

All we know for sure about Madalene is that she was 14 years old in 1911. It appears that she found no necessity to take herself too seriously.

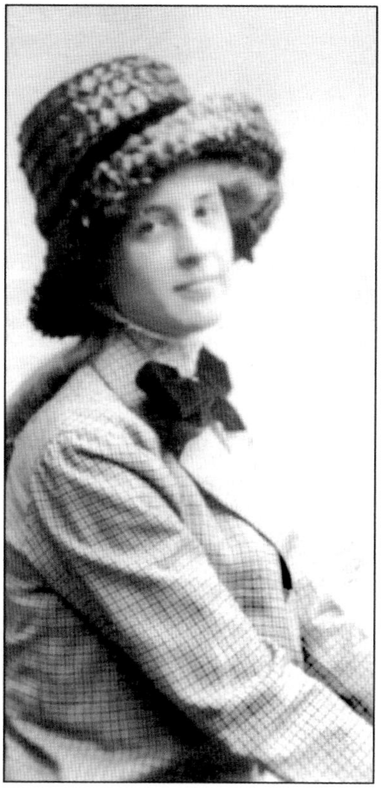

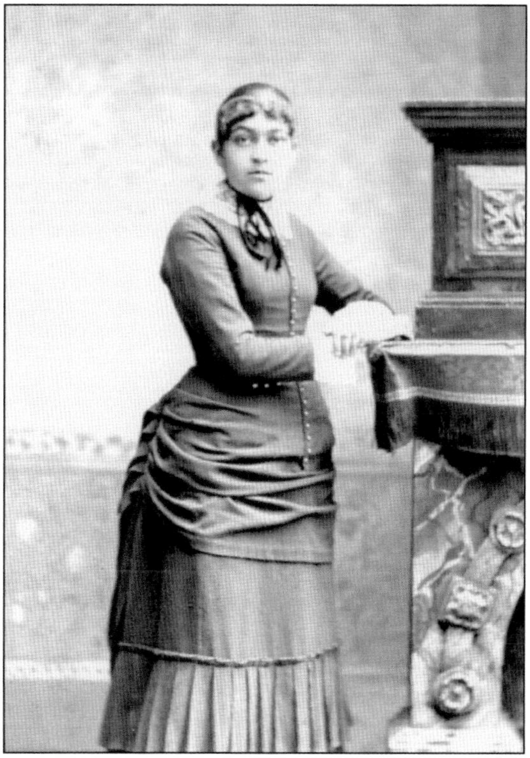

May Lillibridge had herself photographed "in the dress she made after learning her trade" from Emma Perry, a milliner and the wife of O. G. Perry.

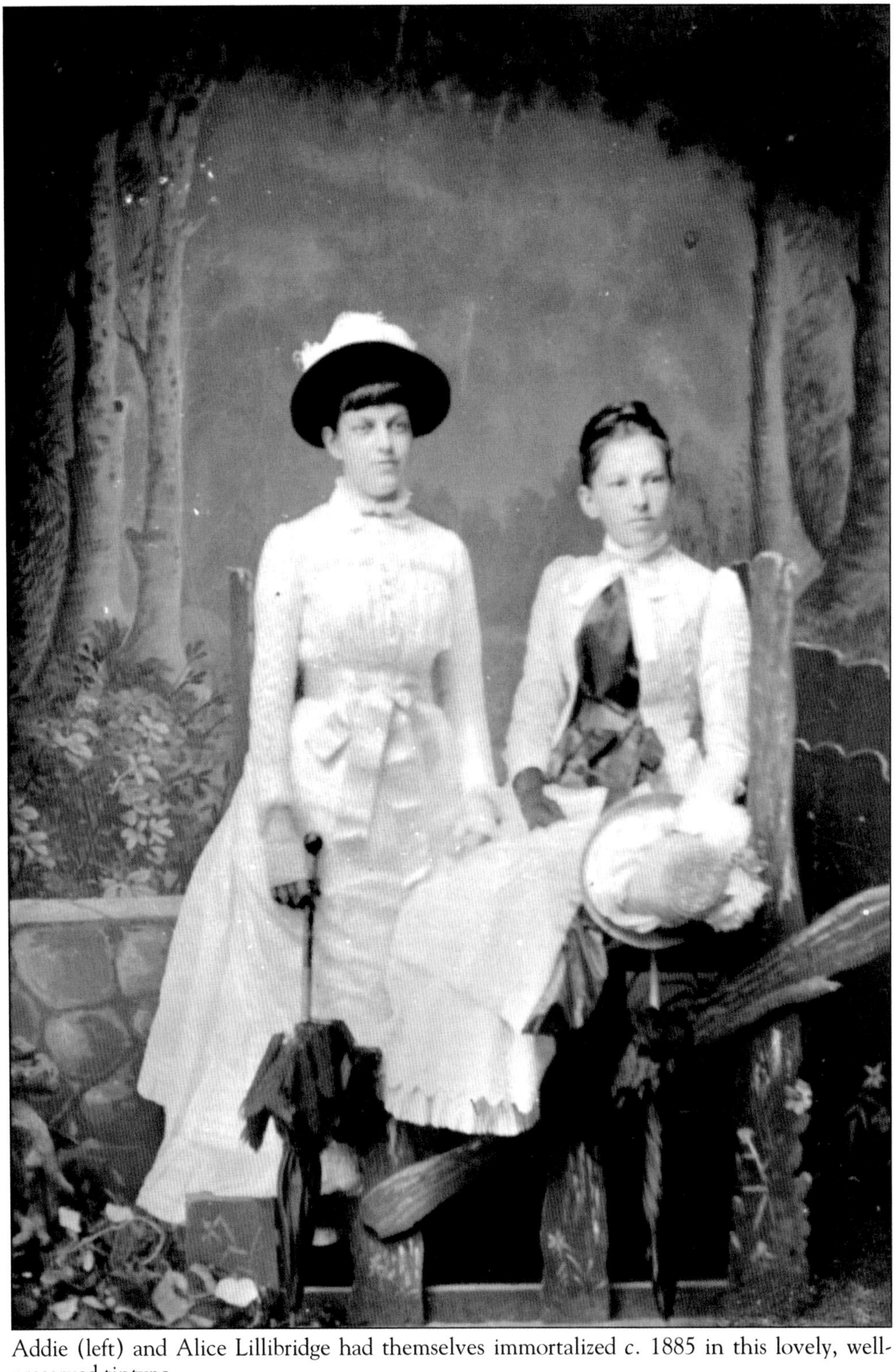

Addie (left) and Alice Lillibridge had themselves immortalized *c.* 1885 in this lovely, well-preserved tintype.

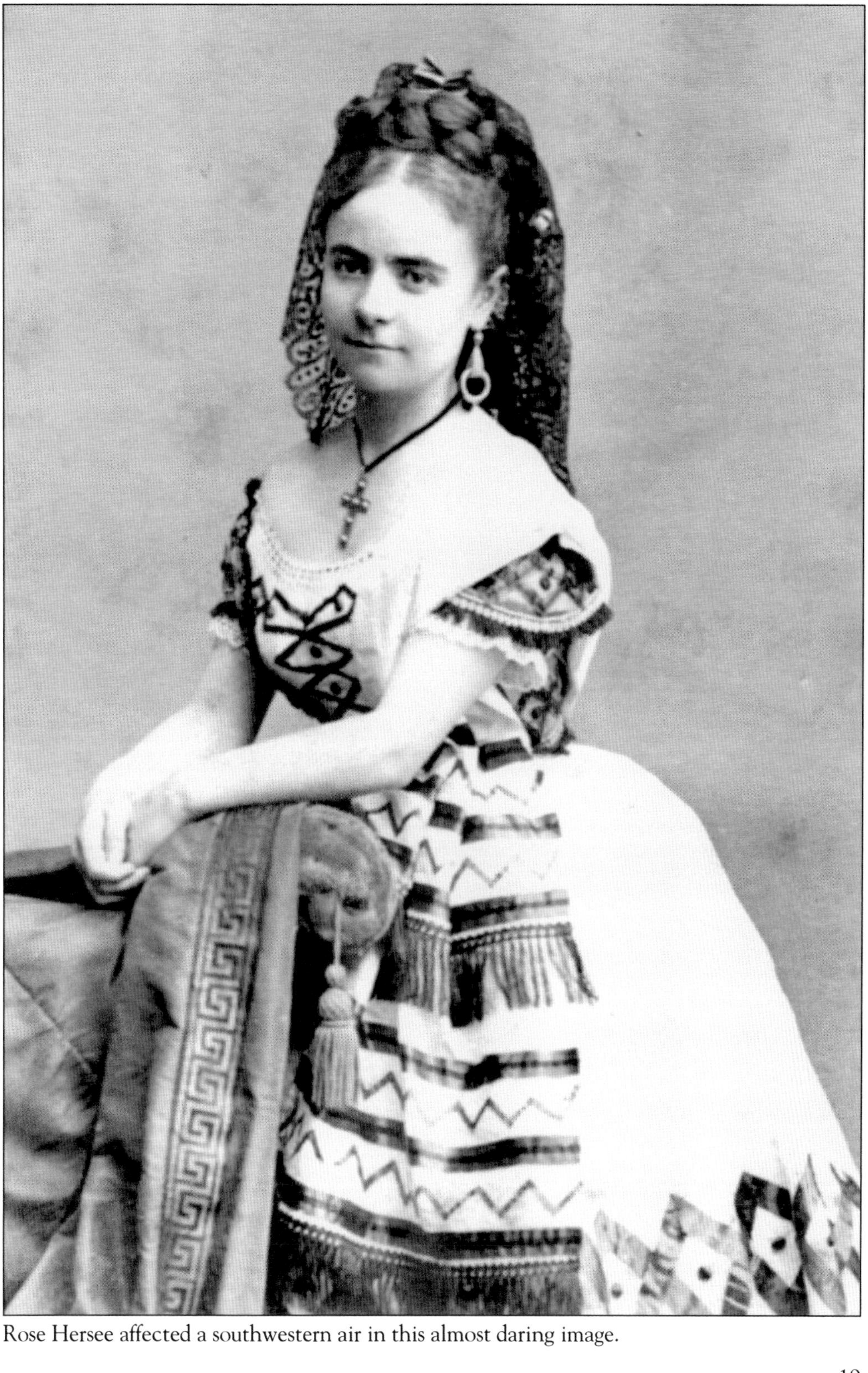
Rose Hersee affected a southwestern air in this almost daring image.

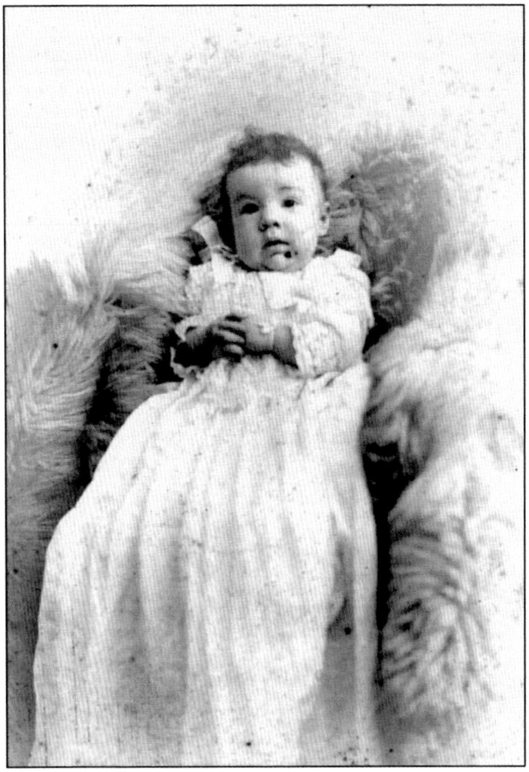

Ruth Allen's family left an unusual photographic record of their daughter.

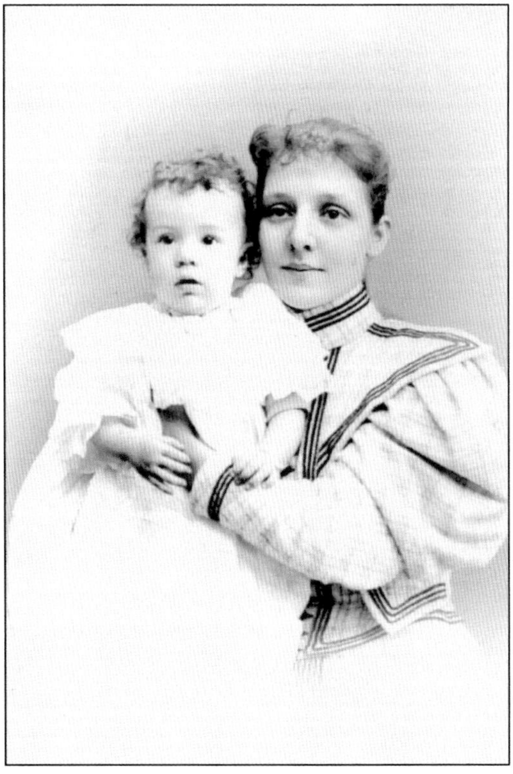

Ruth Allen's parents were Mr. and Mrs. George A. Allen.

By the time of this image, Ruth must have been quite accustomed to having her photograph taken.

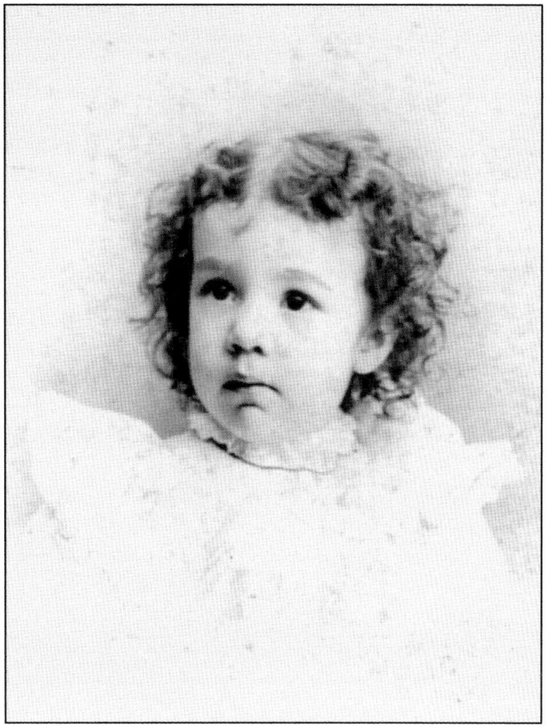

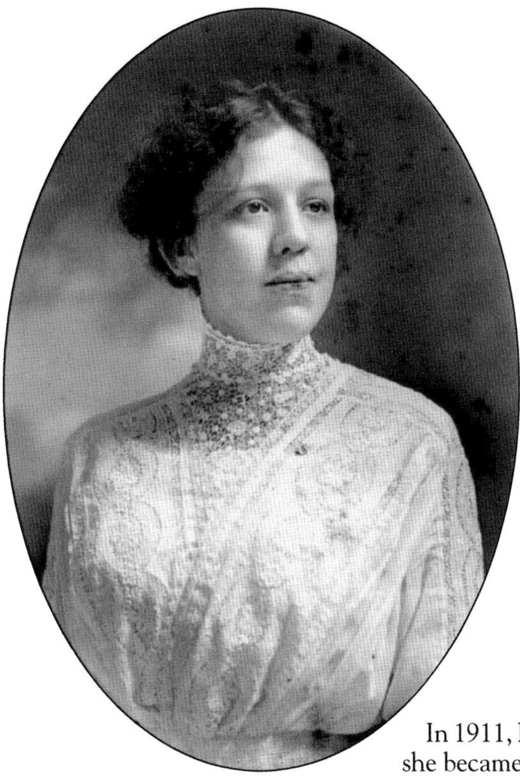

In 1911, Ruth Allen married Dr. William Veal. In time she became the mother of a little girl.

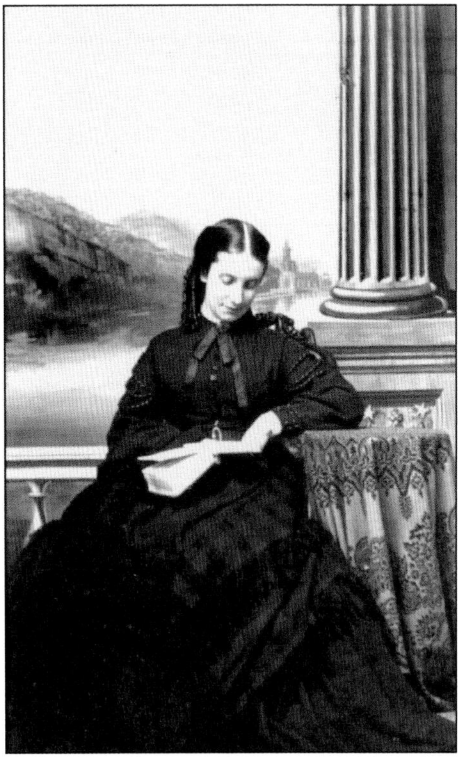

This photograph of Lizzie (Smith) Kenyon displays a typical mid-Victorian setting and clothing style.

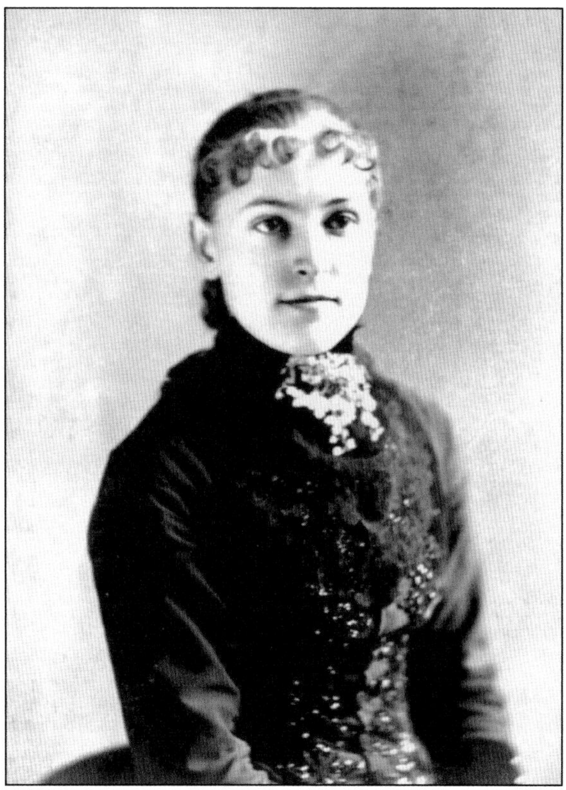

Hallie Langworthy was just about 16 at the time of this photograph. Her serene air and sober dress are betrayed by the exuberant embellishments.

Nellie Pendleton was active with the Sunday school at Hope Valley Baptist Church.

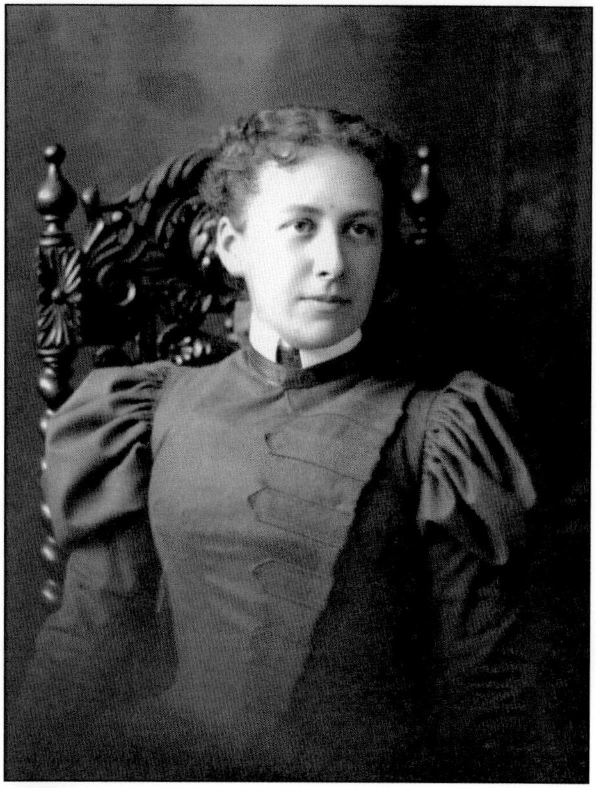

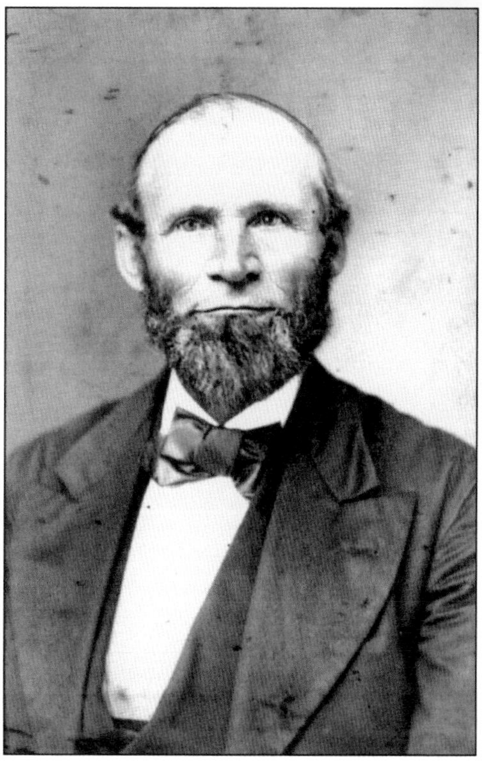

A Methodist Episcopal church started in Canonchet in 1845. Members erected a building in Rockville c. 1846, when Rev. Stanton Austin joined the congregation, which he served for 35 years. They moved the structure to Hope Valley in 1851. The Catholic diocese bought the place in 1922, but it was badly damaged in the Hurricane of 1938, after which the current parish church was built.

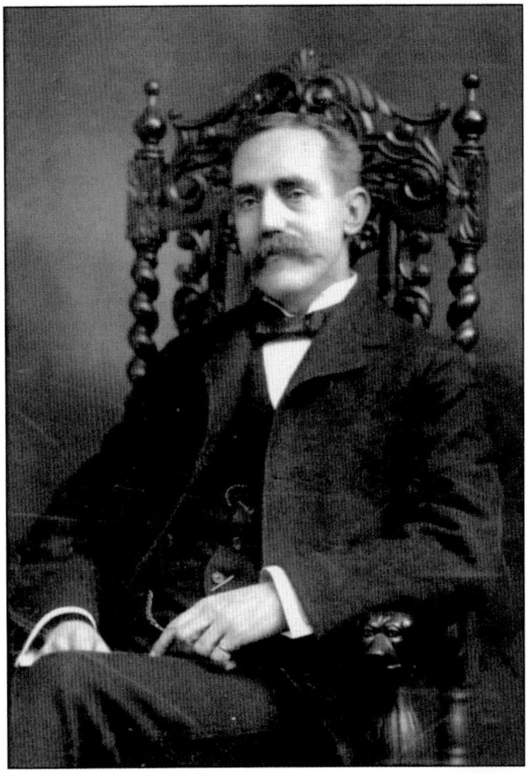

For Christmas 1899, school superintendent Albert Babcock presented his teachers with portrait photographs of himself. They must have been thrilled.

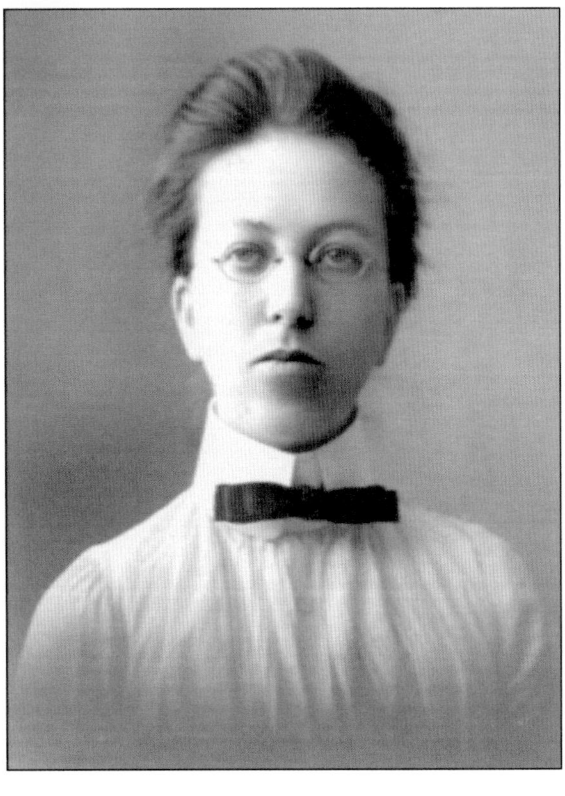

Fanny Yeau taught in Hope Valley School. One suspects that not much got past her.

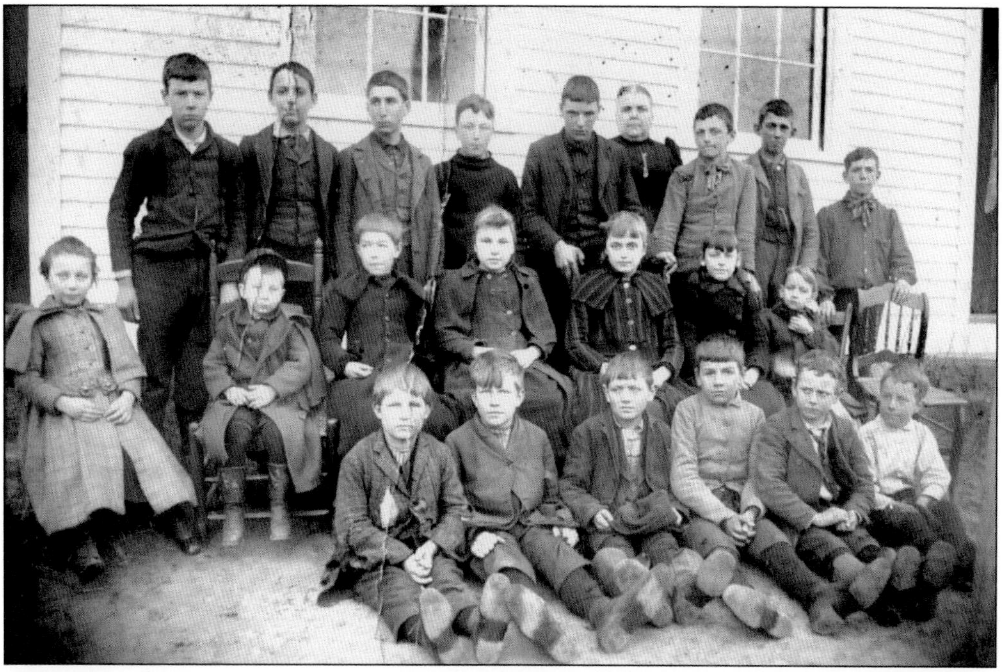

The teacher (back row, sixth from left) at Canonchet school is so short that she is almost lost among her scholars at first glance. It looks as though there is no doubt who is boss, though.

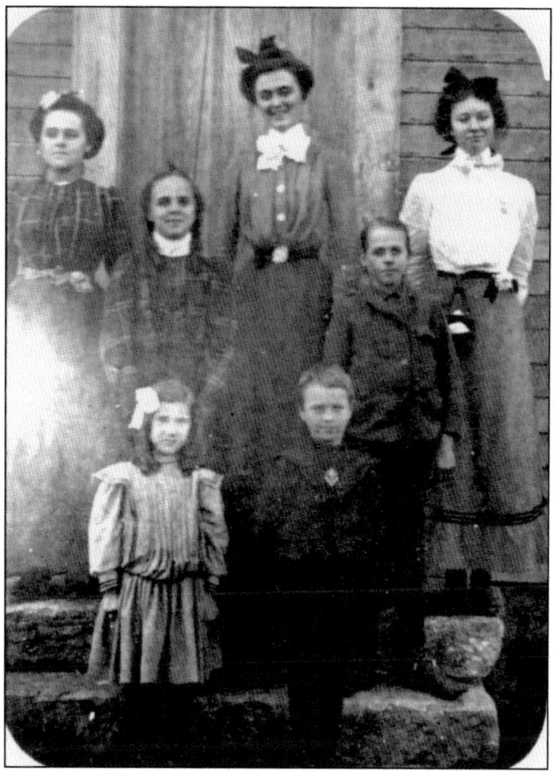

A rather more cheerful Maude Nye Partelo had a much smaller class at her first school, which remains unidentified.

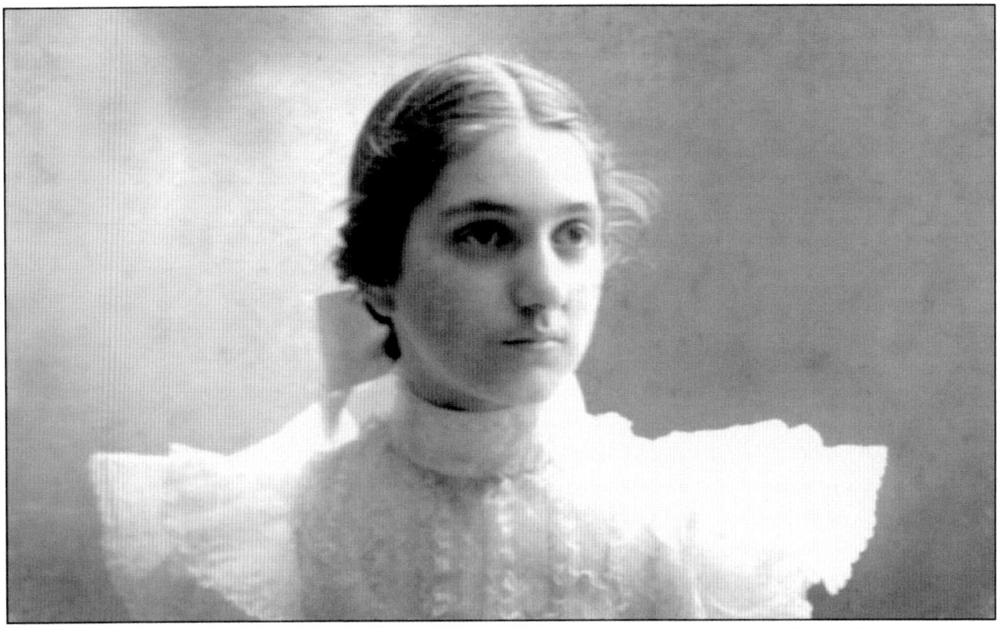

Phoebe Alice (Barber) Smith graduated from Hope Valley School in 1898. She taught at Canonchet and elsewhere, then went to Rhode Island Normal School (now Rhode Island College) with the class of 1904. Barber also taught in Westerly (she was the principal of Avondale and Quarry Hill Schools) and in Yonkers, New York, until her marriage in 1912. She was originally from Exeter.

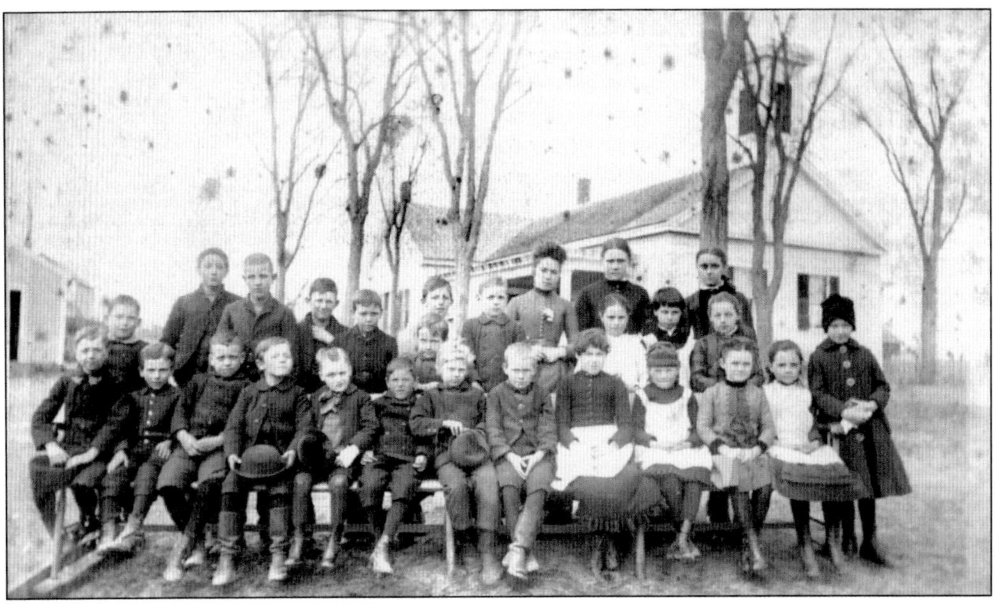

Notice the hats and caps that some of these Hope Valley fellows are clutching.

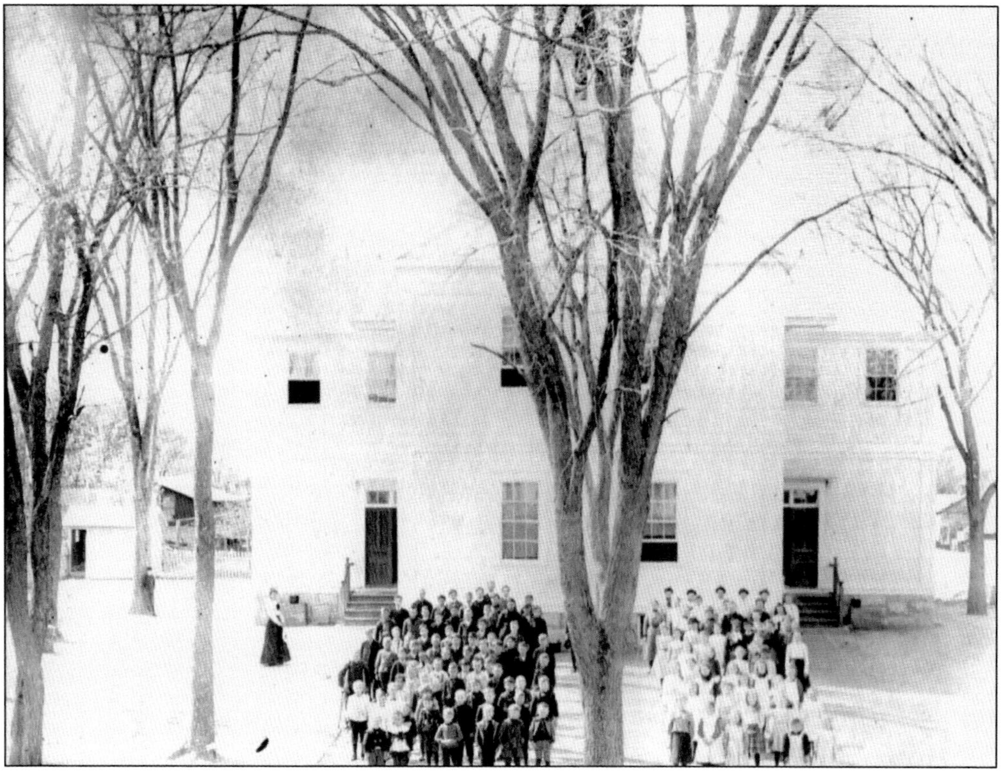

Once the school was enlarged in 1900, it started to dwarf the students.

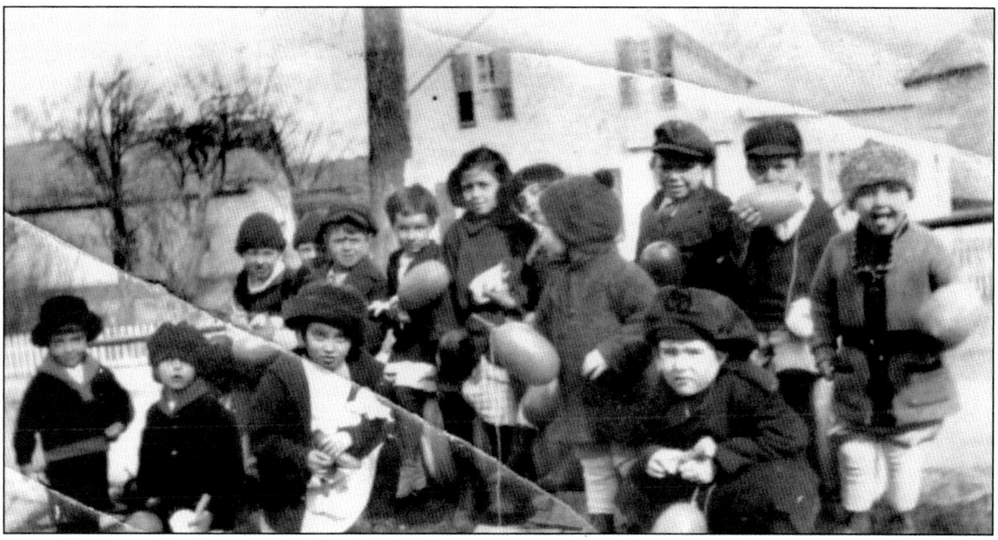

Annie Greene taught kindergarten for decades. One of her classes gathered outside with balloons on a cold day in the 1930s.

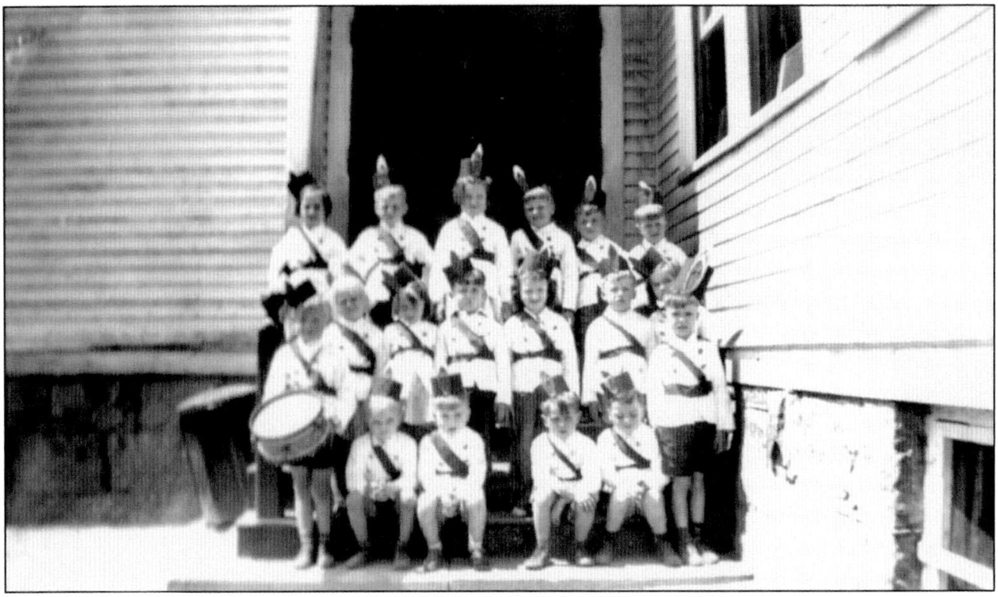

In 1941, Annie Greene got her entire class accoutered alike for some occasion—an exercise most teachers would find quite daunting in these more independent days.

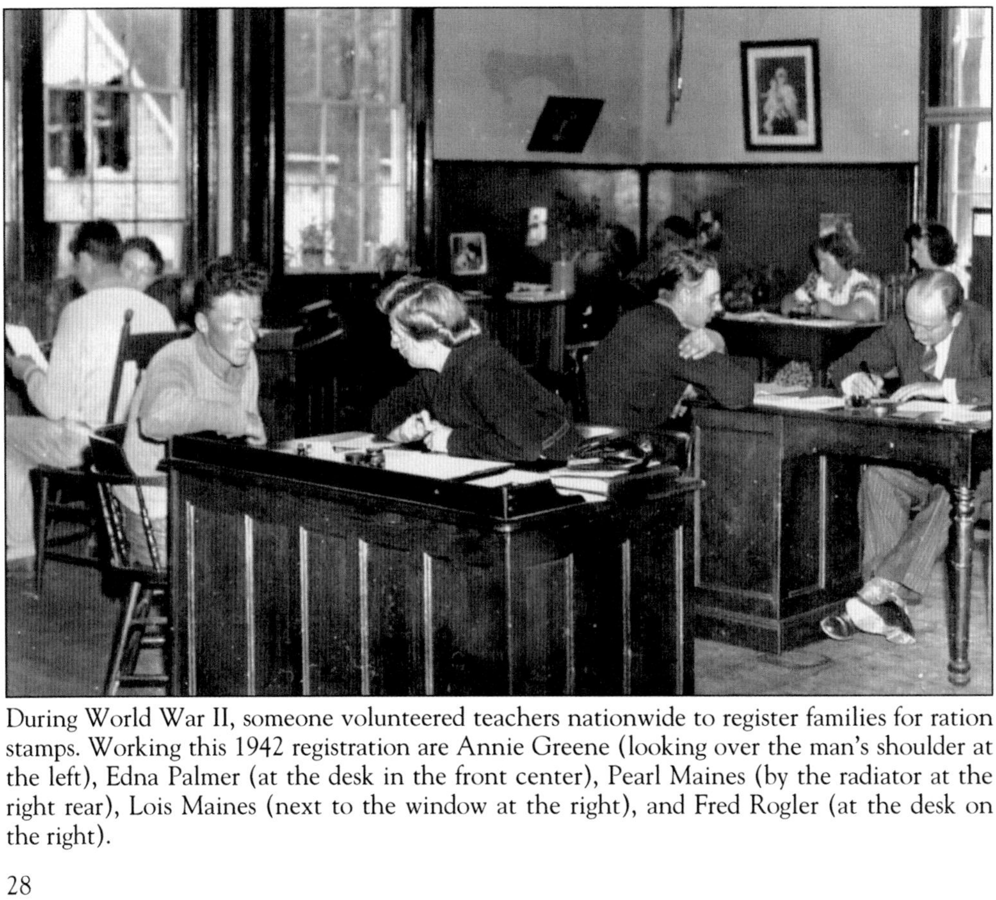

During World War II, someone volunteered teachers nationwide to register families for ration stamps. Working this 1942 registration are Annie Greene (looking over the man's shoulder at the left), Edna Palmer (at the desk in the front center), Pearl Maines (by the radiator at the right rear), Lois Maines (next to the window at the right), and Fred Rogler (at the desk on the right).

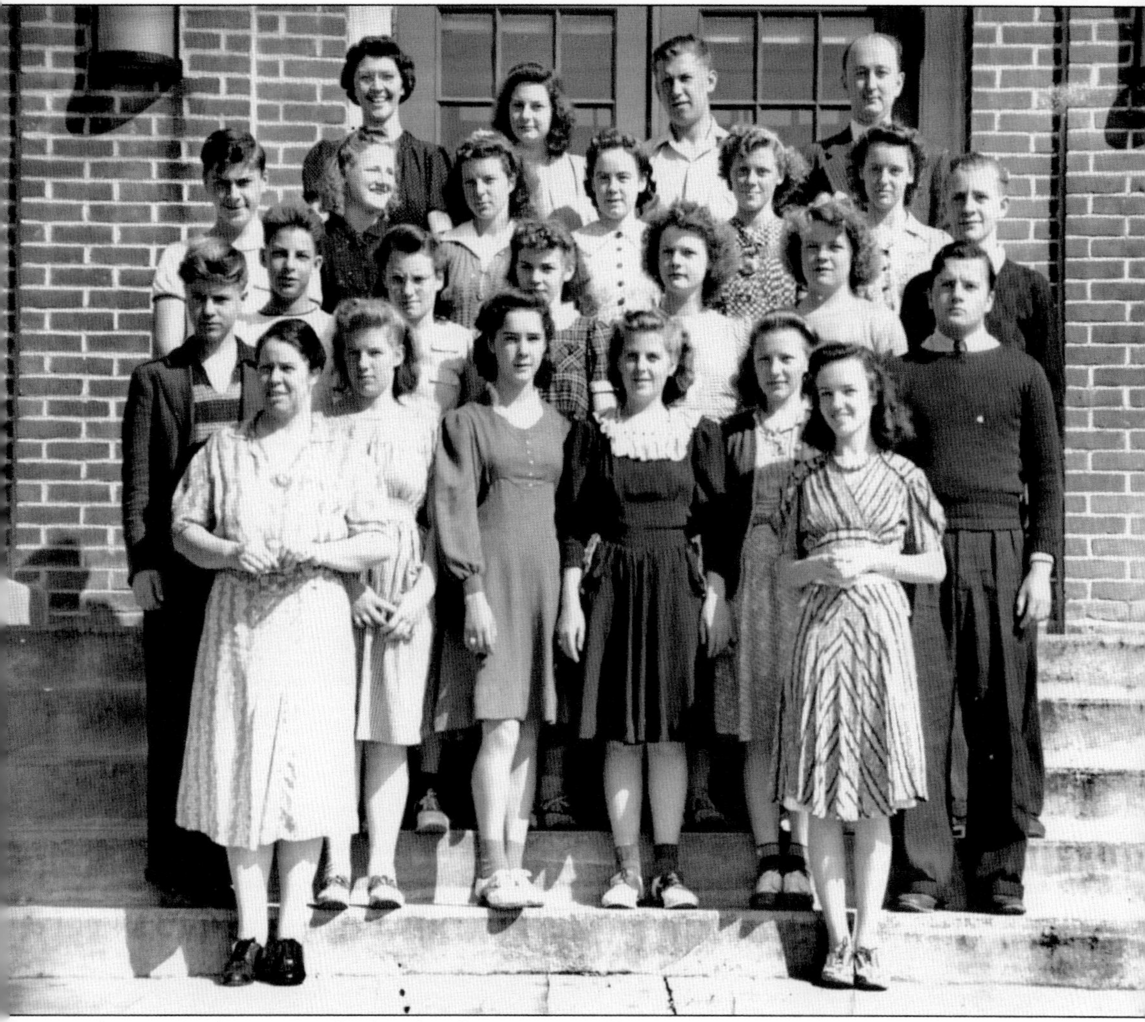

Hopkinton built a junior high school at Hope Valley in 1933, but its program no longer offered 11th and 12th grade; the class of 1942 graduated as sophomores, many of them transferring to Westerly for their last two years of school. A new elementary school was added to the junior high in 1955. Starting in 1960, Hopkinton maintained schools in Hope Valley and Ashaway that offered kindergarten through 6th grade; students in the 7th through 12th grades were sent to Chariho Regional Junior-Senior High School. Schooling for kindergarten through 12th grade, including the Hope Valley and Ashaway Schools, was later regionalized throughout Charlestown, Richmond, and Hopkinton. Seen in the wartime photograph above are, from left to right, the following: (first row) teachers Jane Sherman and Mrs. Rood; (second row) Ray Jordan, Gertrude Kenyon, Ethel Palmer, Eileen Niles, Helen Barszcz, and Raymond Burdick; (third row) Harlan Niles, Charlotte Baton, Marjorie Clarke, Carolyn Spencer, Frances Sherman, and Philip Kenney; (fourth row) Milton Jencks, Dorothy Downs, Hope Greene, Shirley Thayer, Mildred Tefft, and Hazel Sheldon; (fifth row) teacher Mrs. Stafford, Ethel Palmer, Eileen Niles, and teacher Fred Rogler. Eleven students and two teachers pictured here were still living in 2004.

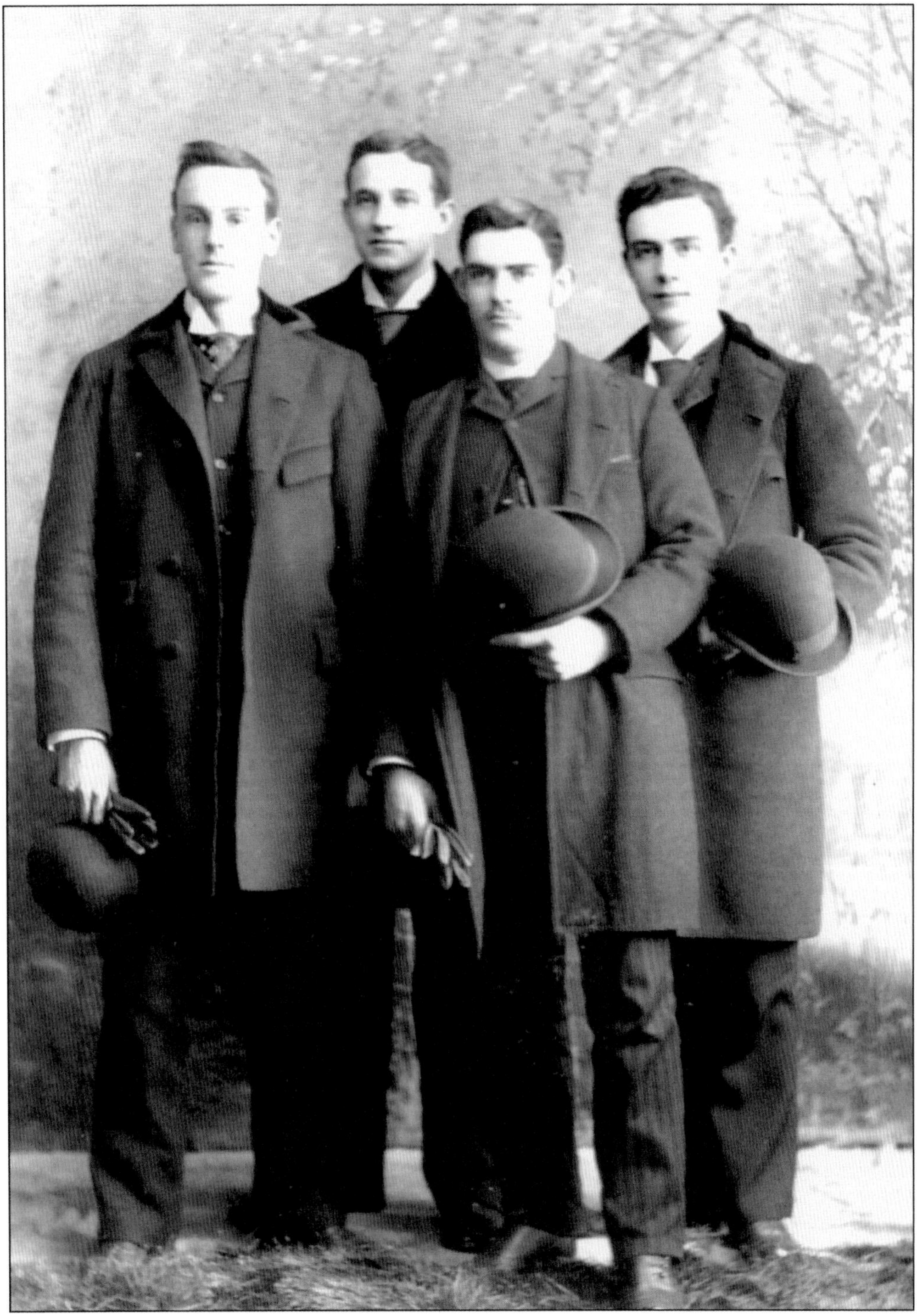

Young women were not the only ones who wanted their pictures taken. The "Dudes" of Hope Valley obviously enjoyed looking their best. The gent on the left is Willis Nichols, who worked in the office at Nichols and Langworthy.

Thad Walker Gardiner, identified as "one of the former 'Dudes' in Hope Valley," was a concert musician in Boston. He looks like he is competing with Oscar Wilde.

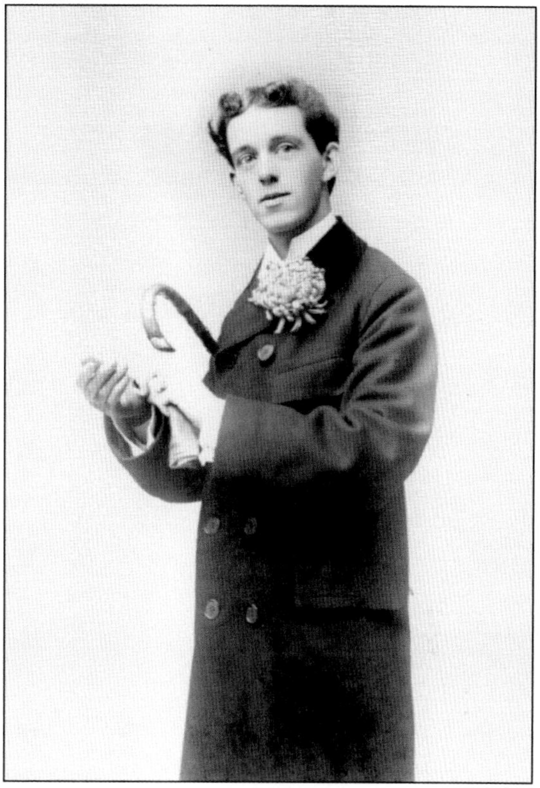

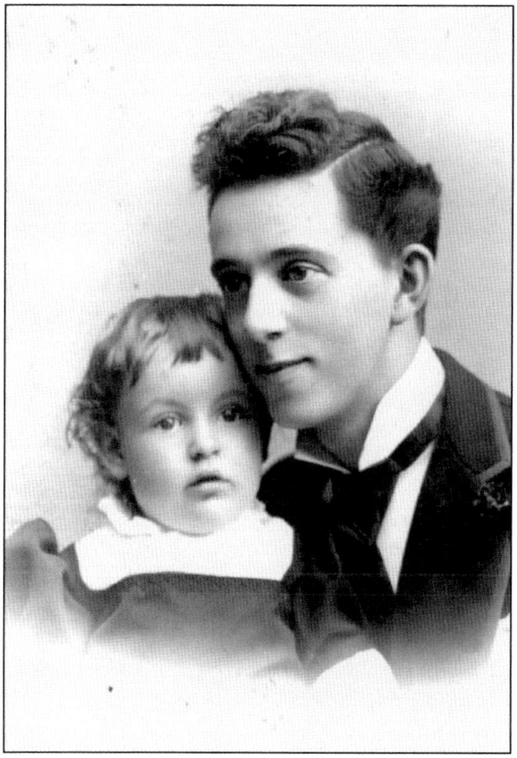

Thad Walker Gardiner appears to have enjoyed posing for this affectionate photograph with his son Merle. Photographs of fathers with small children are rare.

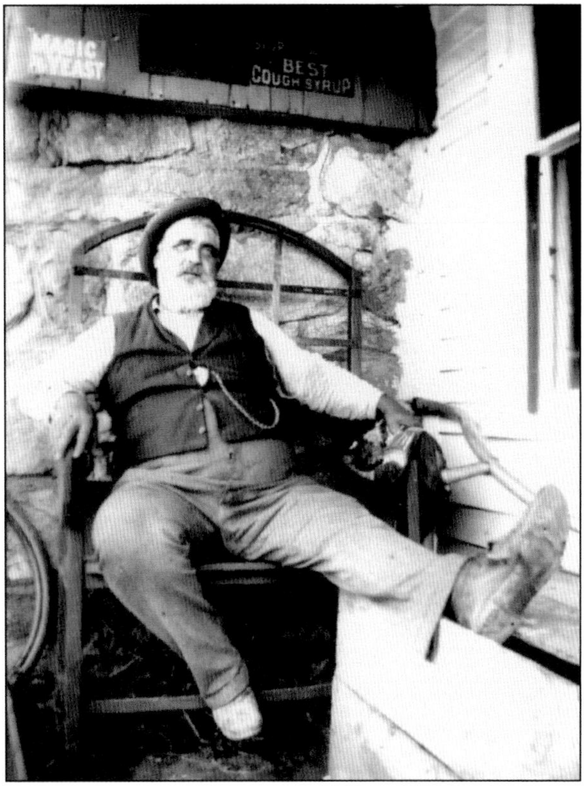

Clinton Crandall kept a store near Rockville.

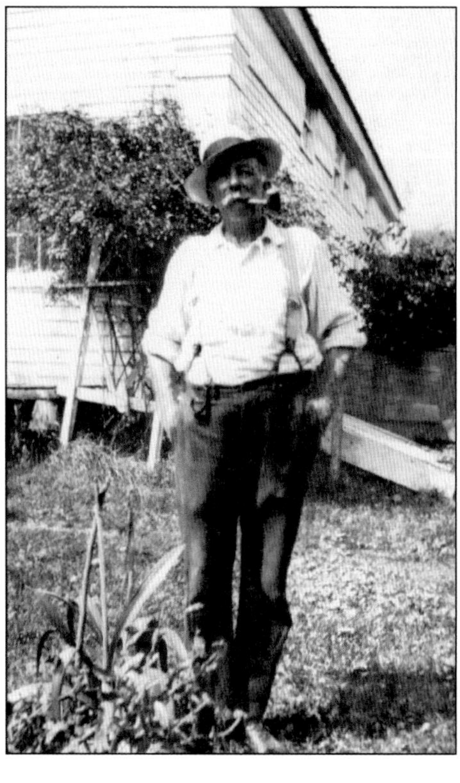

E. G. Boss of Rockville, while keeping casual, still managed to appear distinctive.

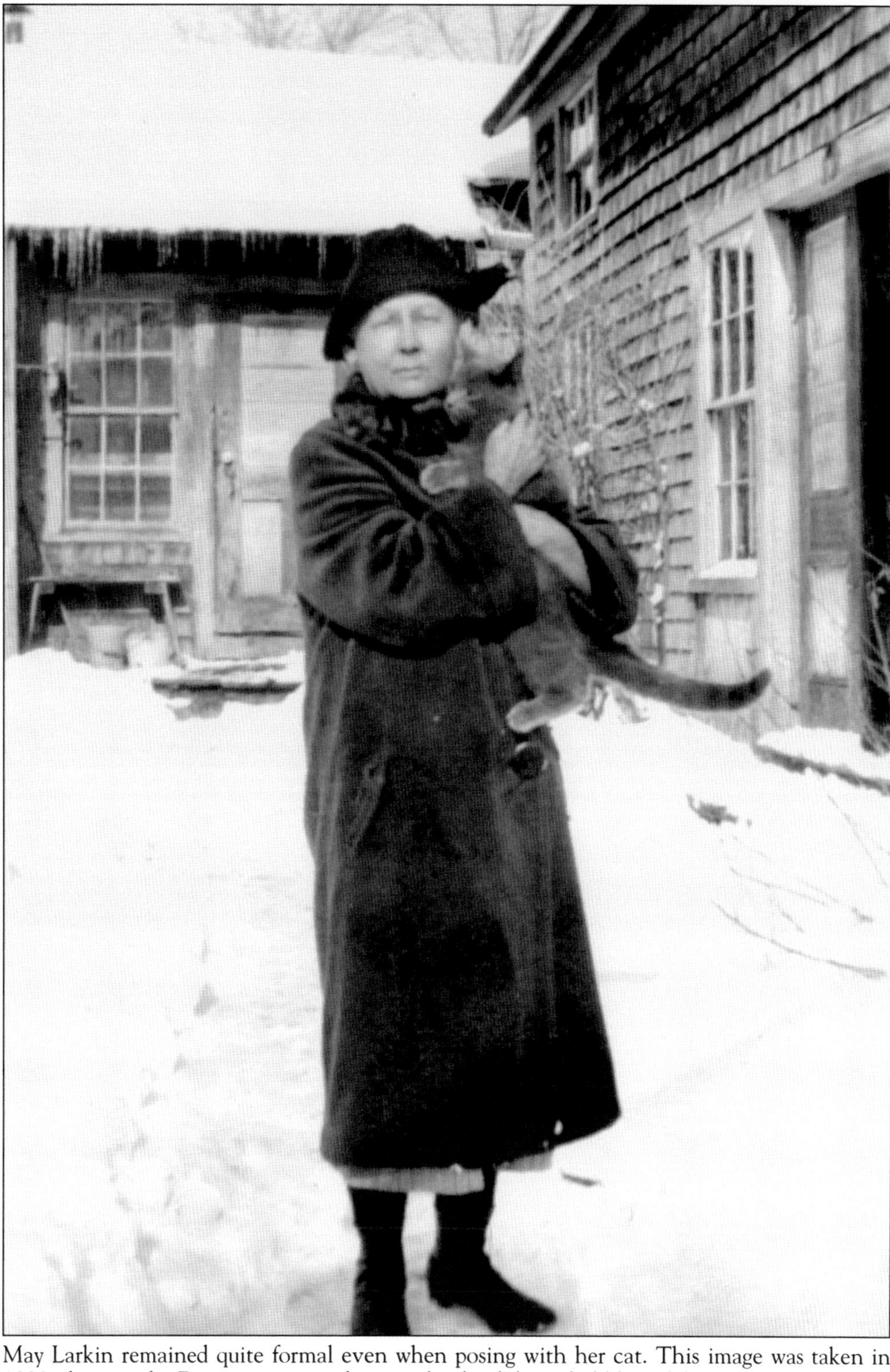

May Larkin remained quite formal even when posing with her cat. This image was taken in 1929, the year the Depression started, so maybe she did not feel like celebrating.

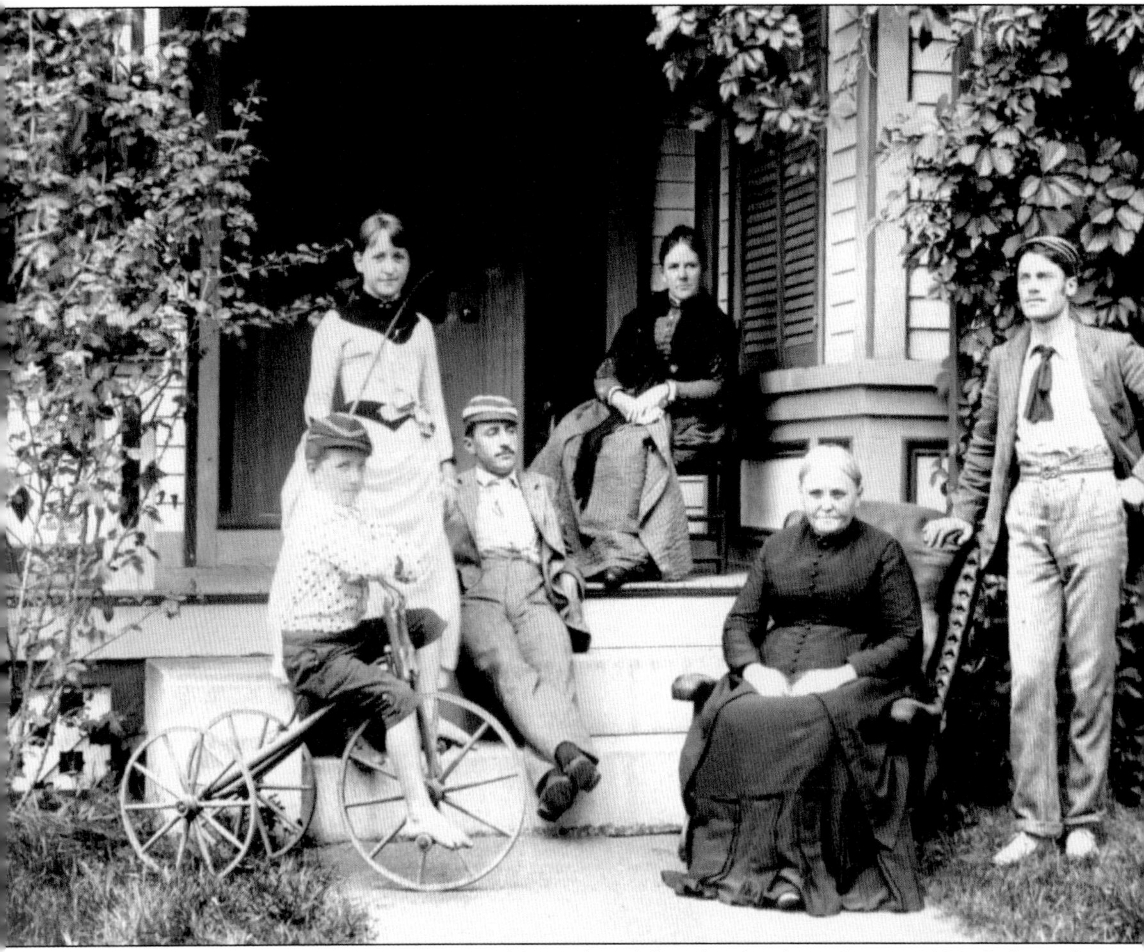

Jona Reynolds, wife of Barber Reynolds, gathered her family about her *c.* 1890. Judging by the caps, these young men may be on a sports team, or at least they are proud supporters. The barefoot boy with cheek of tan has quite an impressive velocipede, but his big sister appears to have a switch.

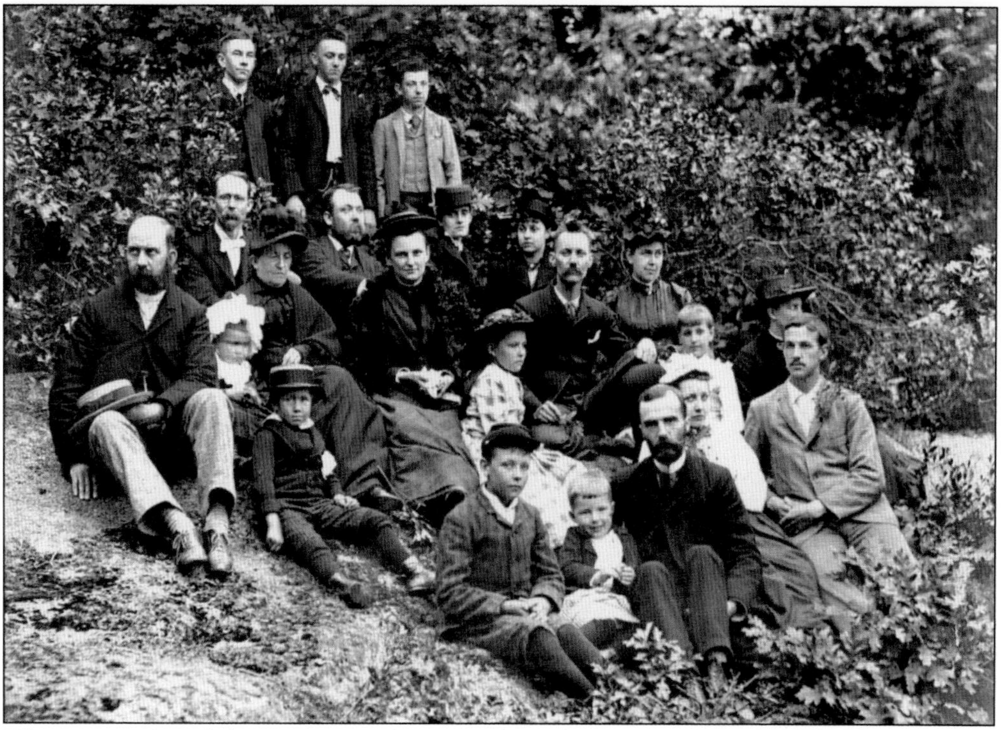

Whatever gathered this group together must have been pretty serious; the only ghost of a smile comes from the lady seated in the center. The boy at the left front wears a Civil War–style army cap.

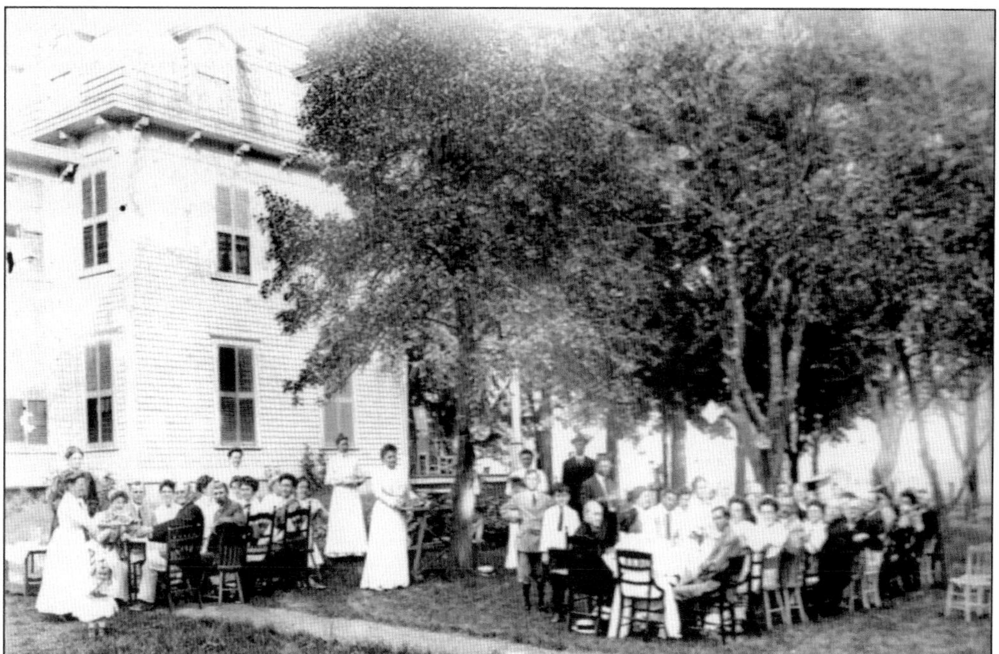

Lizzie and George Henry Spicer hosted quite a mob for a picnic at their home, the old Thomas Barber House on Broad Street in Ashaway.

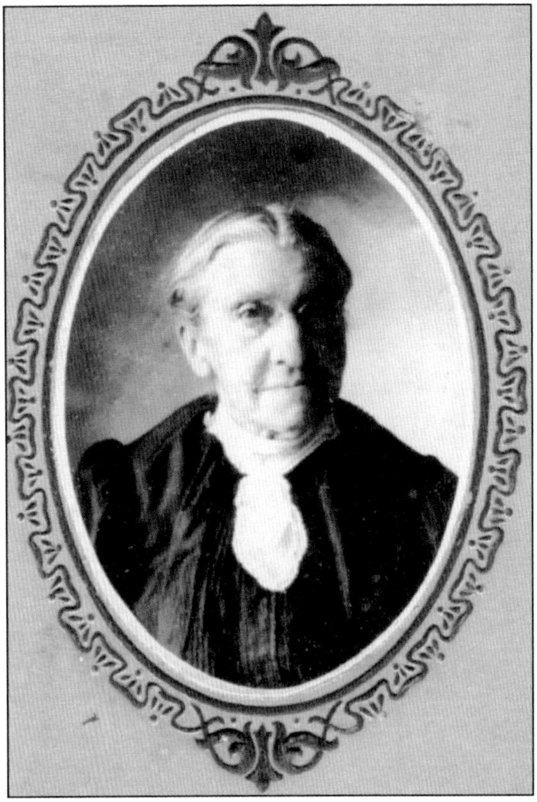

Lucetta Crandall of Rockville was born c. 1827. "Aunt Citty" served as the local self-taught homeopath; "real" doctors were miles distant. Notice the hand embellishing around the mat.

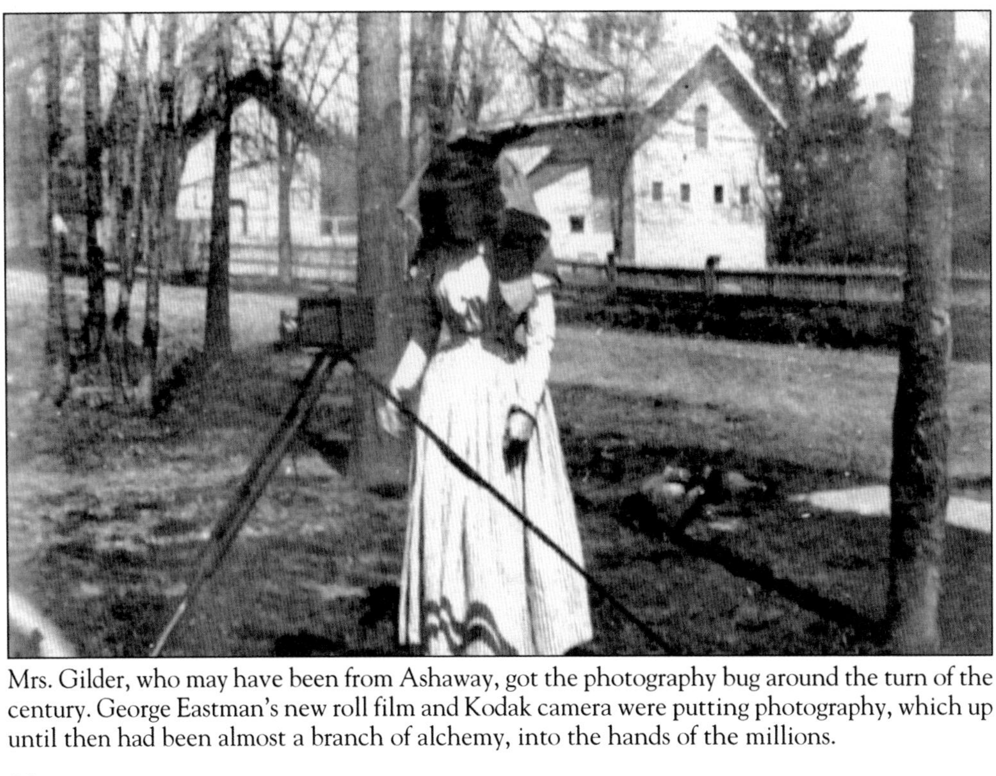

Mrs. Gilder, who may have been from Ashaway, got the photography bug around the turn of the century. George Eastman's new roll film and Kodak camera were putting photography, which up until then had been almost a branch of alchemy, into the hands of the millions.

George Edwin Greene issued postcards of himself, pointing out that he had been the local temperance druggist for 50 years. Lucetta Crandall (seen on page 36) ordered many of her remedies from Greene.

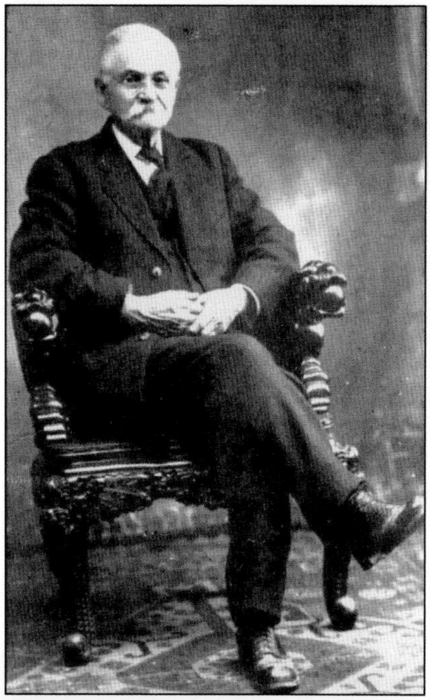

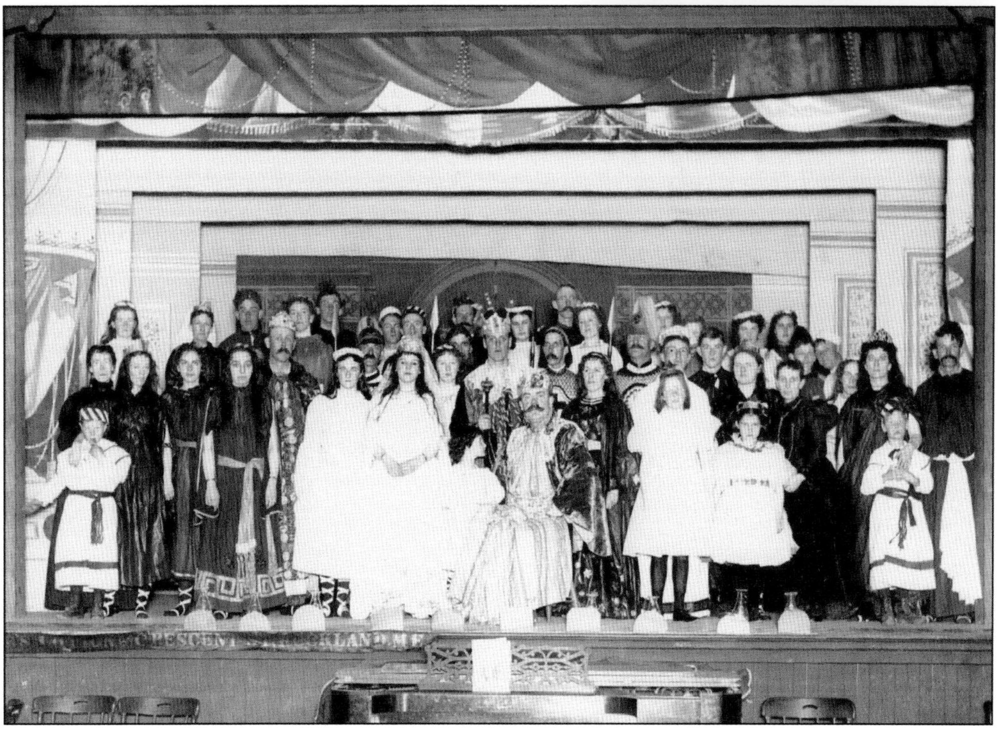

On March 31, 1897, local talent produced the cantata *Queen Esther*. Those interested can verify that this is Barber's Hall (above the old Washington Trust Bank) by climbing to the second floor of Hope Valley Antiques to check the stage, including those brackets at the upper corners. This space was a weekend movie theater known as the Strand through the 1940s. The ticket and projection windows are still in place.

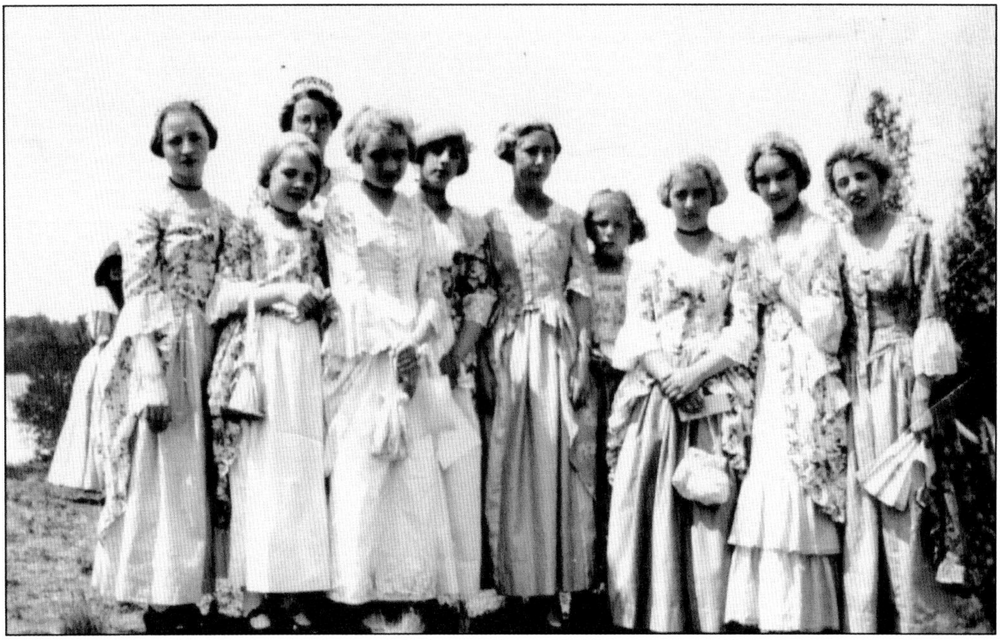

Lucy (Mrs. Roy) Rawlings wrote and directed *A Child's History of Our Great Country* as a Memorial Day pageant in 1921.

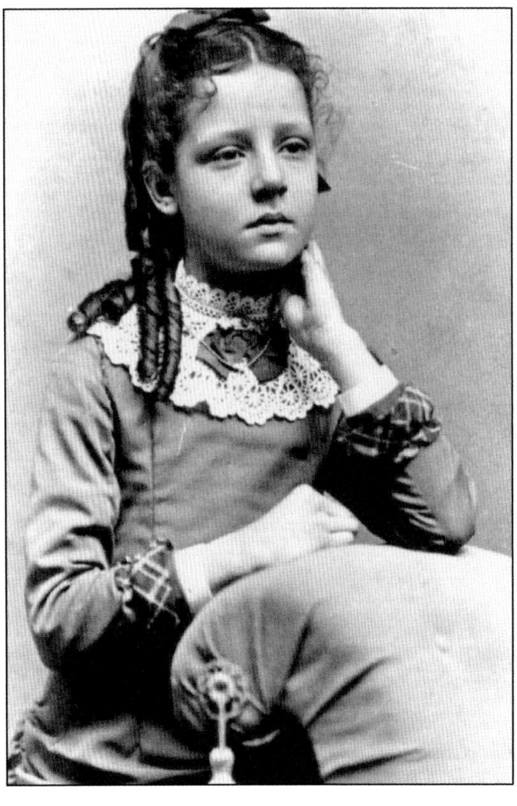

This Annie Greene is not the revered kindergarten teacher, but a girl of the same name from the previous generation.

Nellie Nichols was a telephone operator.

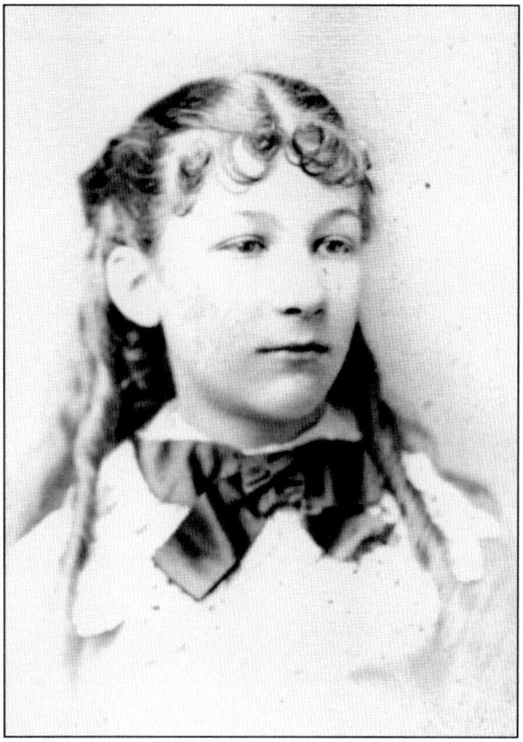

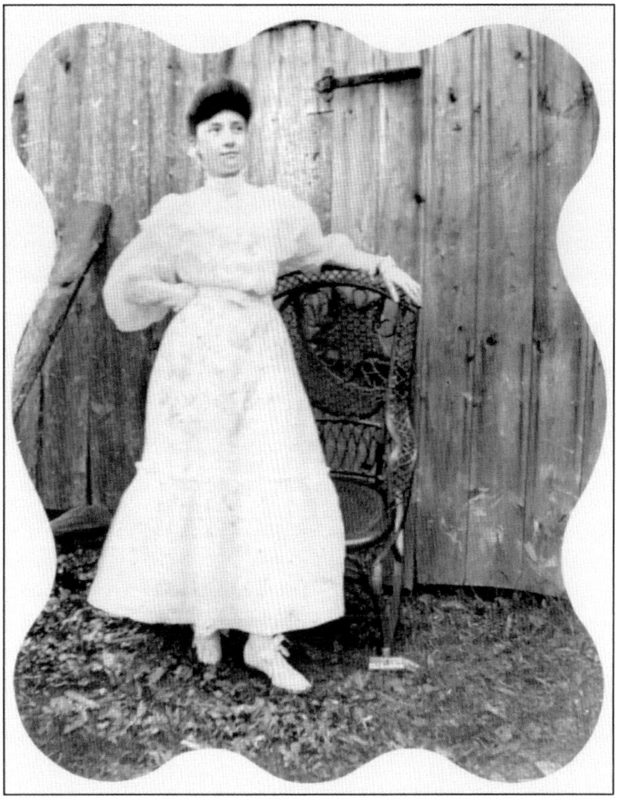

Evelyn Palmer of Rockville married William Taylor. This image, with its creative mat, came from L. Saunders Photos of Rockville.

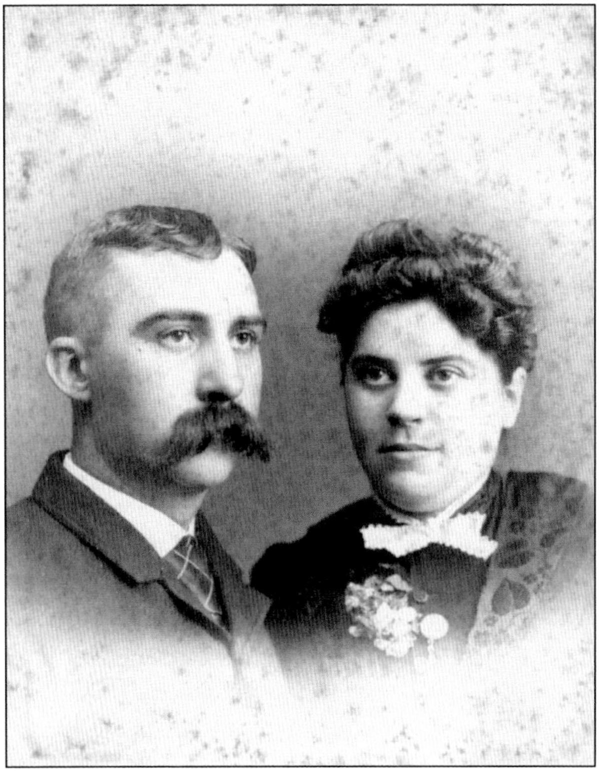

This 1889 portrait of Mr. and Mrs. E. E. Kenyon is unusual in that it shows husband and wife together.

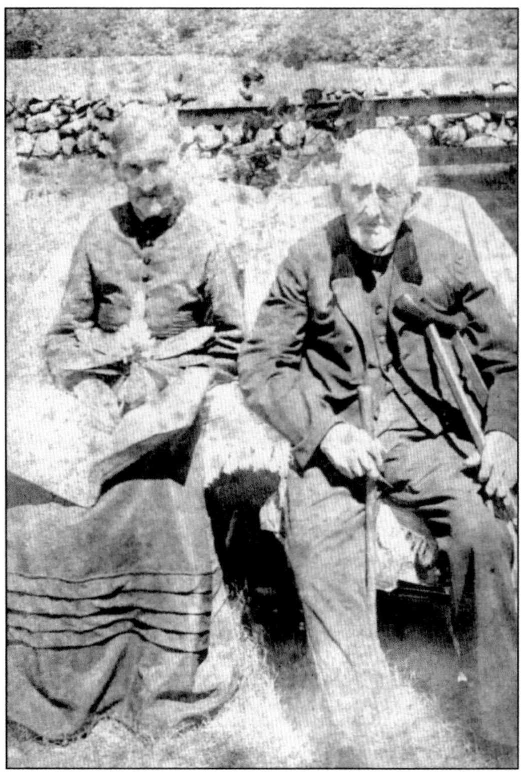

Murfred and Mercy Burdick could never have dreamed of photography when they were born during George Washington's second term. Mr. Burdick was 96 when he died in 1888. Mercy departed this life, just short of 101, in 1896.

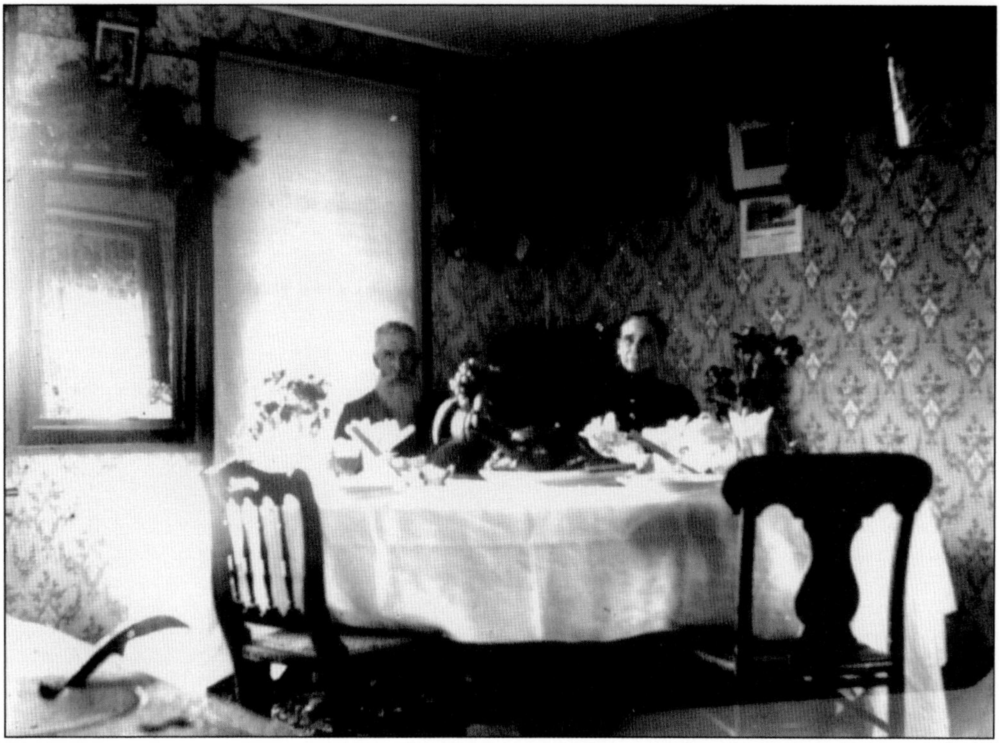

Abel and Julia Kenyon share a holiday dinner in their Rockville home *c.* 1890.

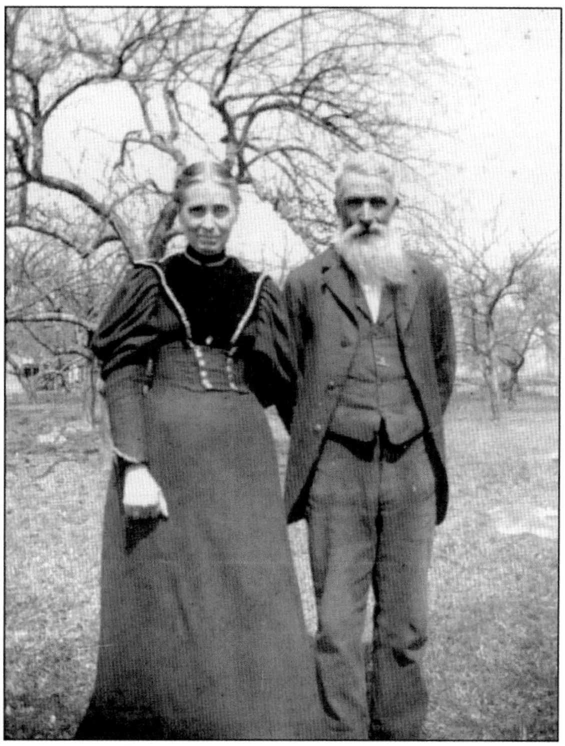

Few couples appear in photographs from this time period. The Kenyons seem to have been both happy and comfortable in each other's company.

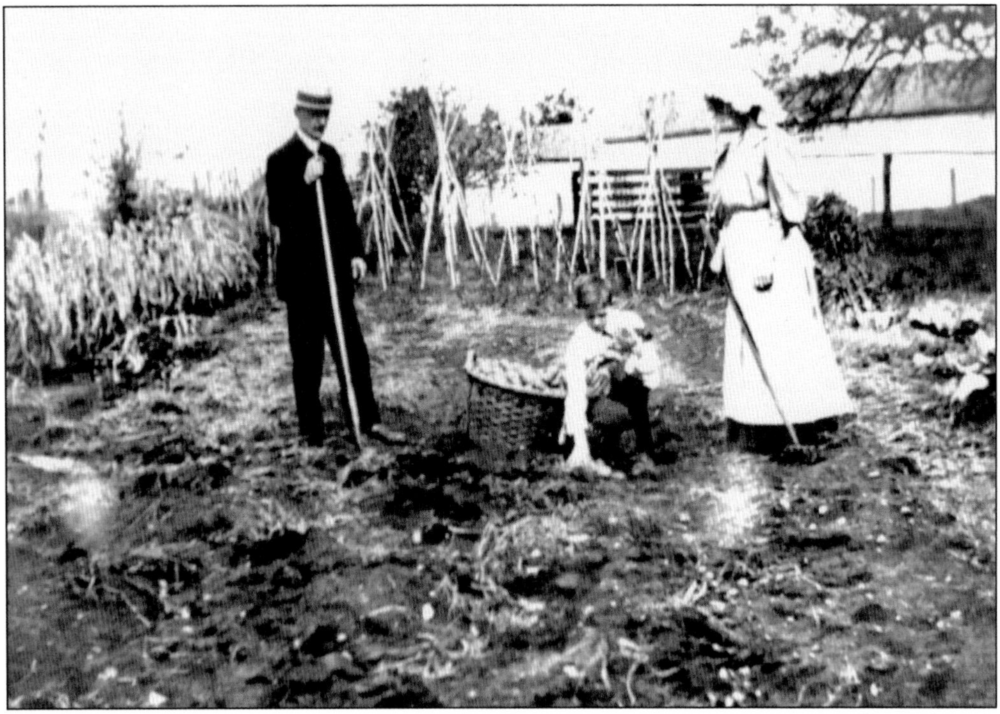

Mr. and Mrs. Christopher are gardening at their home on Main Street in Hope Valley—though it looks like young Master Christopher is doing most of the work. Notice how formally the fellows are dressed.

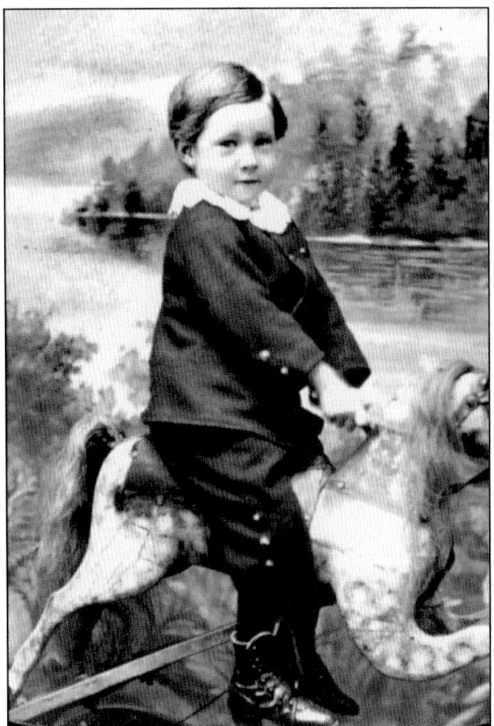

The identity of the child in this *carte de visite* from Pascoag is a little uncertain. While the name of Mary Watrous has been suggested, it is almost certainly May Nichols, who later donated the land on which the Langworthy Library is built.

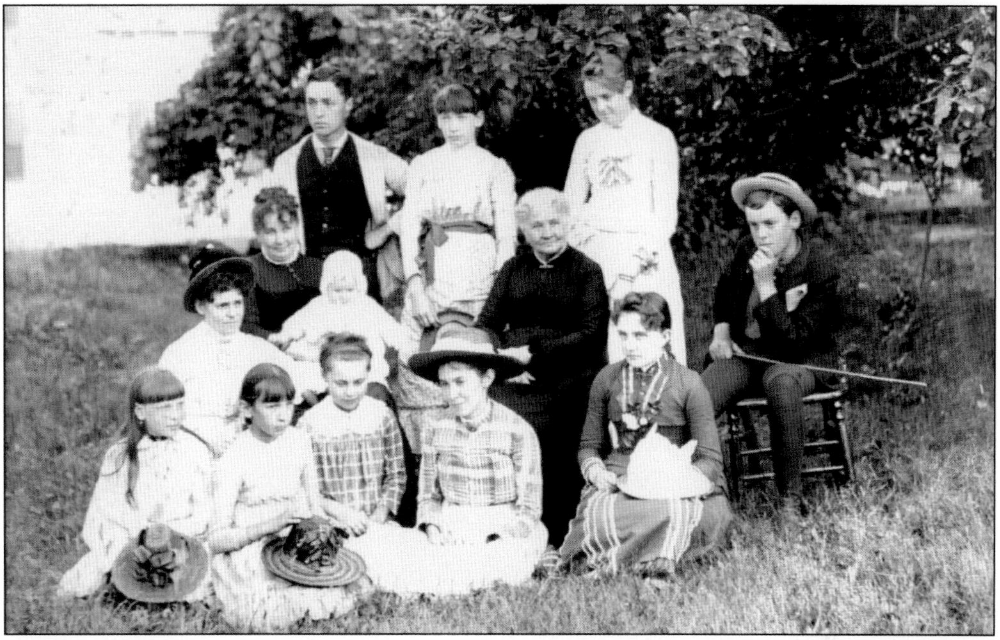

The girl at the front right in this gathering of the A. G. Nichols family is probably May Nichols. The boy at the far right seems to be contemplating exactly what to do with that switch; it is probably best that we do not know.

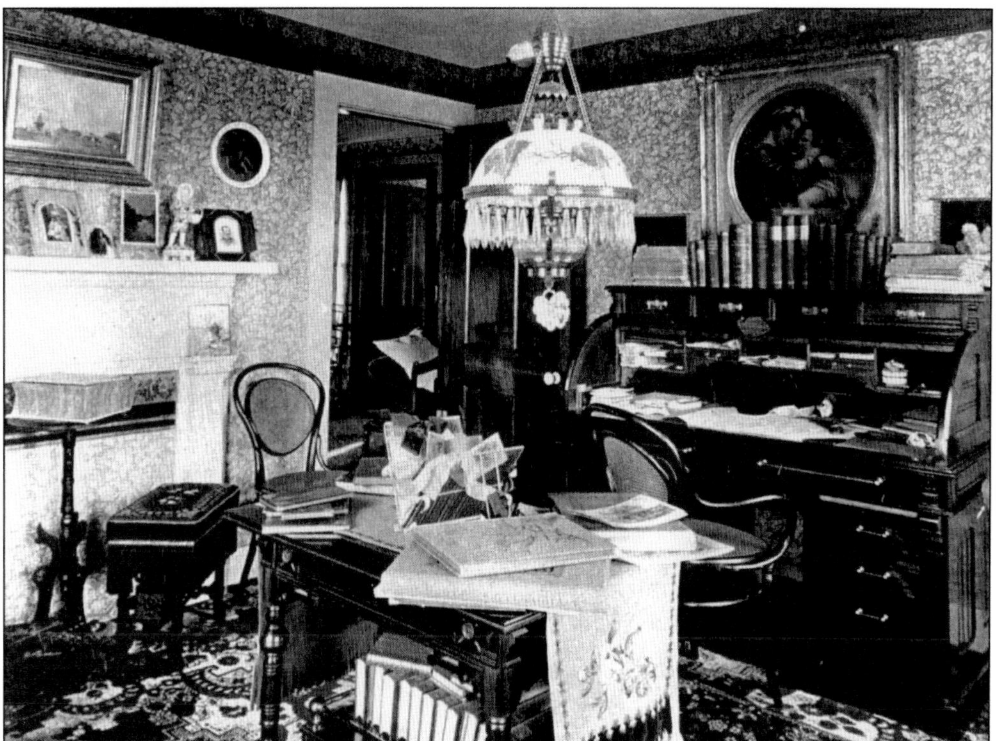

Amos Nichols was a prominent local businessman. His study reflected the traditional Victorian style of cramming every space.

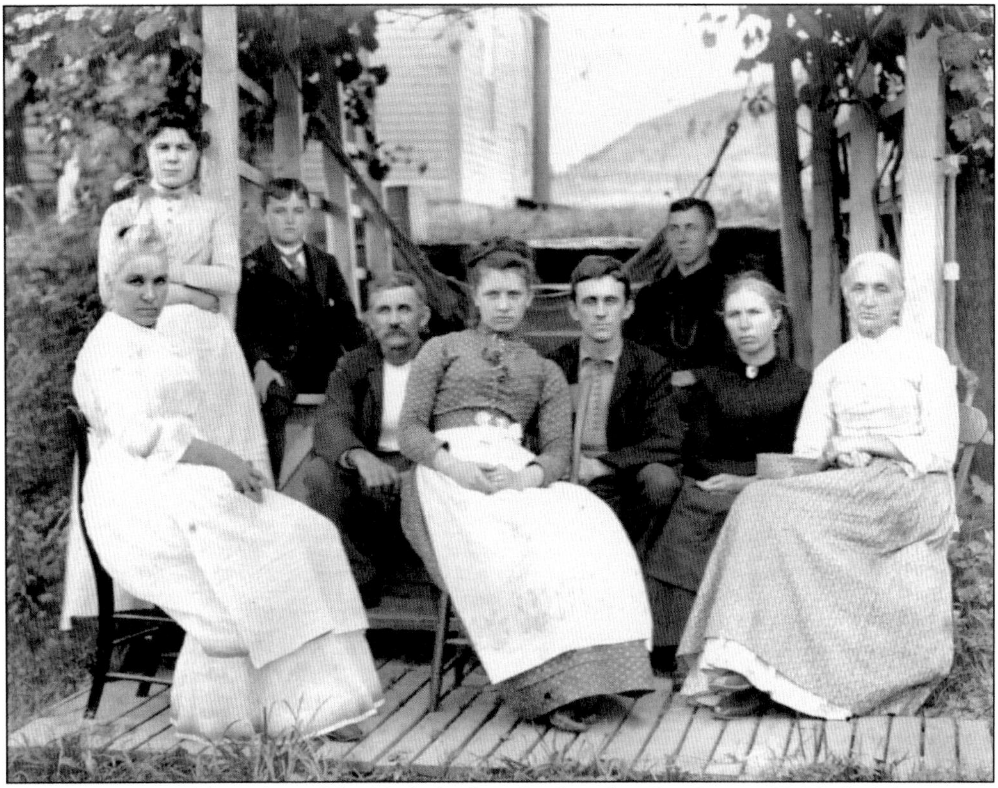

There were several branches of the Nichols clan. Gathered at the George H. Nichols home are, from left to right, Mrs. Jason Rathbun, Carrie Bell Rathbun, Will Wheeler, George Nichols, Cora Nichols, Frank Nichols, Stephen Hall, Mrs. Burdick, and Mrs. George Nichols.

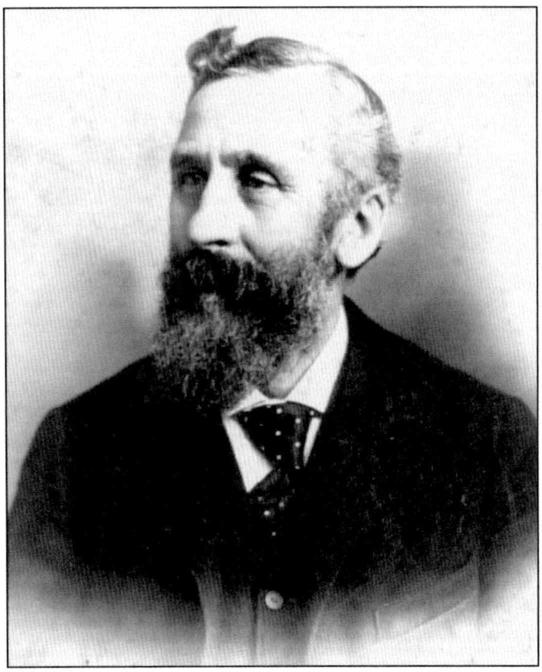

Amos G. Nichols, besides his other work in business and the community, was superintendent of the Hope Valley Baptist Sunday School in 1897.

Rev. C. L. Frost was pastor at the Hope Valley Baptist Church from 1860 through 1867.

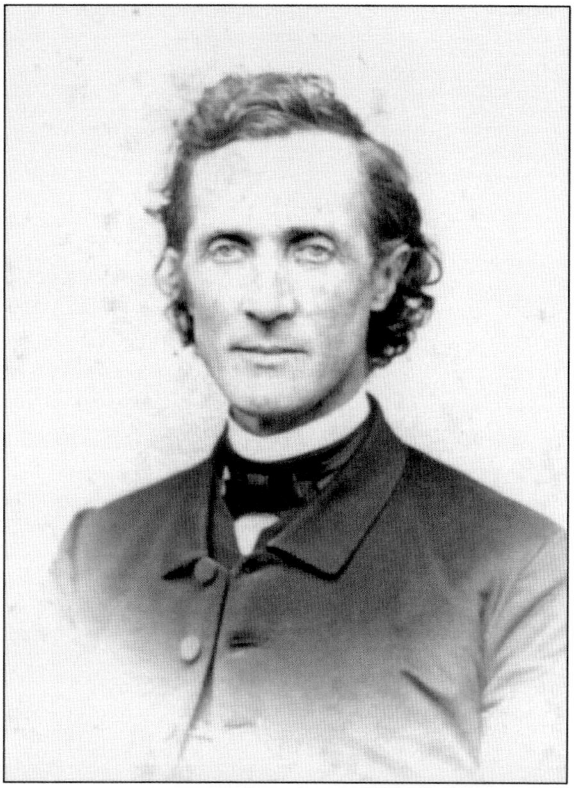

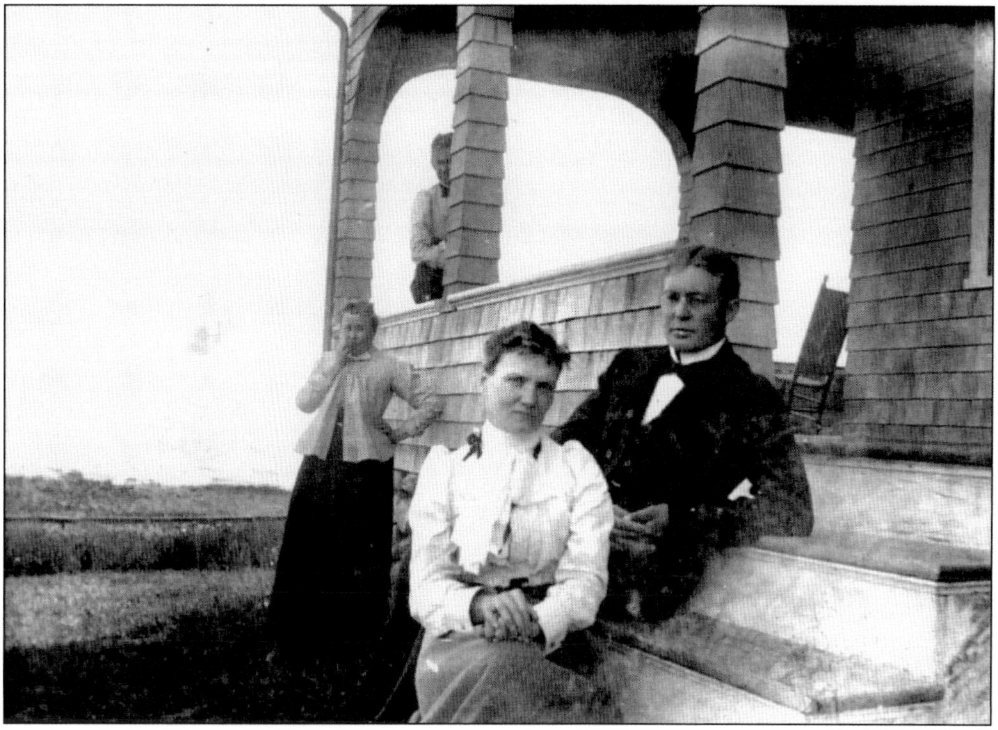

Rev. and Mrs. Eric L. Lindh served the church from 1897 through 1905.

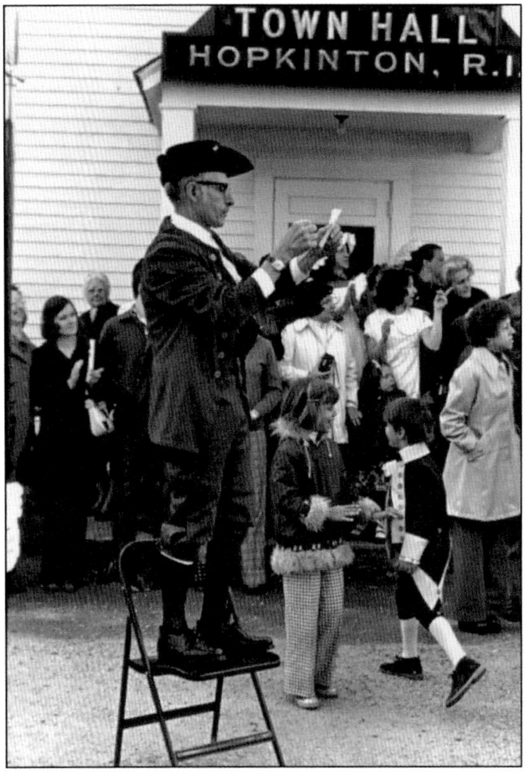

As the decades rolled on, Hopkinton thought more and more about its history. Nathan Kaye recalled the town's early days as chairman of the 1976 Bicentennial Commission.

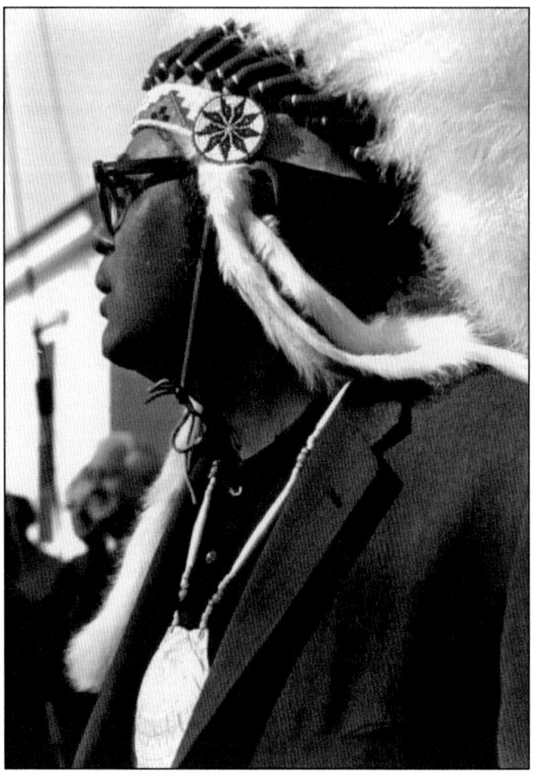

Walter Babcock, also seen at the bicentennial observances, demonstrated the enduring Narragansett presence.

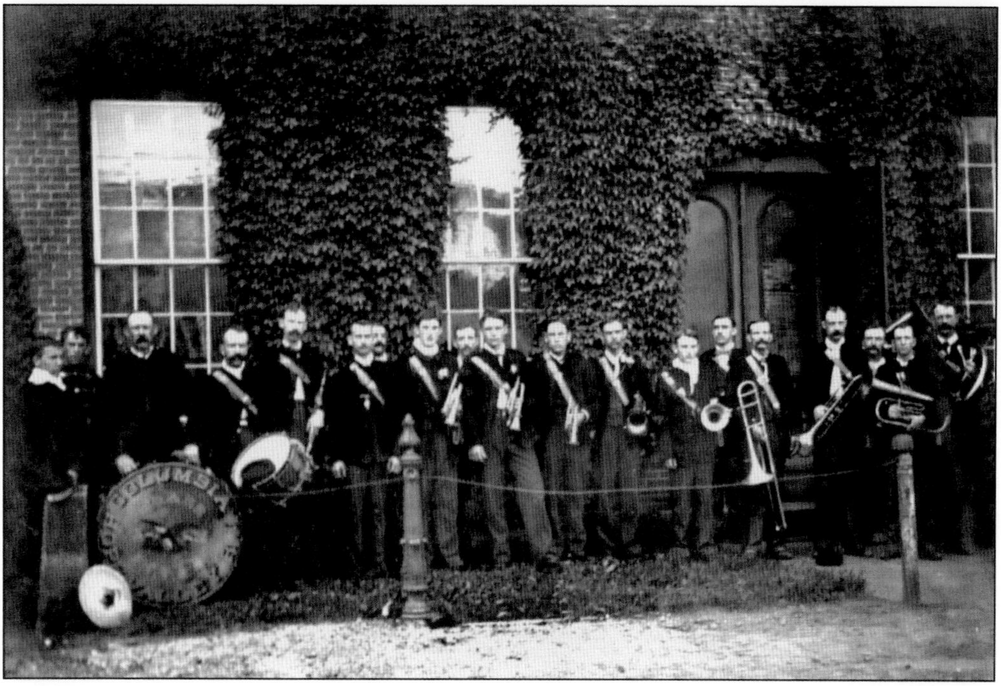

Celebrations are part of any town's life. The Columbia Brass gathered for the Fourth of July in 1897.

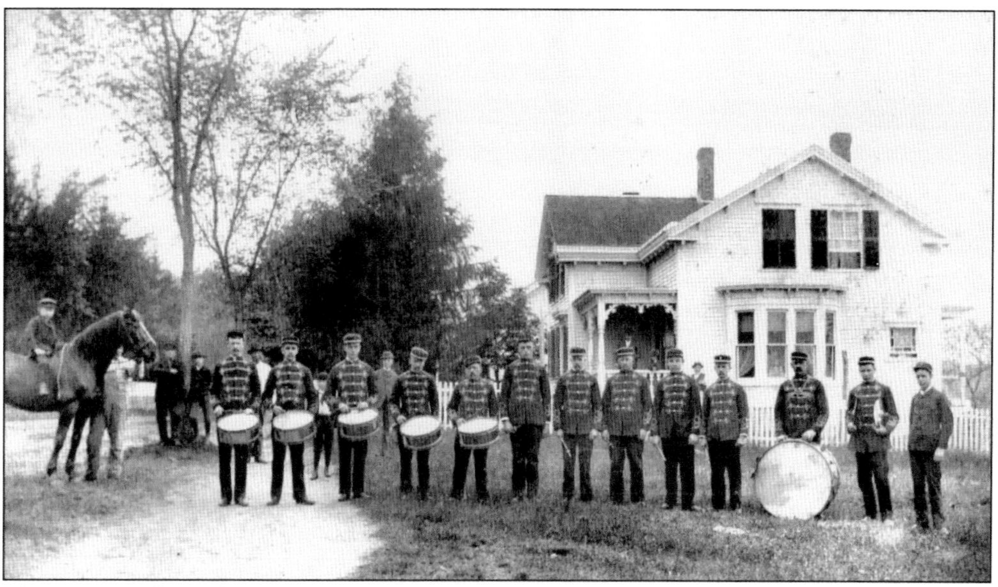

The Hope Valley Fife and Drum Corps gathered on High Street for the Fourth of July. (The year is not known.) With no radios, televisions, or stereos, communities made their own music. Because transportation was limited, people found their social life among their neighbors.

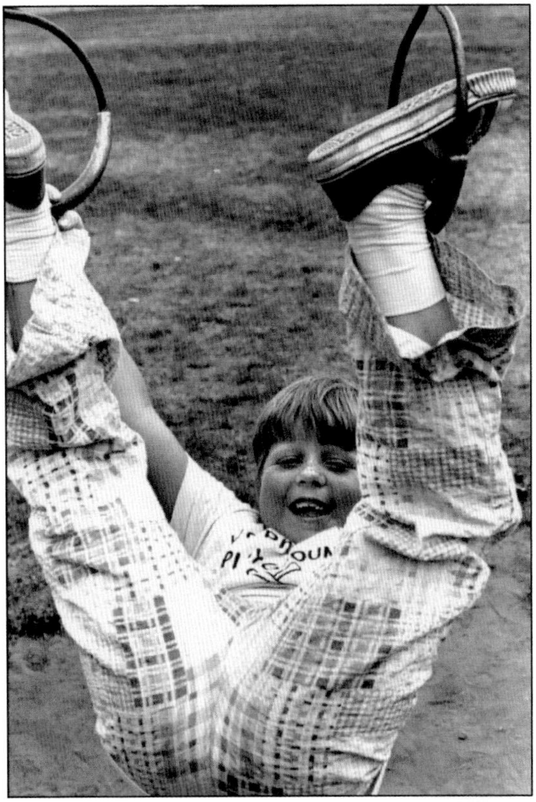

Even in more modern days, places like the playground at Dow Memorial Field (named for Pfc. James Dow, who was killed at Anzio) still attract crowds of kids and grownups.

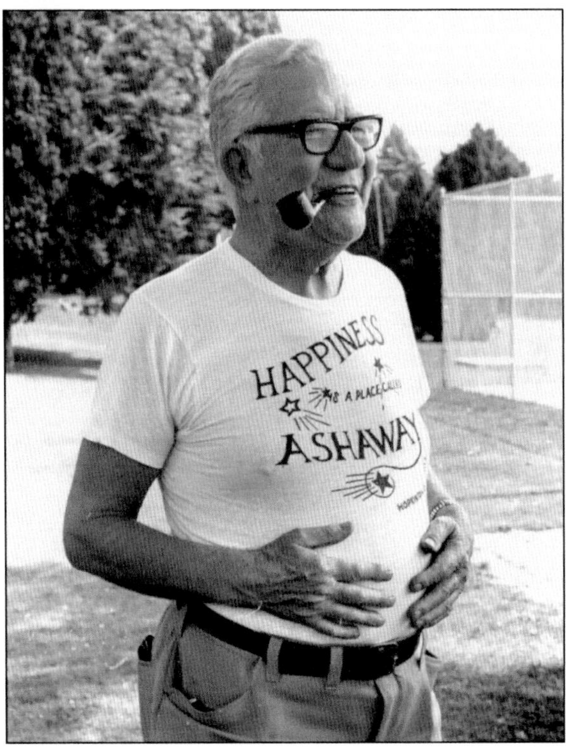

As Julian Crandall's T-shirt proves, in places like Ashaway (or other Hopkinton villages), community is alive and well.

Two

Nature's Traces

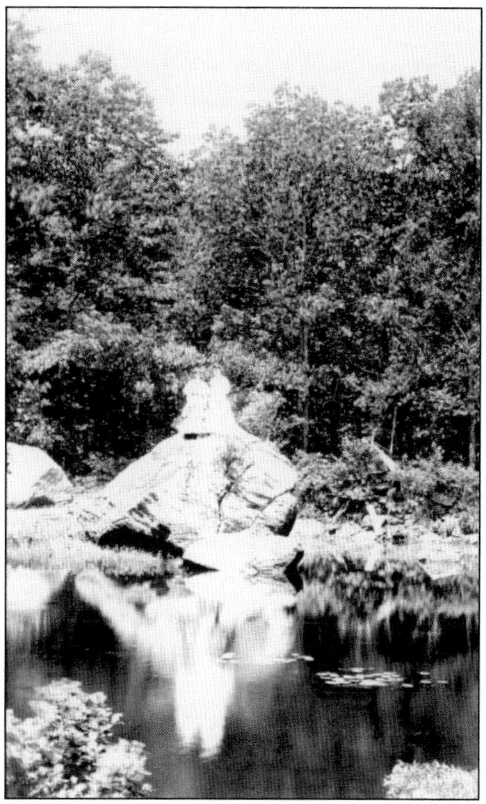

Hopkinton was born in the Ice Age, when the last glacier dumped its terminal moraine. Scraped almost bare of topsoil, Hopkinton got in its place tons of granite rocks and boulders, which were later shaped into foundations and into the stone walls that still crisscross the town. Most farming and grazing has ended, so forests of hemlock, oak, rhododendron, and pine once again blanket the land. Tucked away in that forest are the clefts and gorges in which sleep Long and Ell Ponds. Hopkinton is technically an inland town, but the sandy soil, the passing gull, the daily sea breeze, and the occasional hurricane are traces of the ocean and Block Island Sound, scarcely a dozen miles away. Brooks slide down the rolling hills into Wood River. Here and there a dam widens the river into a millpond, but much of its route is known only by the muskrat, the kingfisher, the bushwhacking fisherman, and the riders of silently gliding canoes.

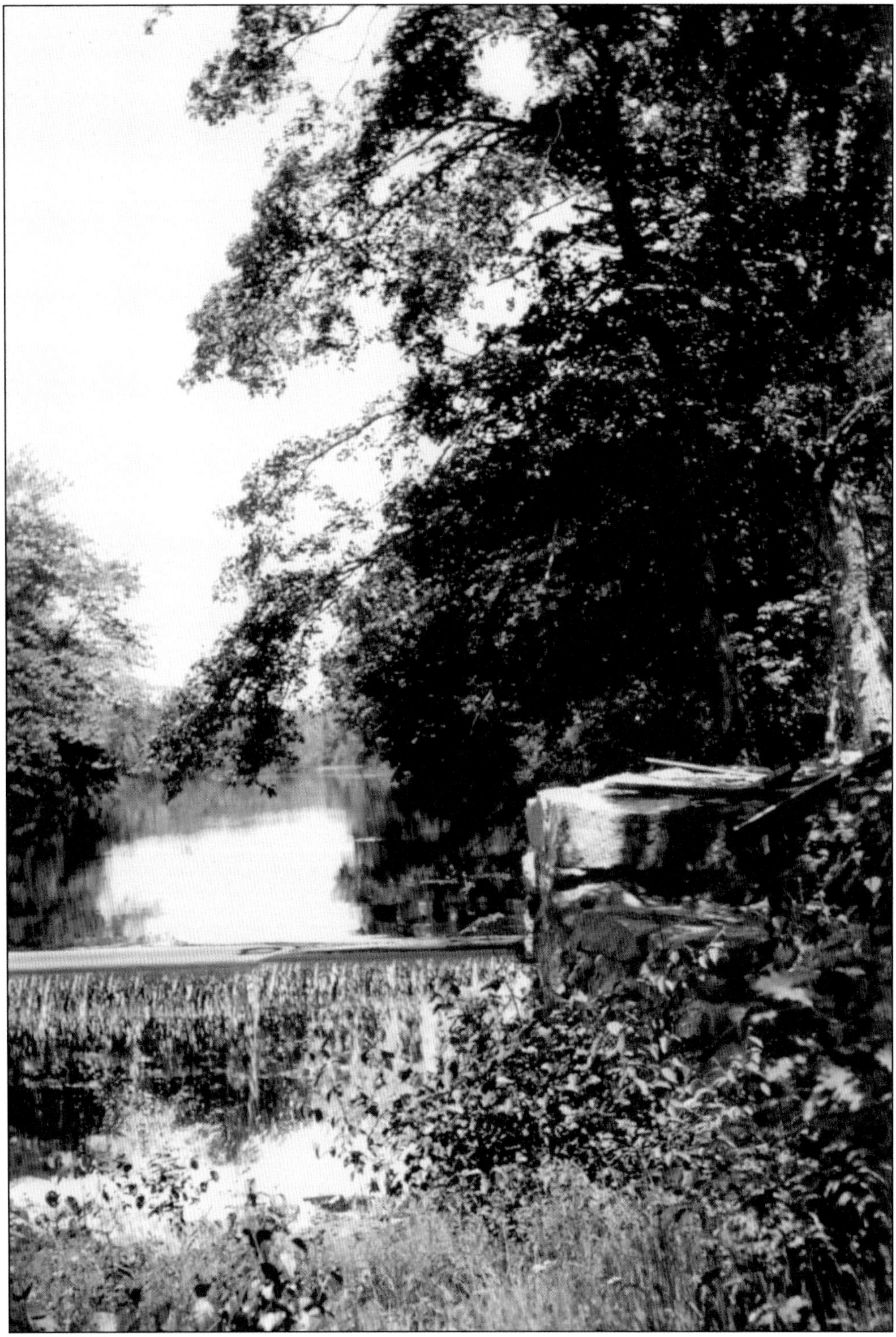

Waterpower brought Hopkinton food and wealth. No stream was too small, and no head too short, to dam.

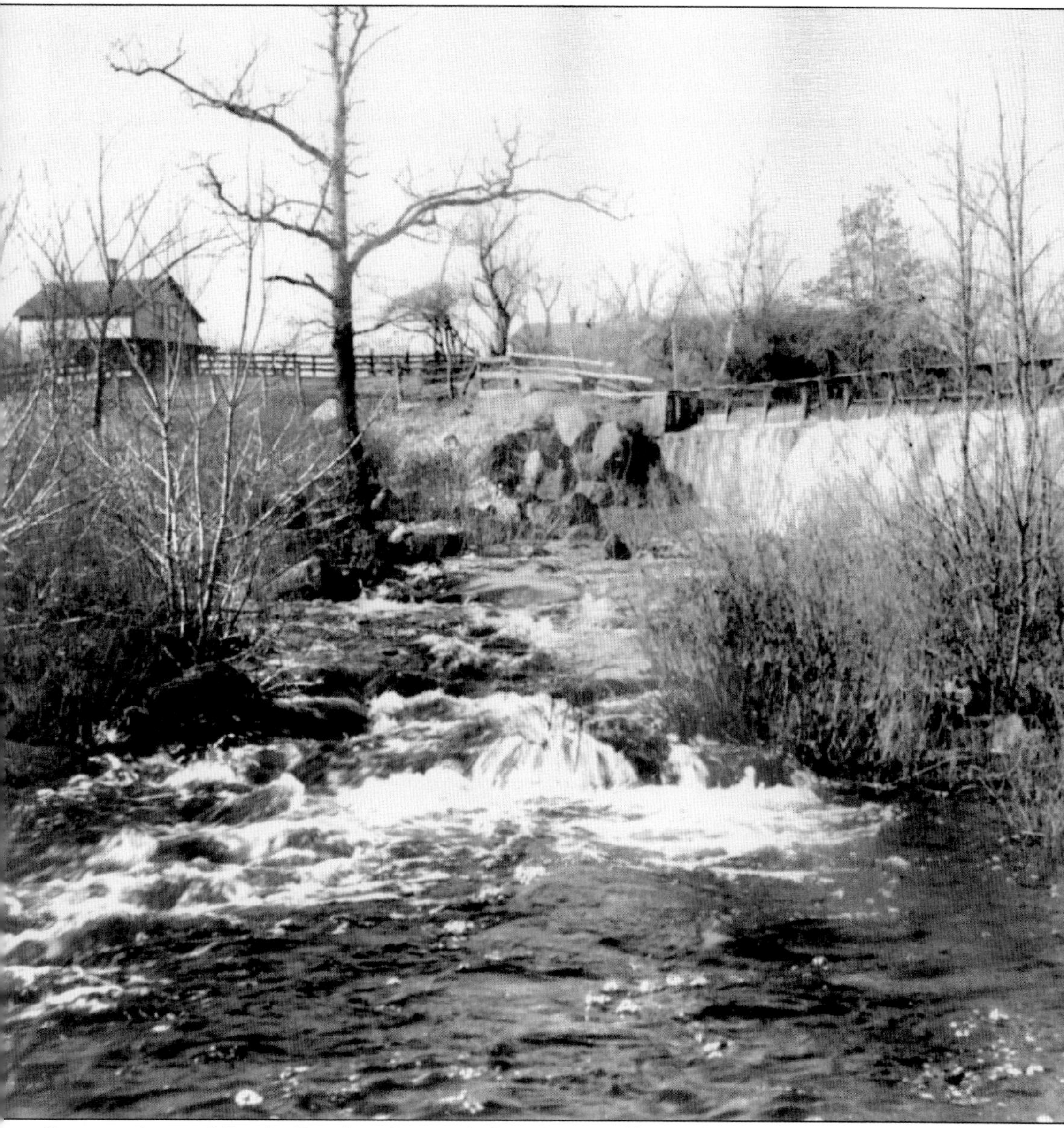

Pioneers dammed Brushy Brook to form mile-long Locustville Pond.

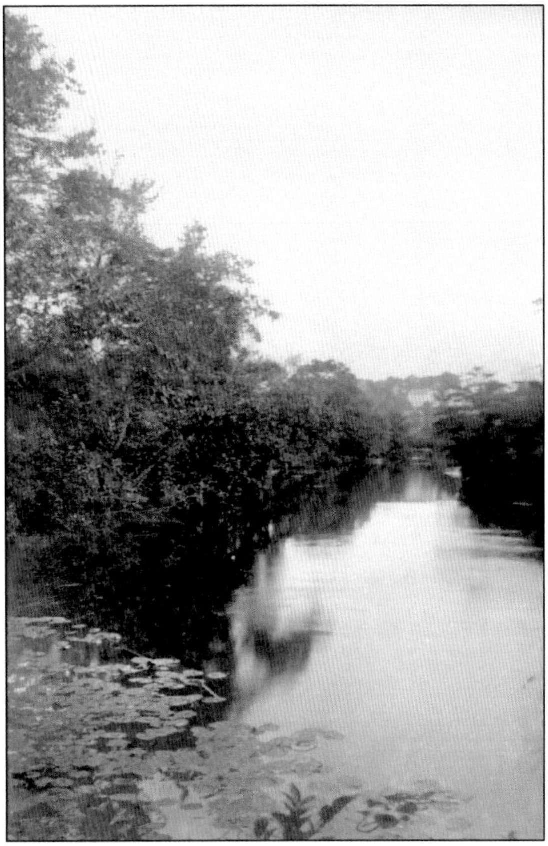

After Wood River receives Brushy Brook, Hope Valley Dam spreads it out and slows it down. Hopkinton's ponds, though lovely, are deceptively placid. Their pent-up power is unimaginable.

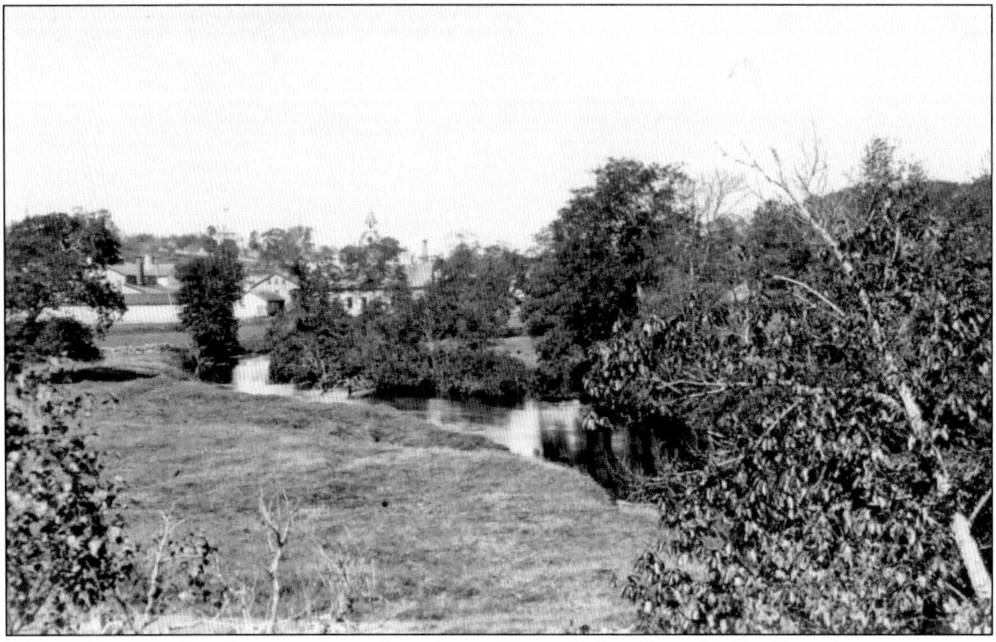

The collection of machine works and woolen mills just below Hope Valley Dam bears testimony to the power of Hopkinton's bodies of water.

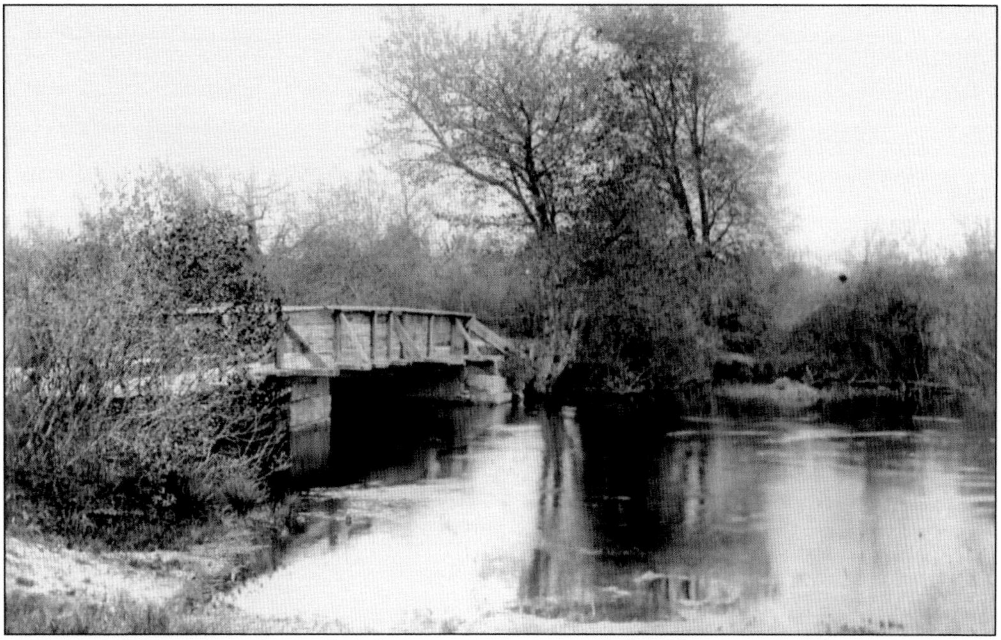

Wyoming Bridge, just a few rods below Wyoming Dam, crosses the town line formed by Wood River without fanfare. Up and down the watercourse, mills, homes, and businesses are clustered along each bank indiscriminately.

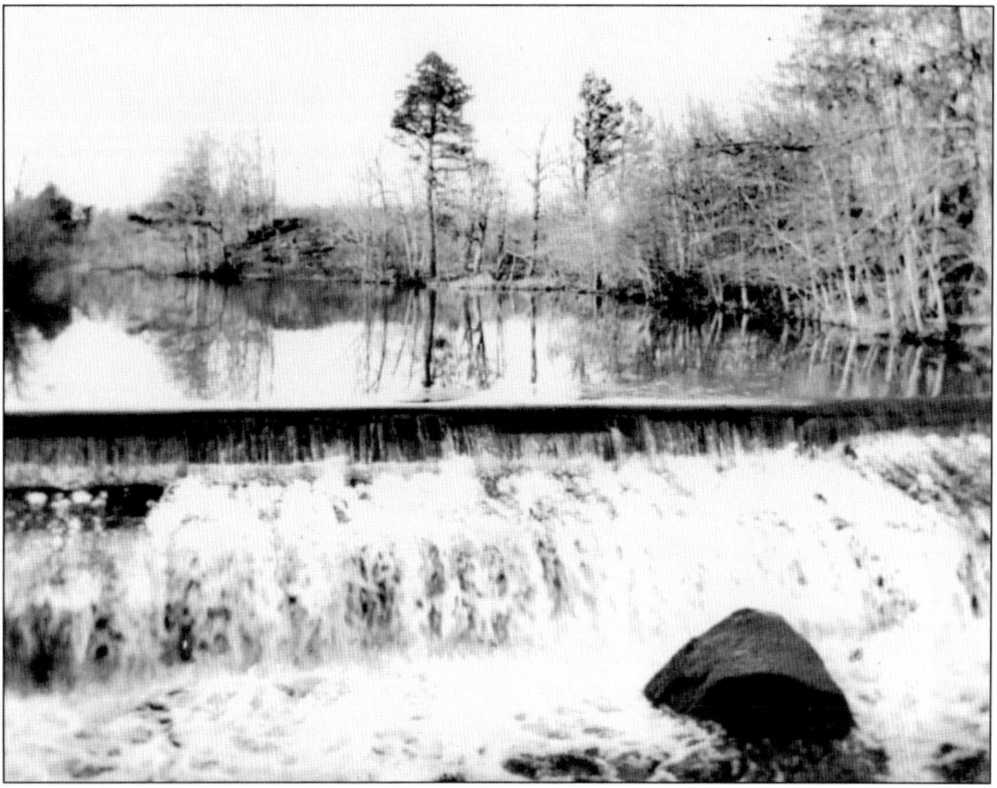

There is decent fishing well upstream, just above Barberville Dam.

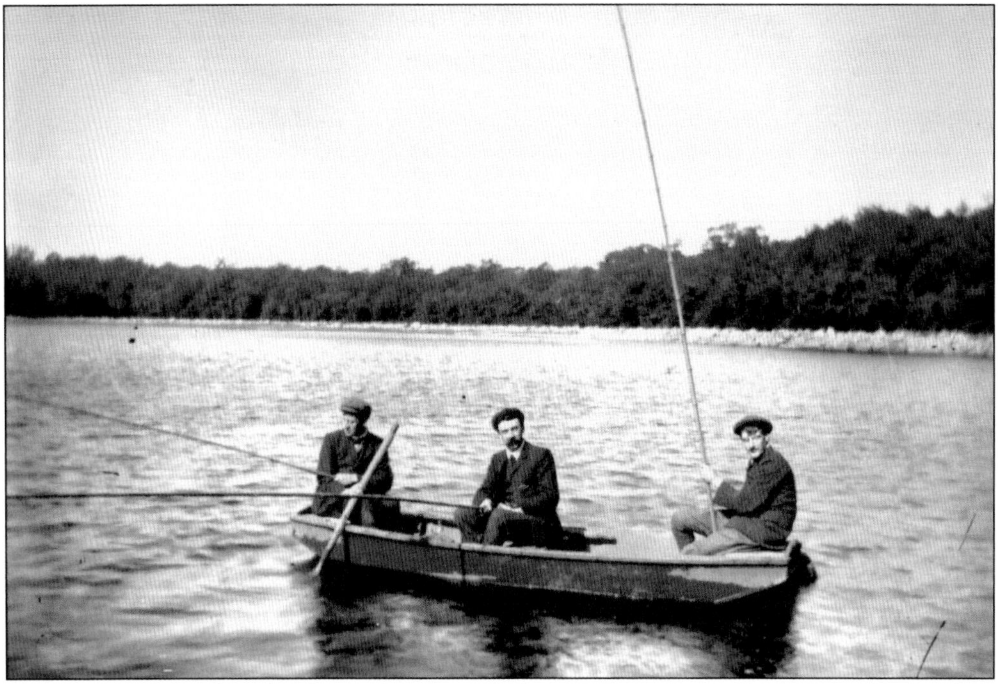

These three intrepid anglers have chosen to challenge Yawgoog Pond in a pram shorter than any of their fishing rods. Notice how formally dressed they are. In a day when few people learned to swim and most folks wore heavy woolen clothes year round, drownings were frequent. Scout camps, like the one that arose here on Yawgoog, helped change that.

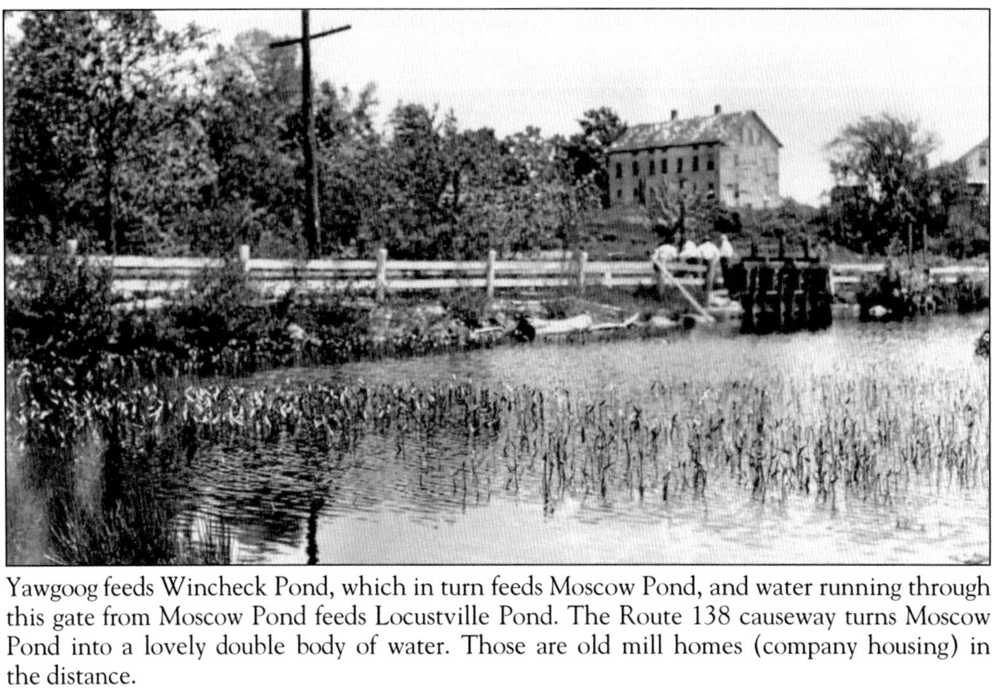

Yawgoog feeds Wincheck Pond, which in turn feeds Moscow Pond, and water running through this gate from Moscow Pond feeds Locustville Pond. The Route 138 causeway turns Moscow Pond into a lovely double body of water. Those are old mill homes (company housing) in the distance.

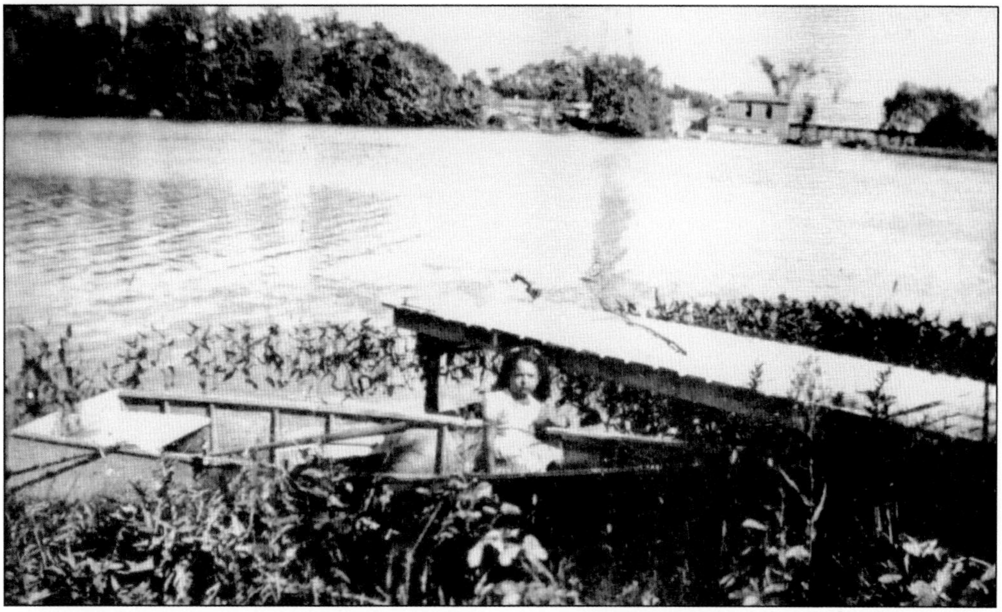

Succeeding mill owners created and expanded Locustville Pond in stages over the years by damming Brushy Brook. The shore in the foreground lies behind the Eva Sheldon Wright house and Langworthy Library. Locustville Mill, just beyond the dam with its since vanished water tower, is now Ure Outfitters. (Postcard from the author's collection.)

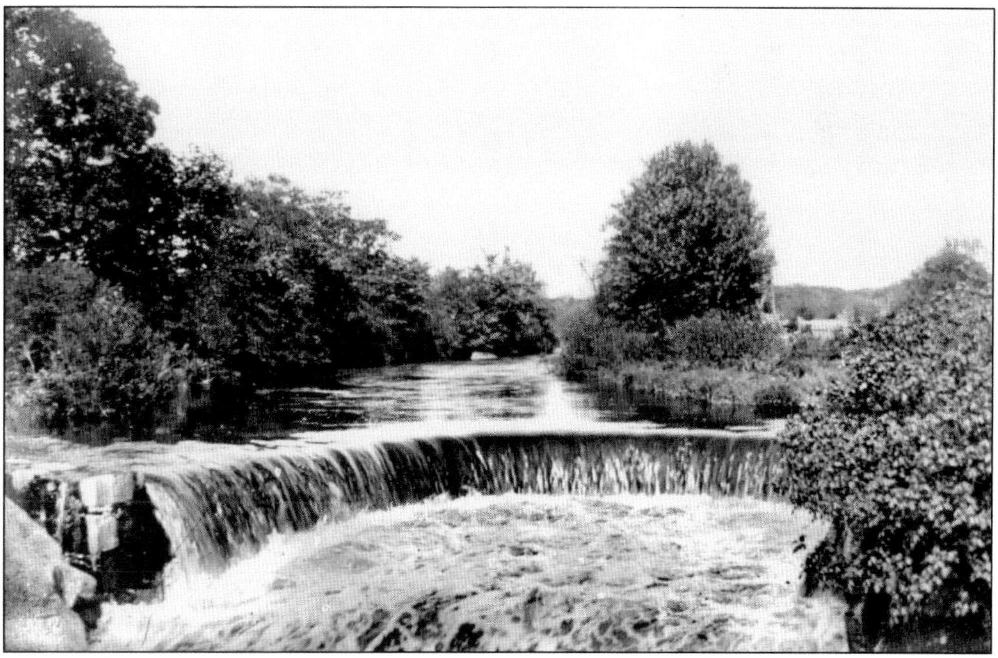

Horseshoe dams relieve some of the stress on the structure.

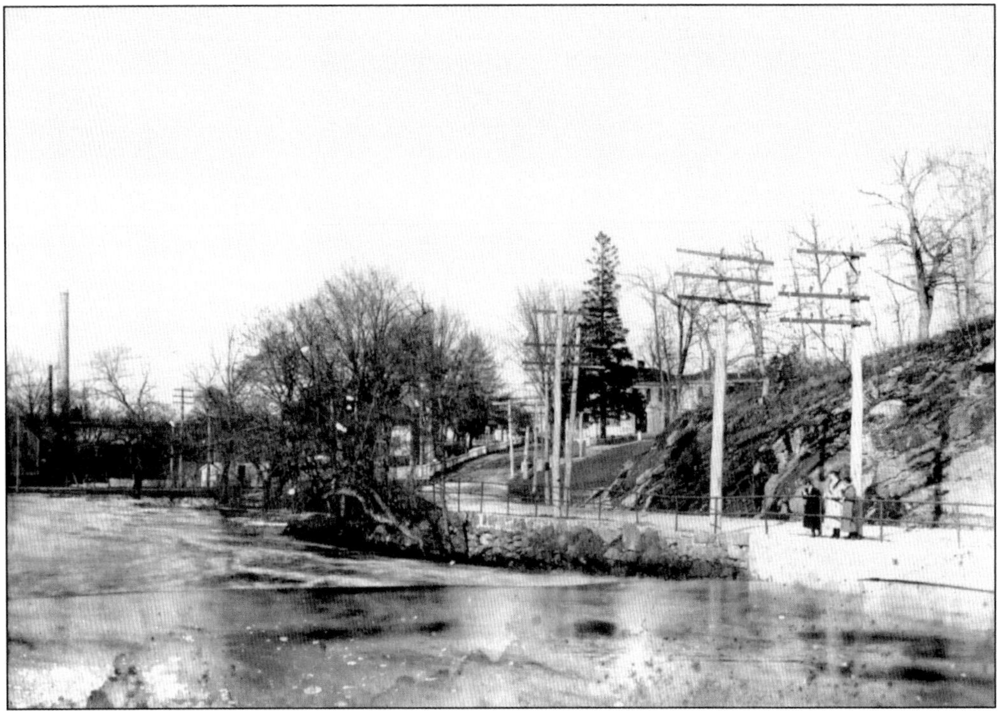

The Ashaway River, though not especially large, can be impressive in a flood; judging from the state of the trees, this particular flood probably resulted from snowmelt or heavy spring rains. *Ashawog* means "cold spring" in Narragansett.

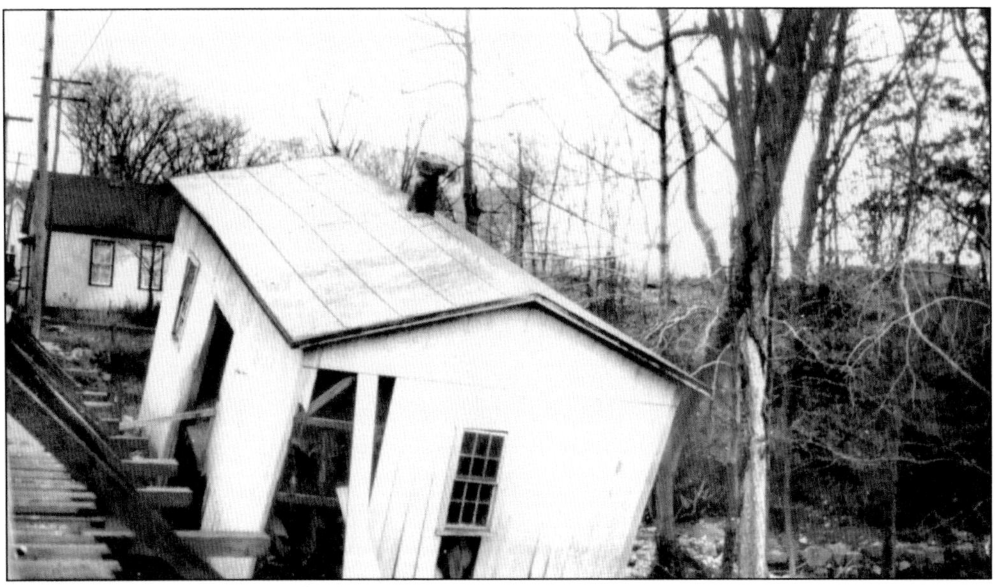

This 1927 flood was extremely destructive.

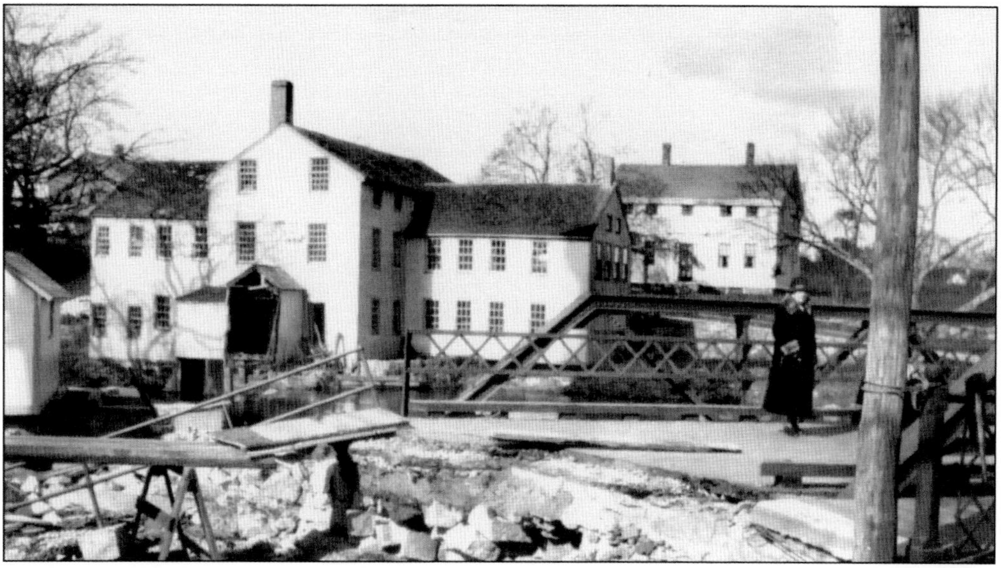

The heavy engineering of the bridge to the right is an interesting contrast to the makeshift bridge on the left.

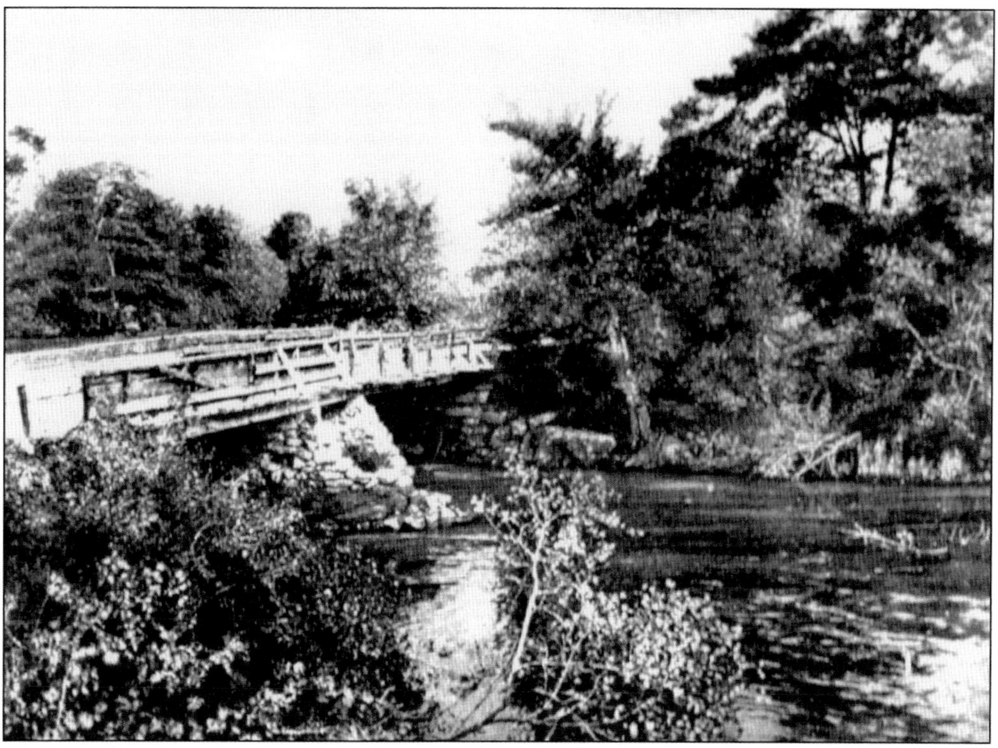

Meeting House Bridge near Ashaway helped satisfy three prime concerns of early settlers—felling the trees, bridging the brooks, and clearing the stone.

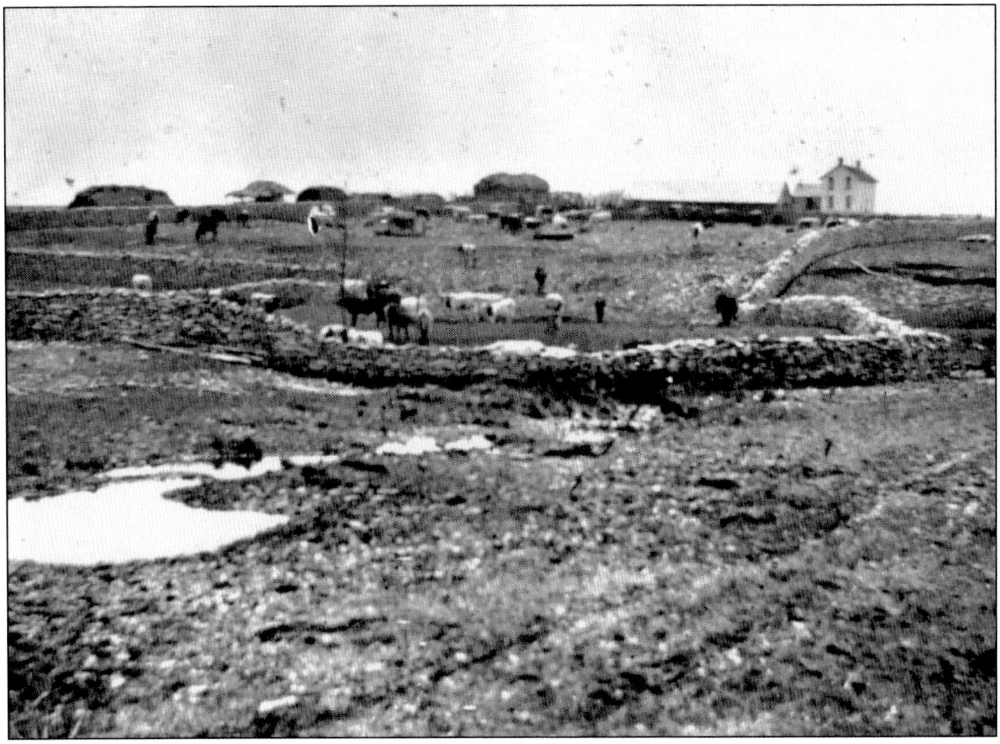

At Dr. Joseph Kenyon's home outside Ashaway, fieldstones were put to use as stock pens.

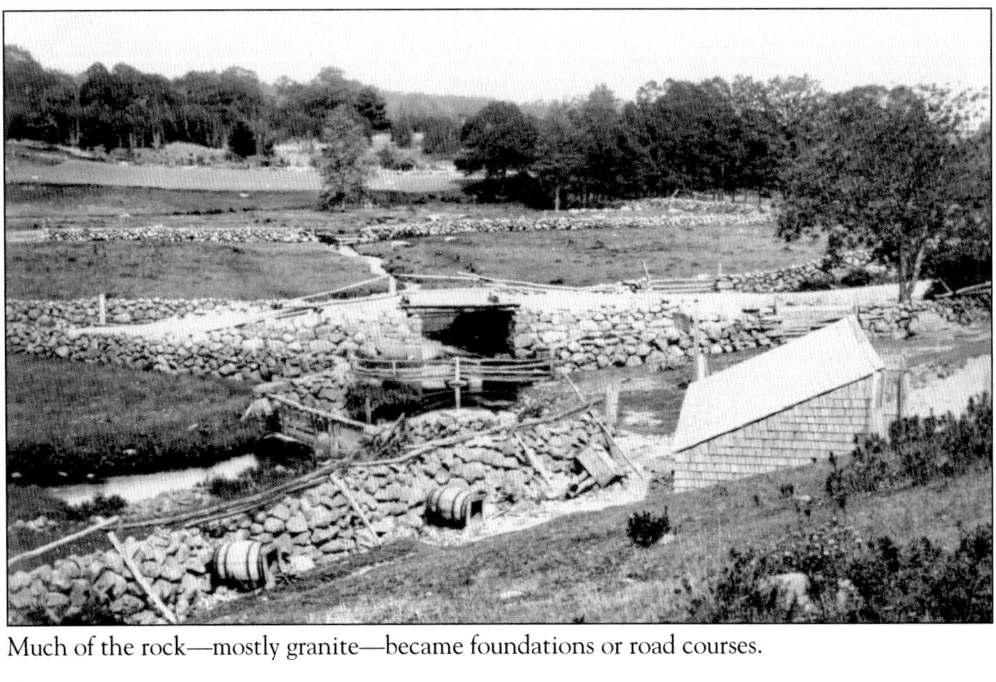

Much of the rock—mostly granite—became foundations or road courses.

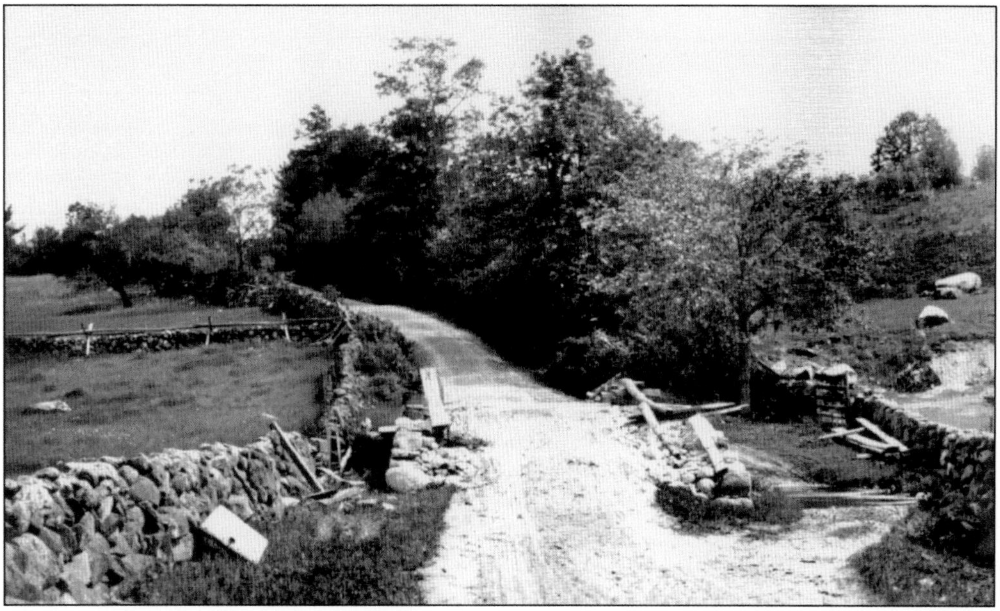

The ubiquitous New England stone wall was, as much as anything else, a measure of desperation on the farmer's part. All that rock had to go *somewhere*.

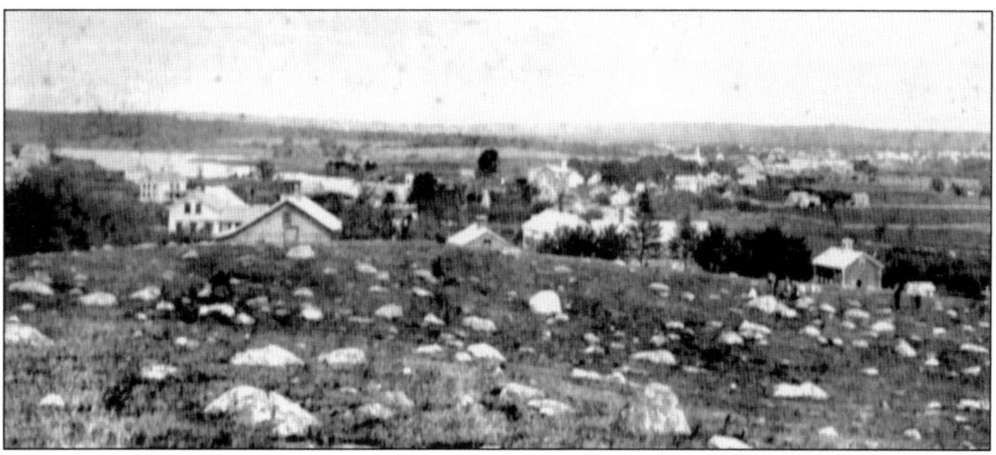

This view of Hope Valley from Highview Avenue makes one wonder, Since they pulled so much stone out, how can there be so much left?

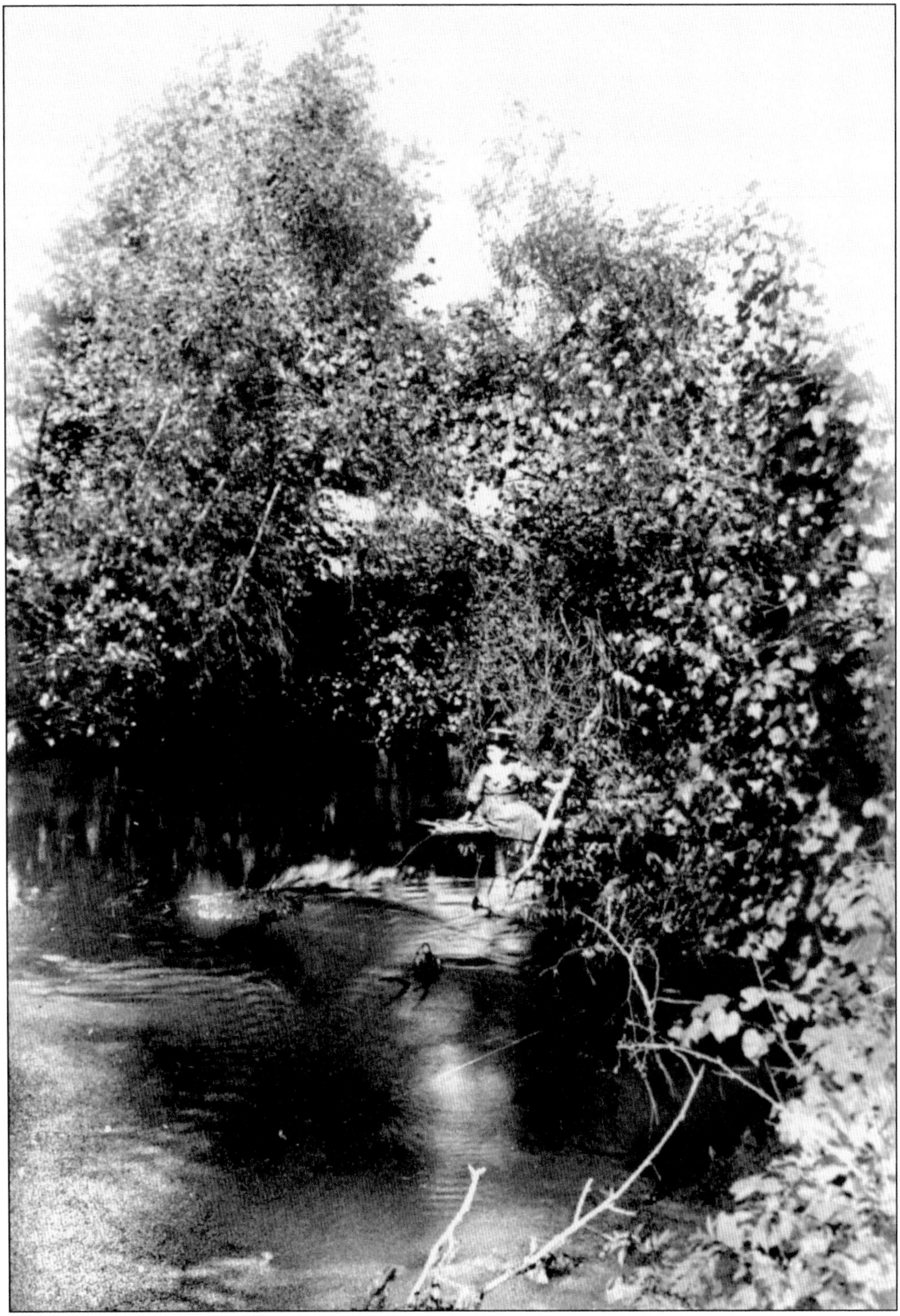

In some ways, nature has been rough on Hopkinton; in other ways, townsfolk have grappled with nature and turned it to their advantage. But there have always been children to remind us that nature also offers playfulness and peace.

Three

Cherished Spaces

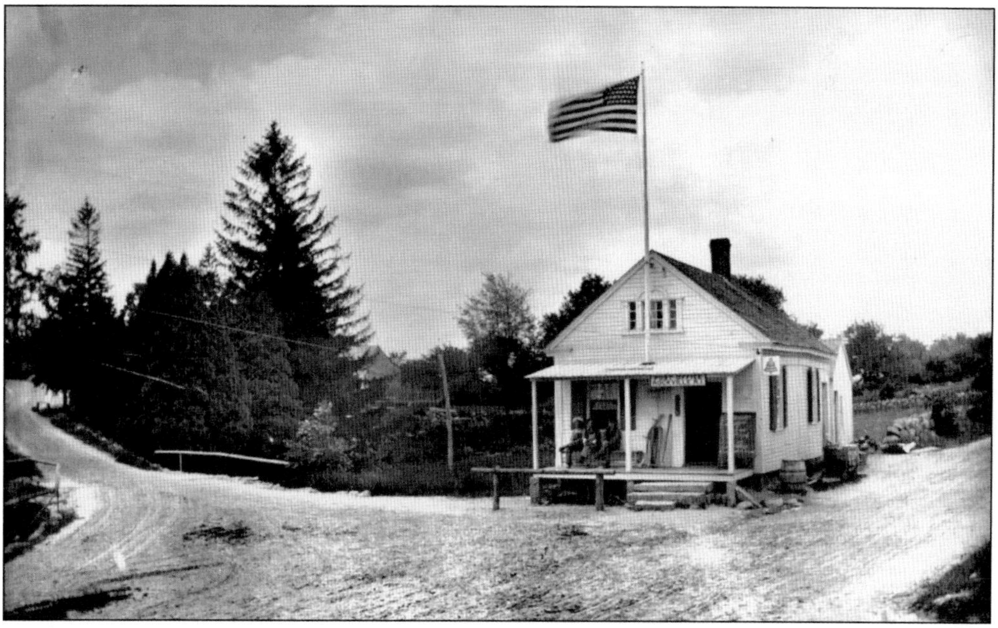

Hopkinton's villages have only unofficial names, although the names may be centuries old, and residents may assure you that adjoining houses stand in distinct villages. Hope Valley and Ashaway anchor the northern and southern ends of town. The only real "center" is tiny Hopkinton City, home of the town hall. Because communities grew up around dams and because town lines ran along rivers, Wyoming, Hope Valley, Woodville, and Alton spill into two municipalities, bewildering out-of-towners. Names have shifted over the years. Hope Valley was once Middle Iron Works, and before that was Carpenter's Mills. The name swallowed up Grantville, Locustville, and part of Wyoming. Rockville may do the same to Centerville, as Ashaway has to Bethel, Laureldale, and the Hopkinton part of Potter Hill. Off-the-track Canonchet seems safe, as does Hopkinton City. Will Tomaquag, Burdickville, and South Hopkinton endure? Each village has its own flavor, and however small each may be, there are those that love it.

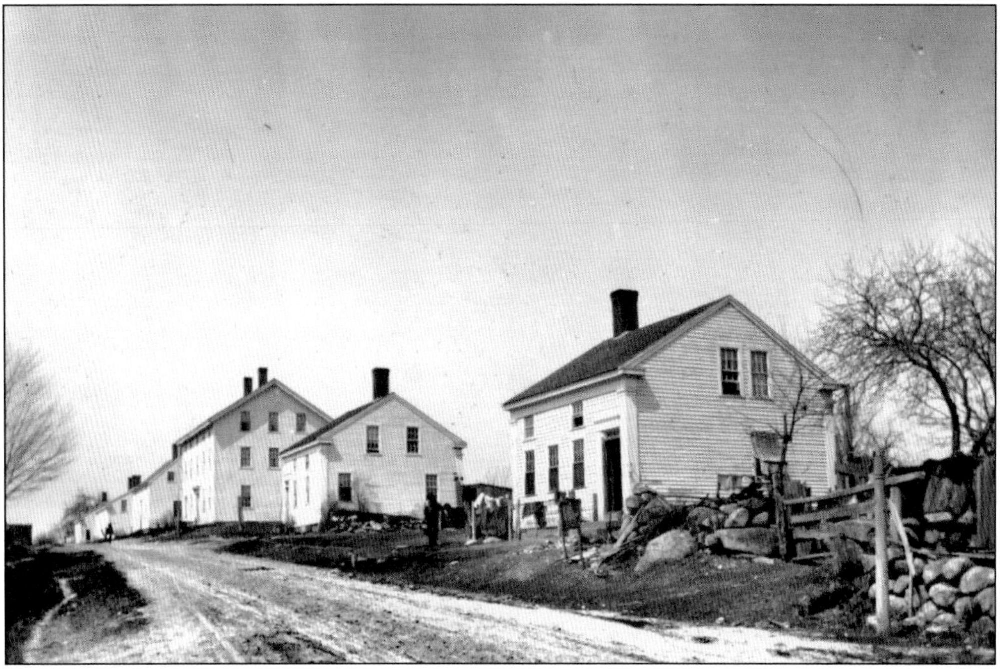

These mill homes, which varied according to an employees' rank in the company, still welcome visitors to Rockville.

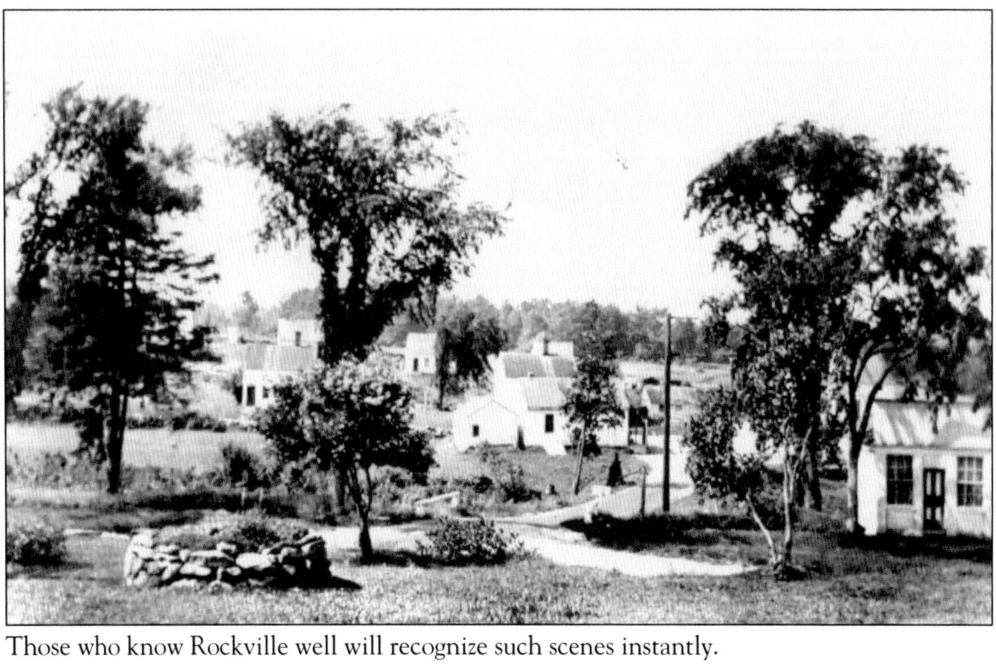

Those who know Rockville well will recognize such scenes instantly.

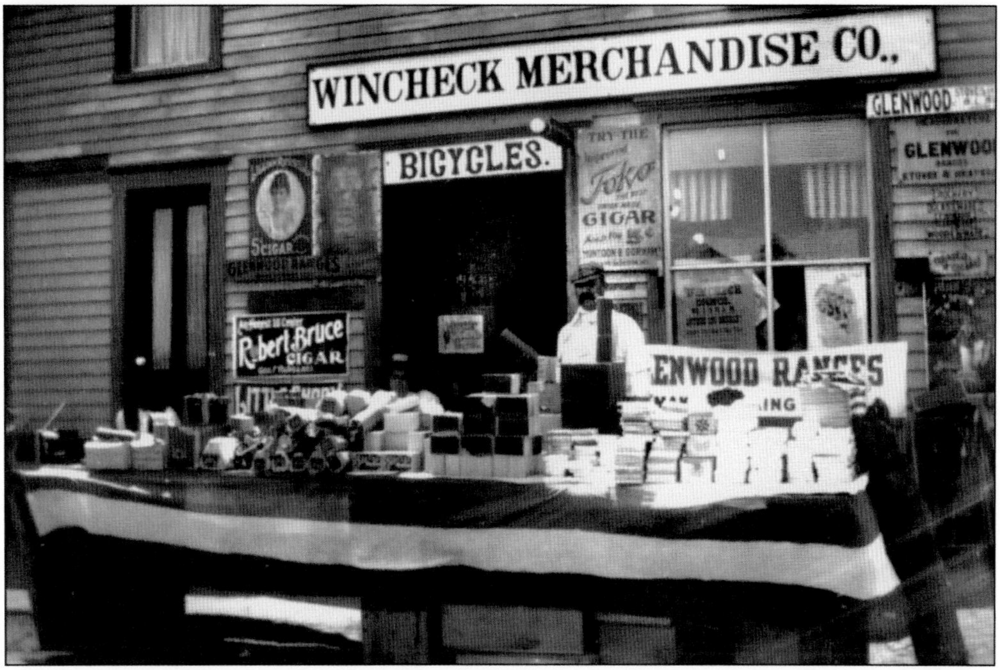

Small stores in small towns had big jobs, selling everything from stoves, cigars, and bikes to crockery, tinware, woodenware, and fireworks.

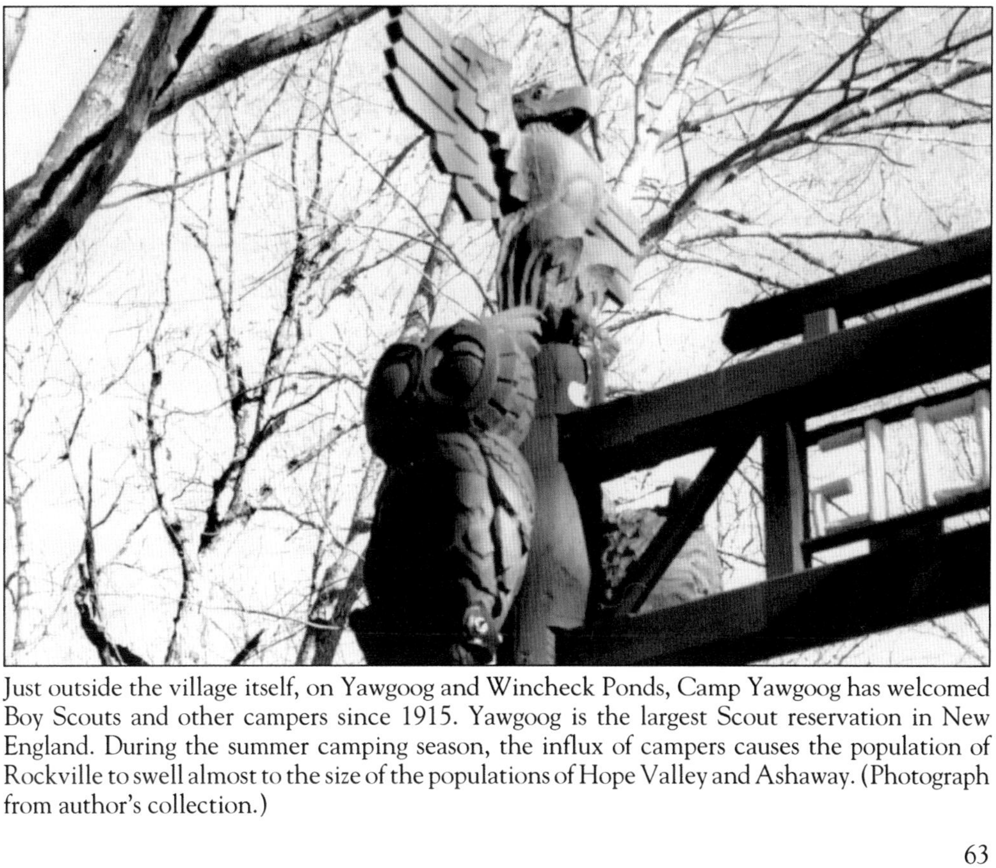

Just outside the village itself, on Yawgoog and Wincheck Ponds, Camp Yawgoog has welcomed Boy Scouts and other campers since 1915. Yawgoog is the largest Scout reservation in New England. During the summer camping season, the influx of campers causes the population of Rockville to swell almost to the size of the populations of Hope Valley and Ashaway. (Photograph from author's collection.)

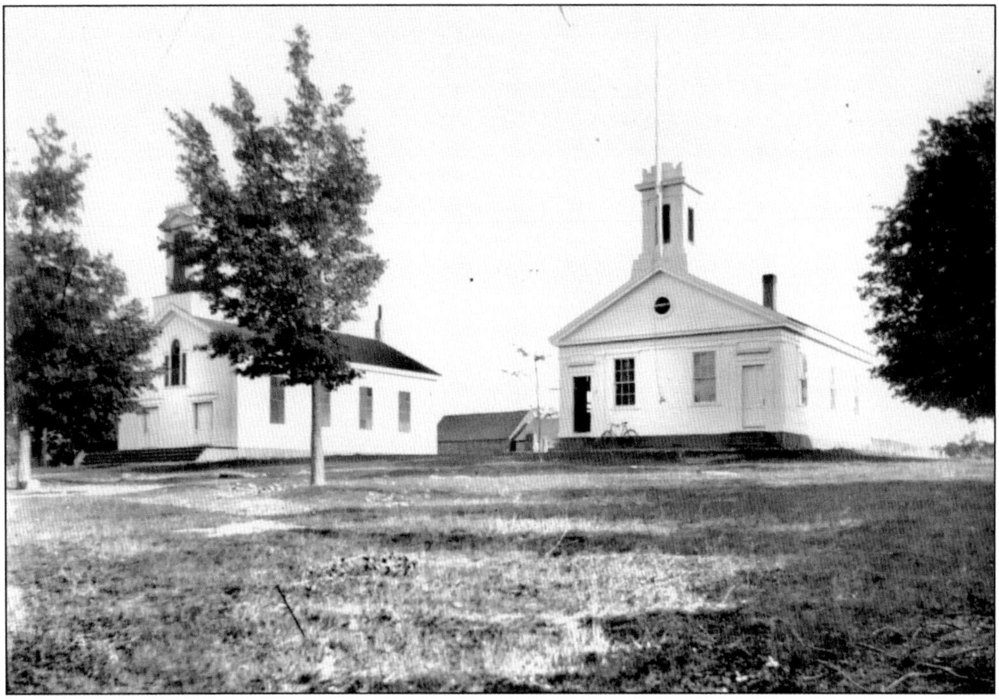

On the road to Centerville, the Rockville Seventh-Day Baptist Church (left) still holds forth the word, but the Rockville schoolhouse (right) is long gone. The Rockville congregation descends from a 1680 church established near Potter Hill. Although not as common as they once were, Seventh-Day Baptist churches remain a definite presence in the region.

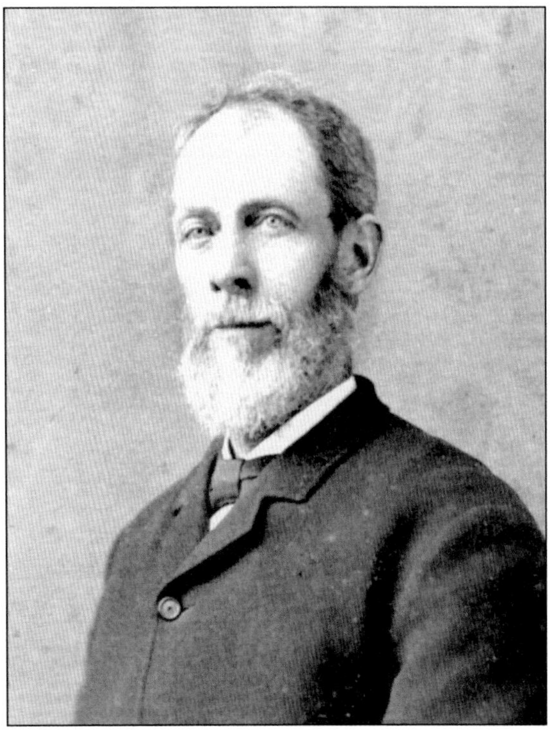

William Woodmansee was treasurer of the Rockville church.

No doubt Mrs. Woodmansee was very active in the church as well.

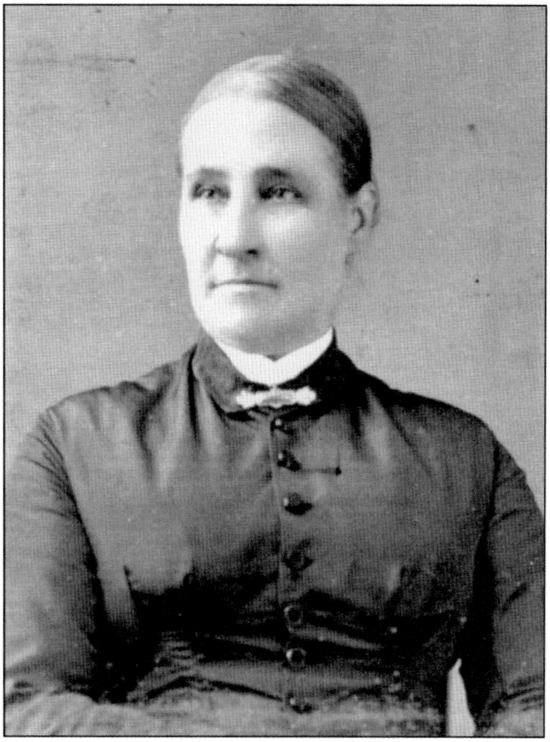

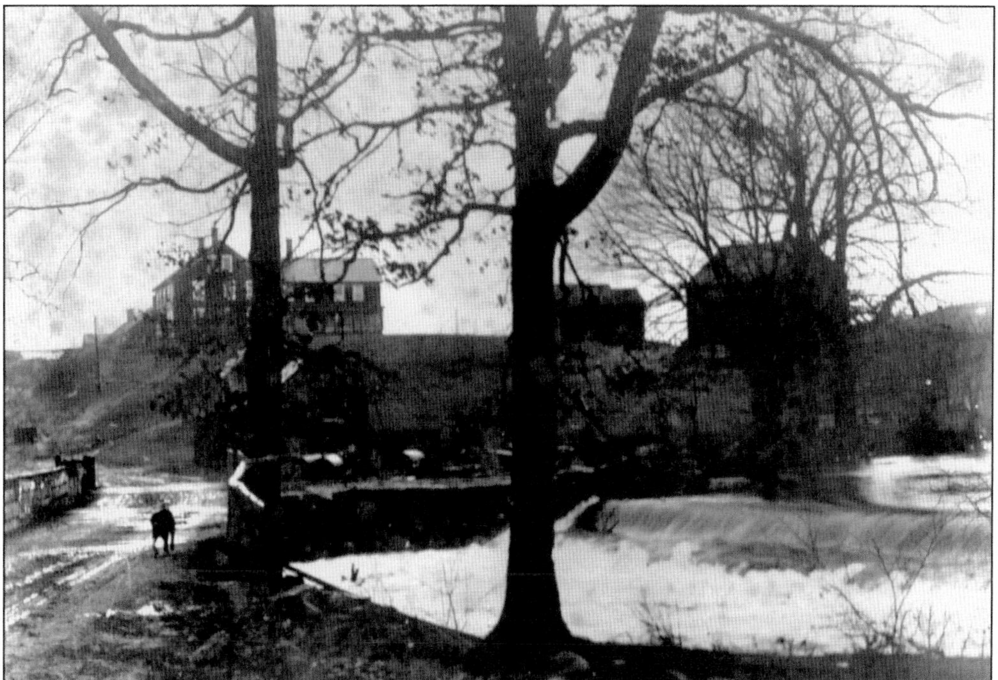

Tiny Barberville on Wood River got its start when Joseph T. Barber and his brothers erected a dam and sawmill in 1829.

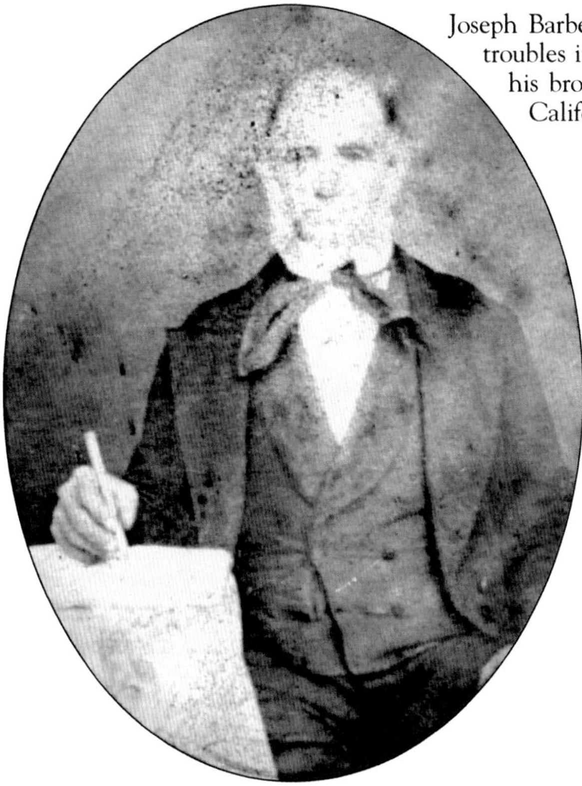

Joseph Barber, born in 1802, was facing financial troubles in 1851. Turning his properties over to his brothers, he departed with his family for California in the wake of the gold rush.

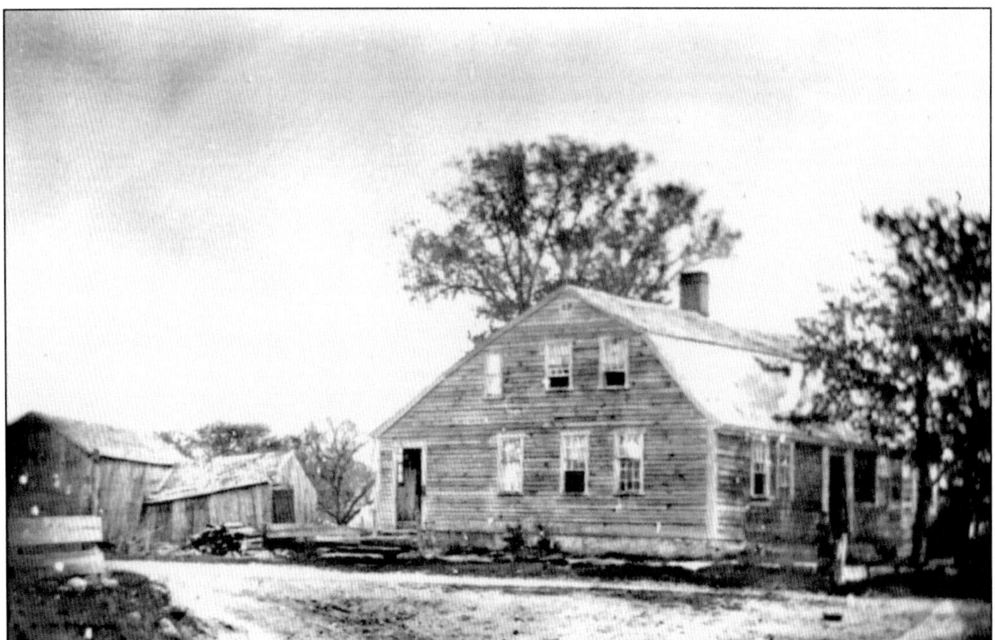

The "red house at the corner of the ways" in Ashaway was the Polly-Thomas Wells home. Homeowners often created the saltbox construction, with its long roof slant, by adding on to an existing high-walled home. A fairly common New England style, it also reduced snow buildup.

Judging by the chimney in the little addition to this structure, located on Dr. Joseph Kenyon's place near Ashaway, the addition may be a summer kitchen. Even a fairly short time ago, our ancestors lived lives radically different from our own.

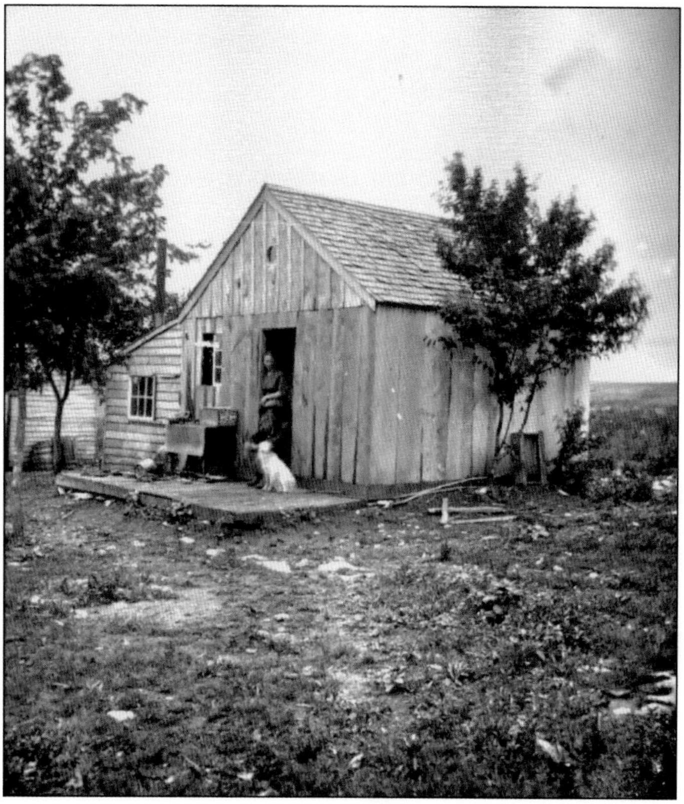

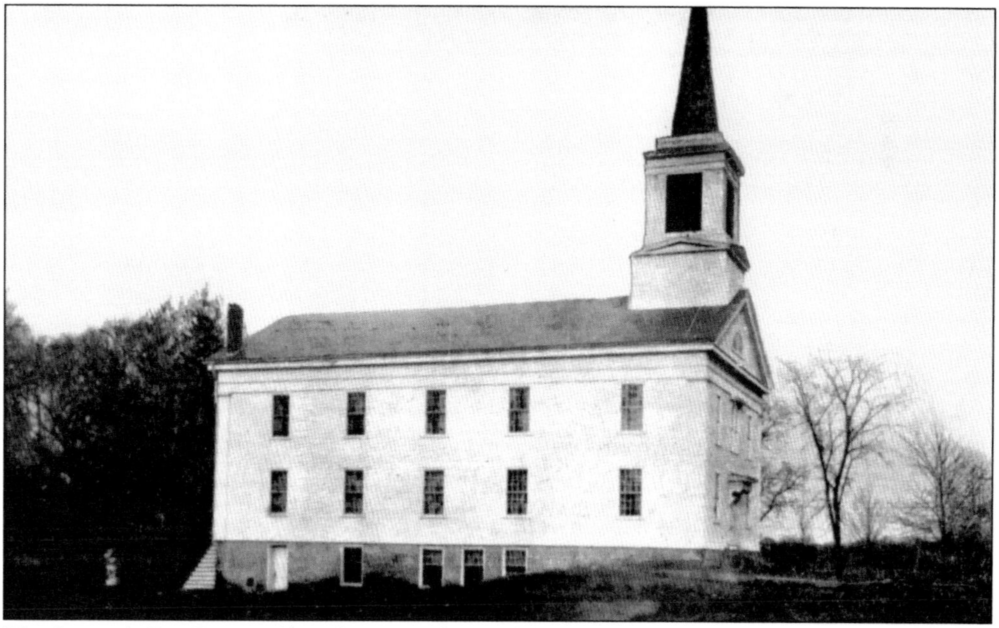

The Seventh-Day Baptist Church is one of several churches standing close together in Ashaway. The oldest part of the building was erected at Hopkinton City in 1835, then moved to Ashaway in 1858. It has had considerable alteration since.

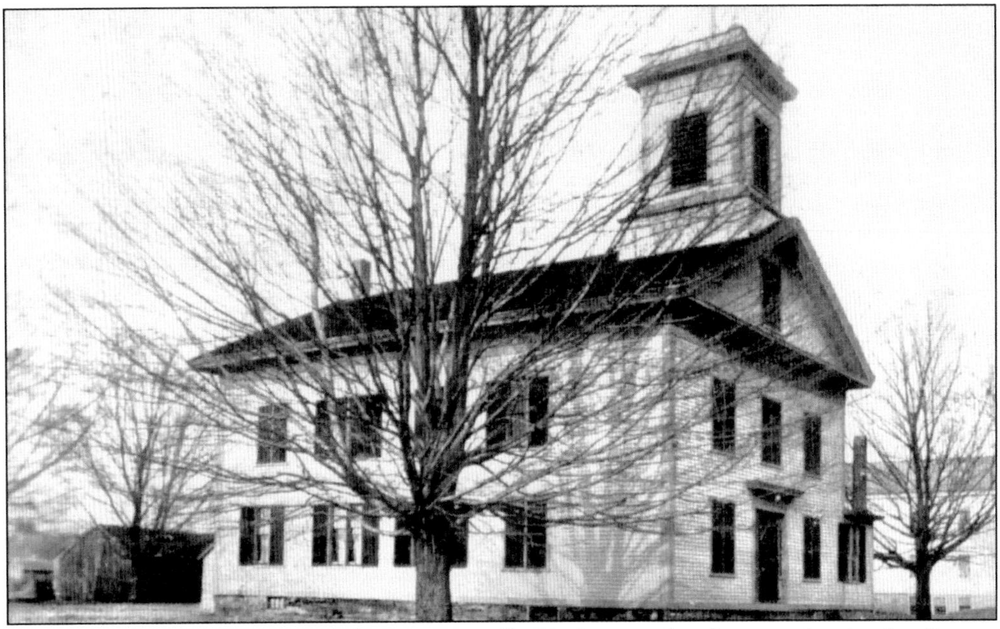

The Seventh-Day Baptist parish house, originally Hopkinton Academy, is the site for dinners and activities apart from worship.

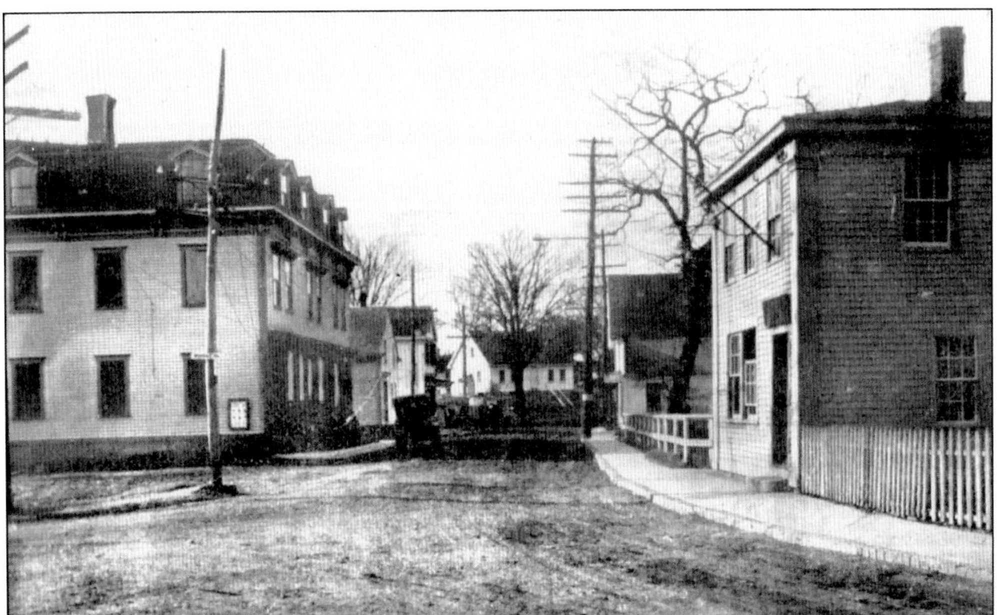

Photographers a century ago seemed fascinated by dismal hours in dismal seasons, giving viewers absolutely the wrong impression of, for instance, Ashaway's High Street, a far busier district than this photograph suggests. Notice how many crosspieces most of the utility poles bear; telephone and electric systems of the time were less efficient than ours, requiring more lines to service fewer customers. The pole on the corner is rough-hewn and bent, obviously not much more than a trimmed tree.

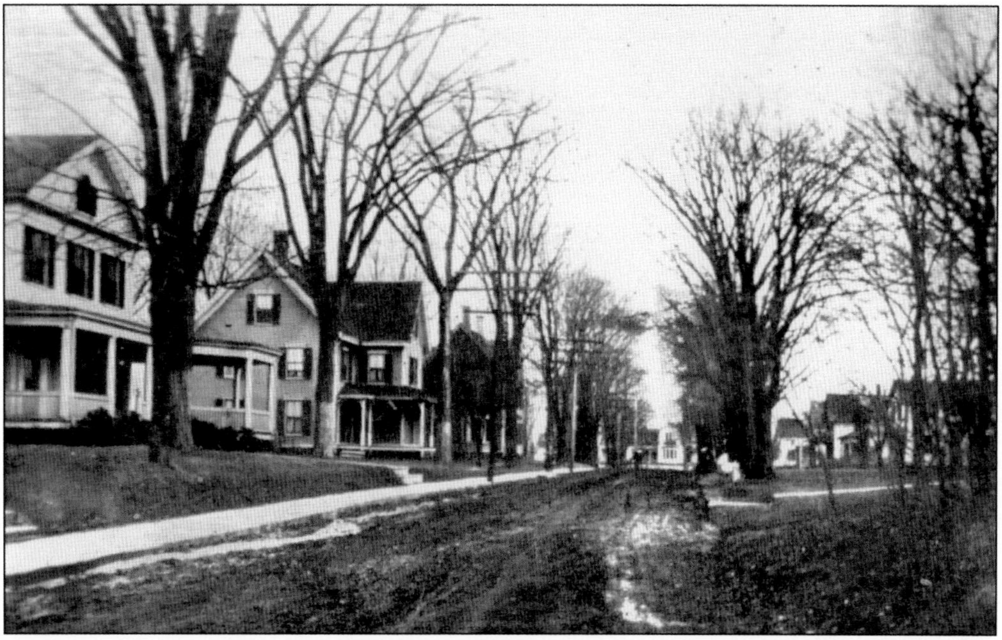

With its own busy mills and businesses, in addition to its proximity to the prosperous larger town of Westerly, Ashaway has long been known for charming, elegant homes, such as these on Main Street.

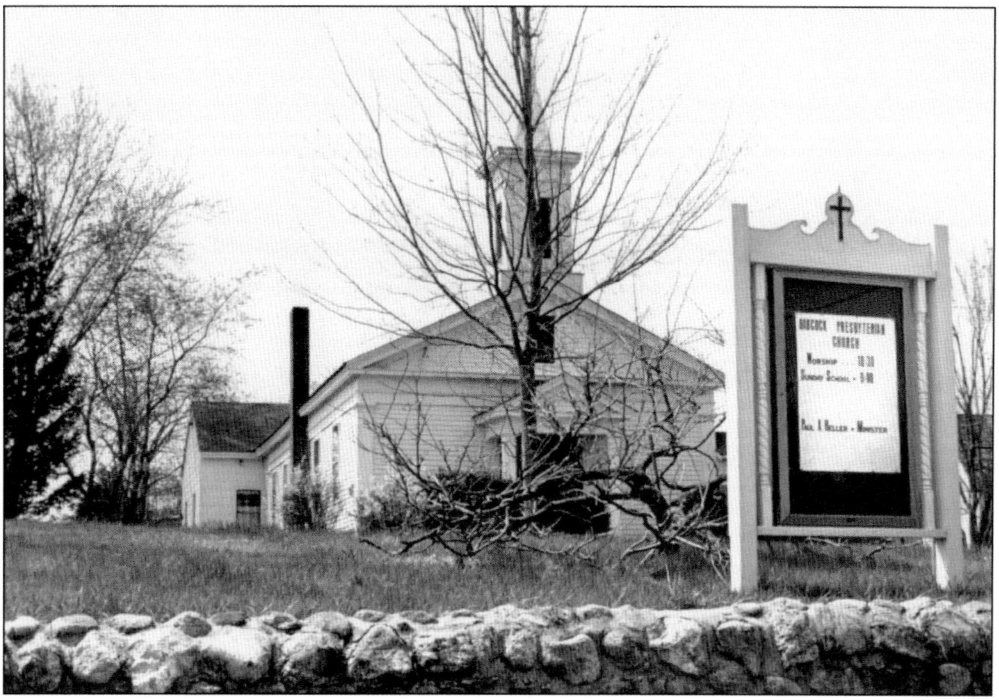

The Westerly YMCA started the Union Sunday School in 1869 at an Ashaway schoolhouse. Olivia Babcock bought the structure when the schools consolidated in 1874, and the congregation continued its nondenominational services. The members elected to affiliate with the Presbyterians in 1966.

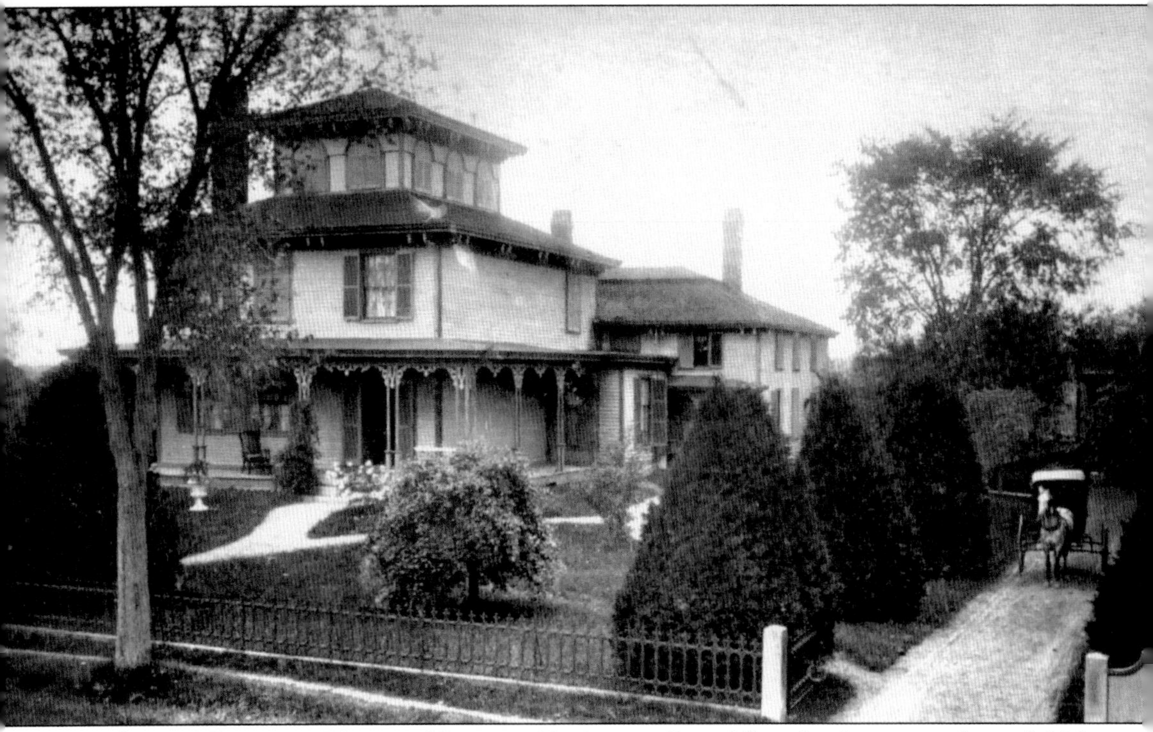

The 1848 Benjamin Thurston House, in Hopkinton City, fell on hard times in the mid-20th century but was later returned to the state it richly deserved. Thurston, who served as lieutenant governor and as a U.S. representative, sold the place to carriage manufacturer Augustus L. Wells in 1864. The porches, added at about that time, have since been removed.

While traditional New England architecture (as in this Ashaway home) favored an austere beauty, it also ventured on softly spoken grace notes.

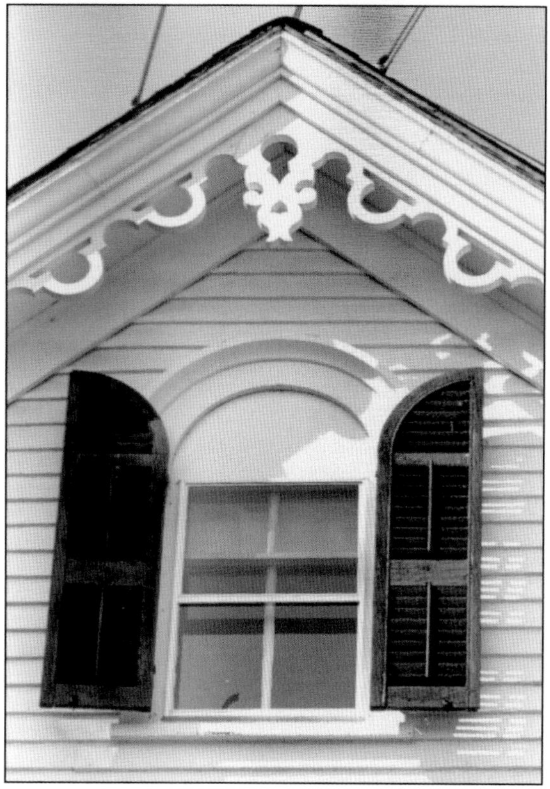

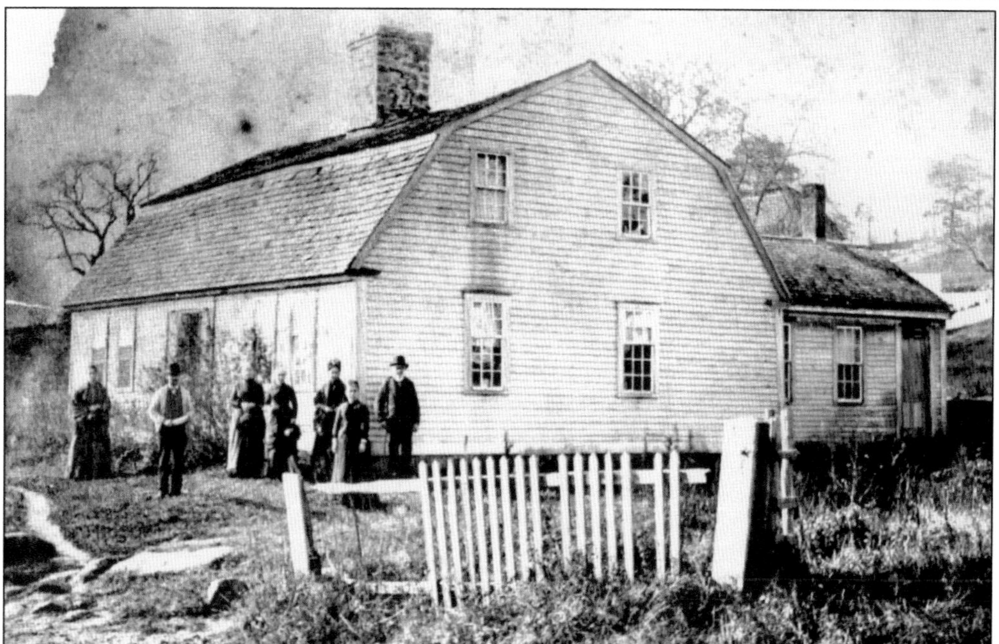

Ironworker Samuel Brand lived on Mechanic Street in one of the earliest houses in Hope Valley. In 1786, he moved up the road to what at that time became known as Brand's Iron Works (now Wyoming).

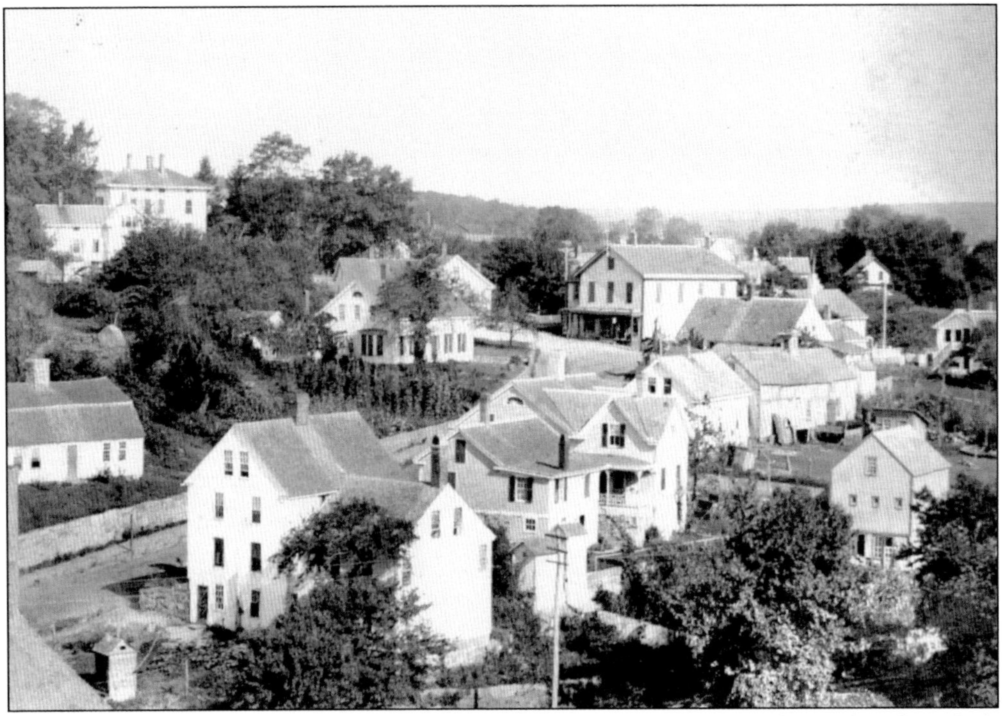

Mechanic Street in Hope Valley ran from the depot down to the Richmond and Nichols machinery works. The large building in the center with the covered porch, located at the intersection with High Street, was the post office. That site, later the Polish-American Citizens' Club, is now Polish Park.

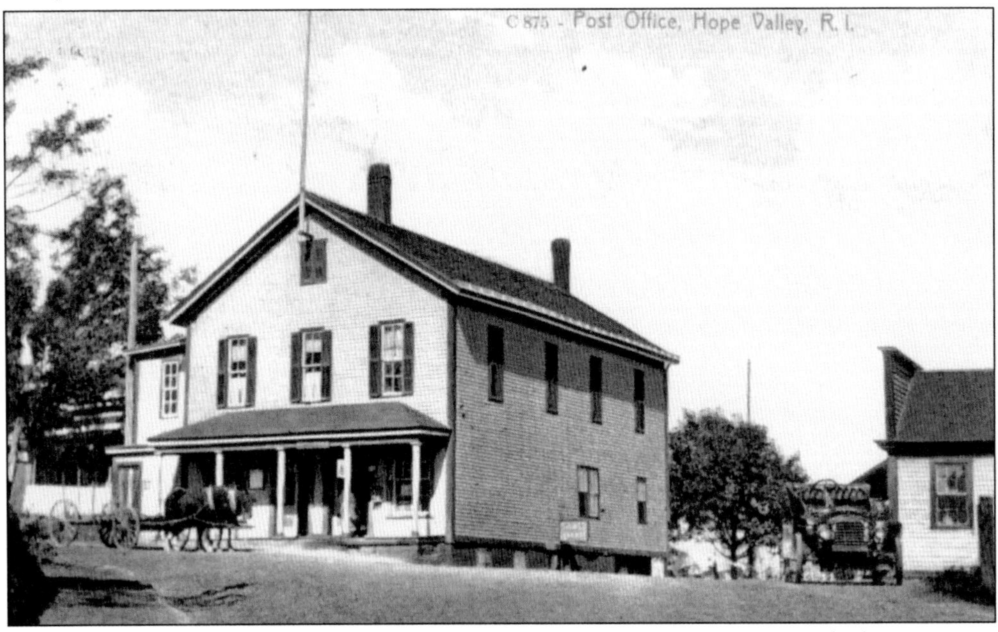

This postcard view reveals that the post office had a public phone on the Bell Telephone system. Notice the automobile (with the steering column on the left) and the dray. The sender stated that she had ridden 15 miles on Tuesday and 4 miles on Wednesday.

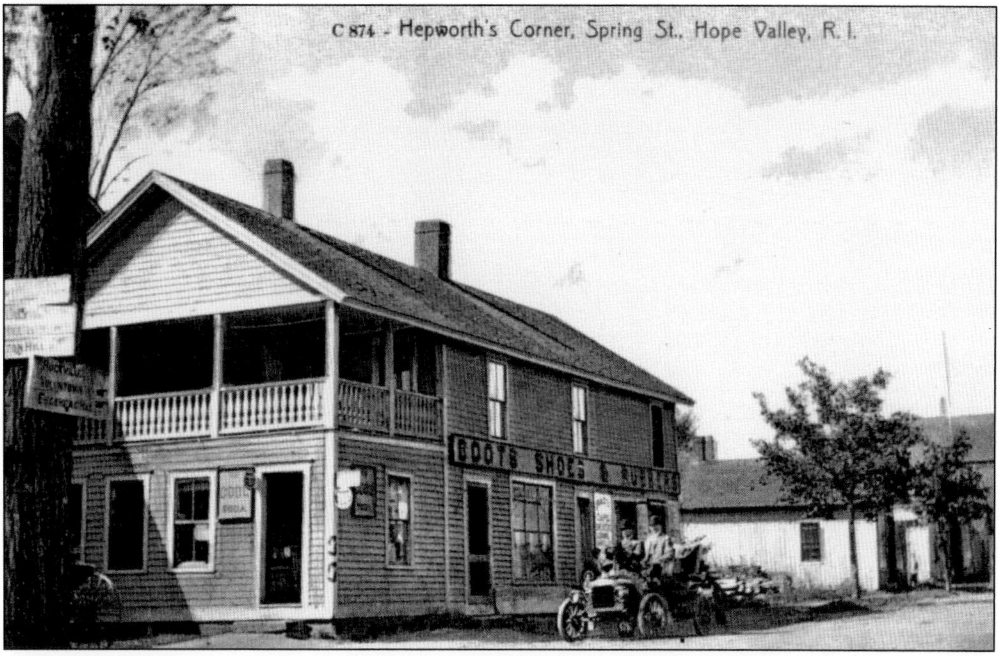

Hepworth Corner, somewhat altered, is today the Spring Street Market. It does not carry boots, shoes, or rubbers anymore, but cool soda is still an important part of the business. The unnamed sender noted that she "bought the postal" (postcard) at Hepworth's in 1909. The automobile seems to be the same one that appears on the previous postcard, suggesting that it is the photographer's vehicle.

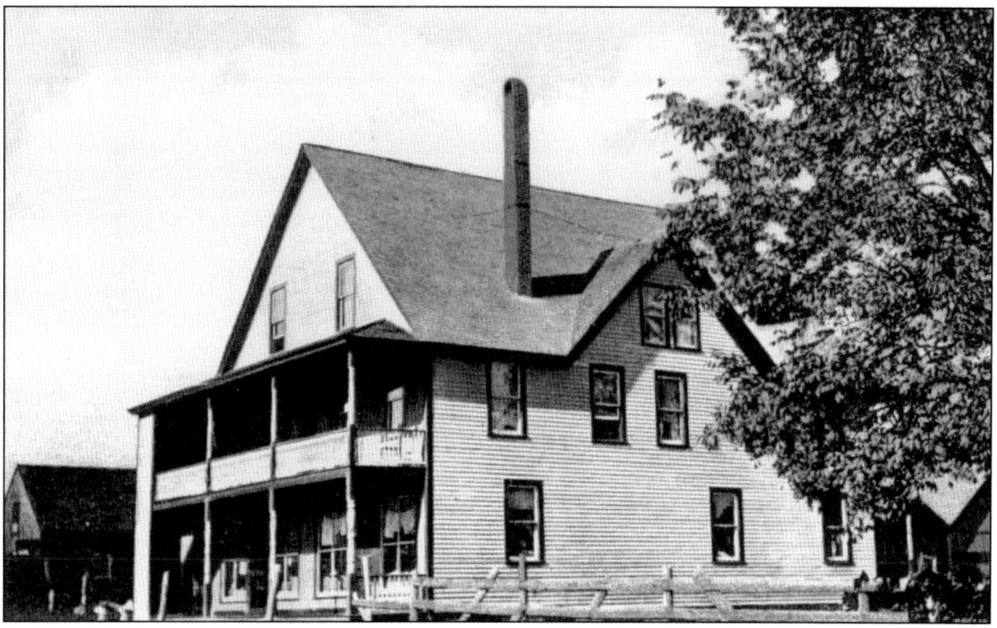

"Cutie" sent this postcard to Mabel Cole of 45 Furnace Street in Providence in 1909, noting that there were two shops in the now vanished Kenyon Block. The sender writes, "One is a five and ten cent store. The other is the leading milliner of the town where you get all the latest importations and our own designs." The building was later home to the A & P.

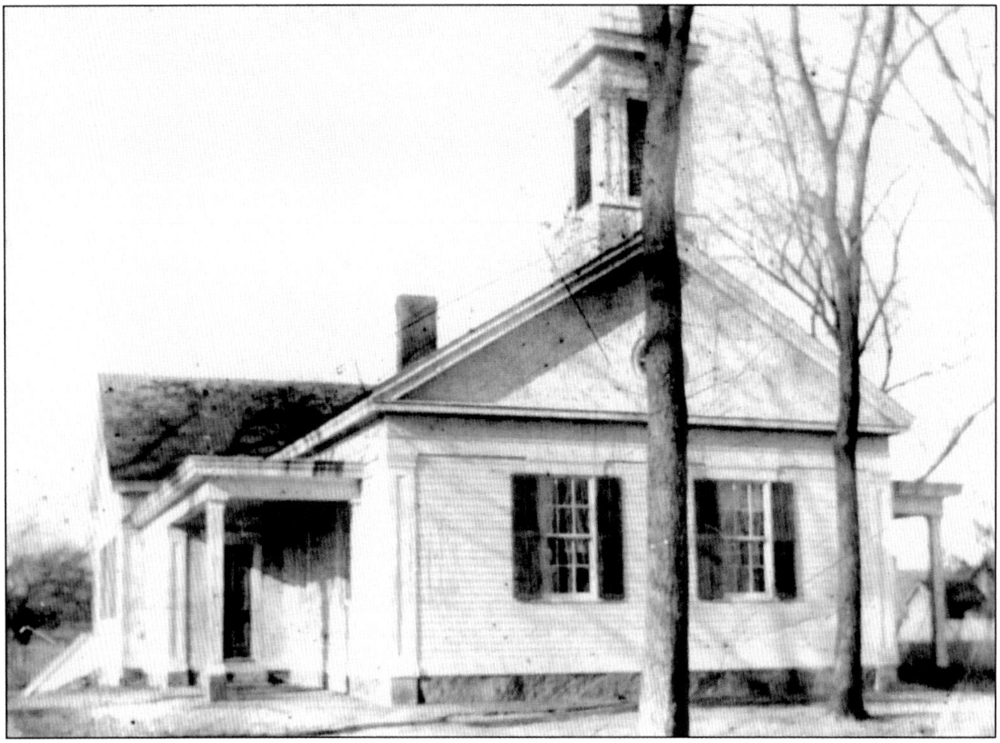

Hope Valley School replaced an earlier Locustville School in 1852. The school was in place on its hill before Main Street was.

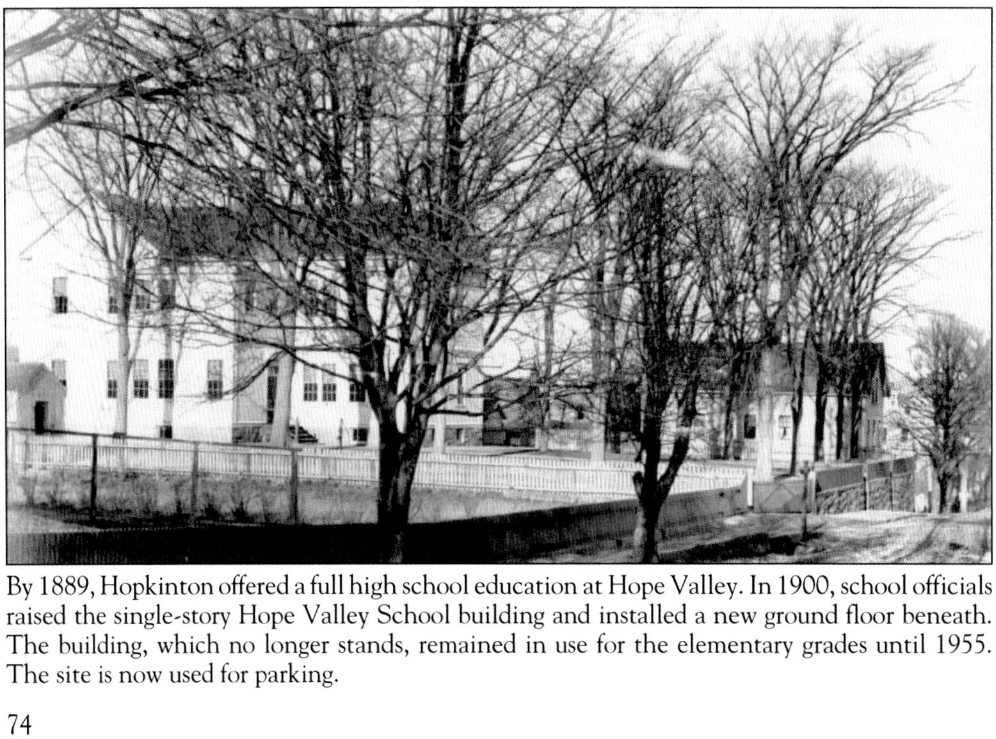

By 1889, Hopkinton offered a full high school education at Hope Valley. In 1900, school officials raised the single-story Hope Valley School building and installed a new ground floor beneath. The building, which no longer stands, remained in use for the elementary grades until 1955. The site is now used for parking.

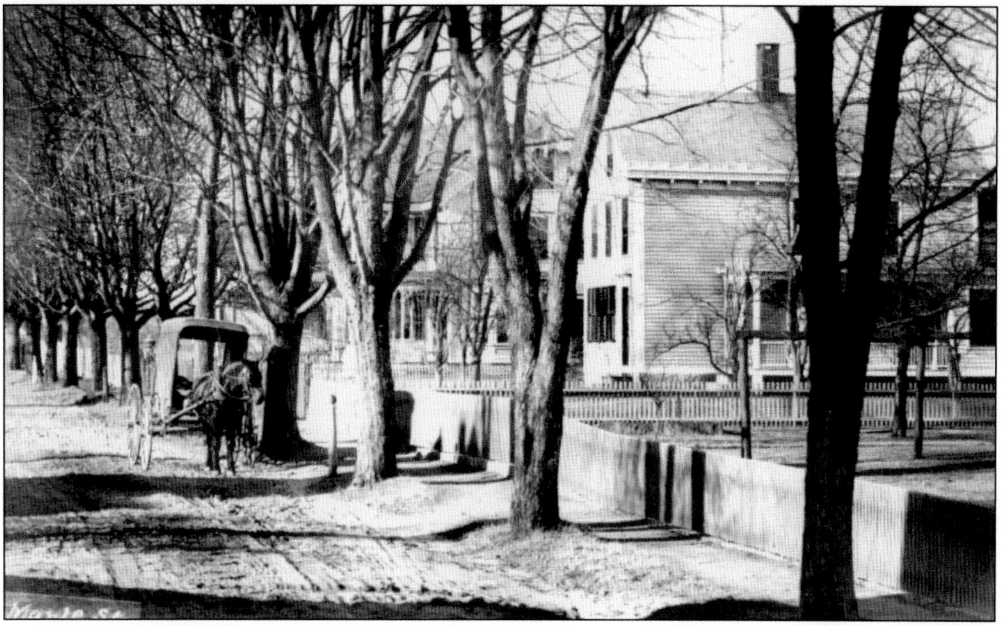

Maple Street makes two sides of a rectangle around tiny Chipman (or Barber's) Pond, with Main and Spring Streets forming the other sides. Since Maple Street has never been a through street, it retains its quiet charm.

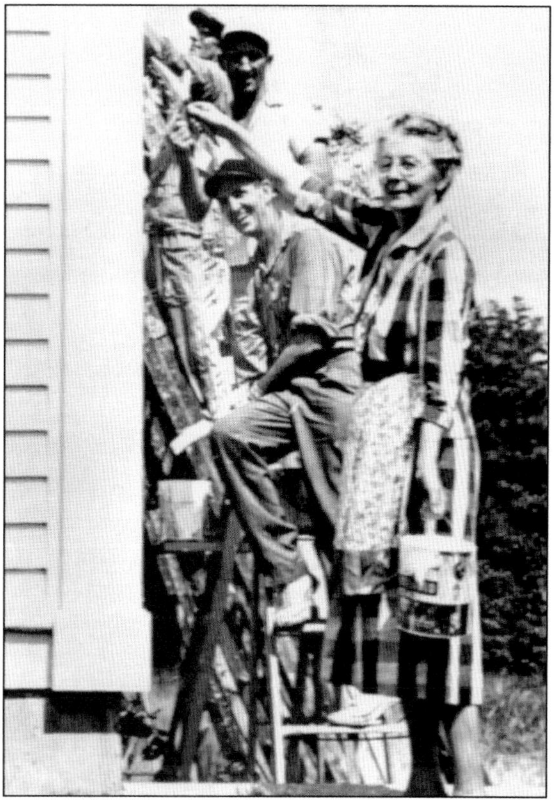

The libraries in Ashaway and Hope Valley, created in 1871 and 1888, respectively, have been important parts of Hopkinton life for over a century. In this view, volunteers team up in Hope Valley to paint the Langworthy Library. From left to right are Bill Kay, Joe Welch, Fred Rathbun, and Ida Gardiner.

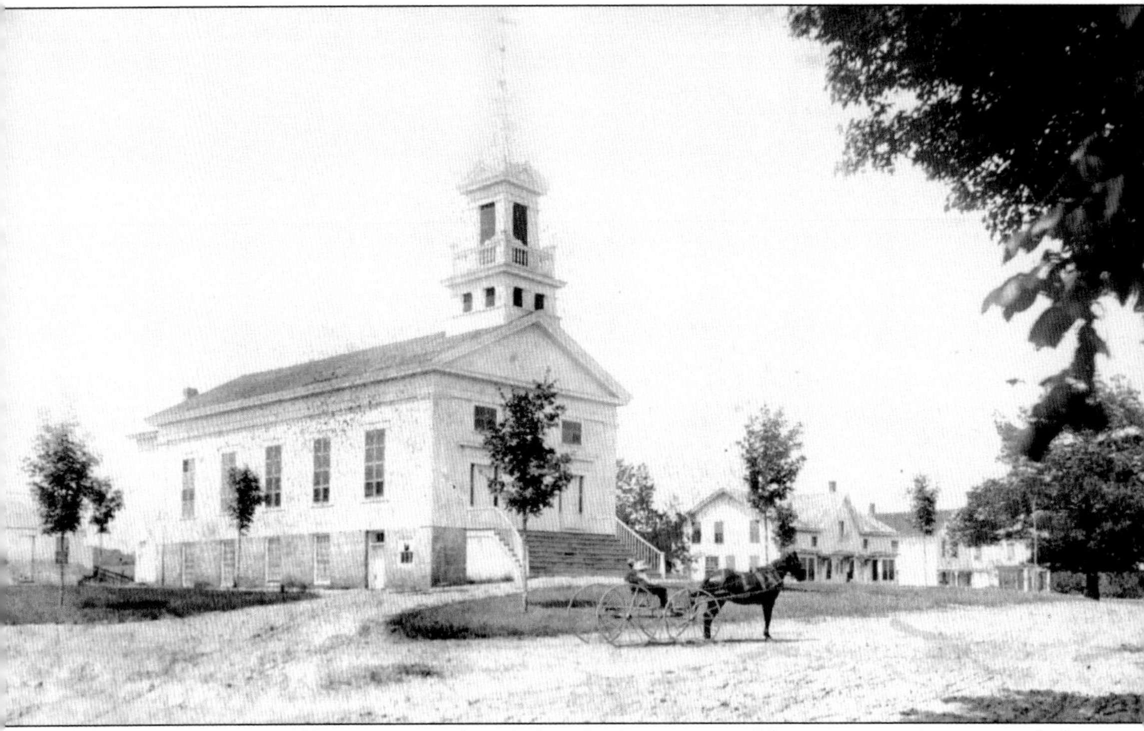

Though Hope Valley Baptist Church has had a major addition since the time of this photograph, church planners carefully preserved most of the 19th-century building. The double front doors—leading to two side aisles, rather than a single central aisle—were used fairly frequently in New England.

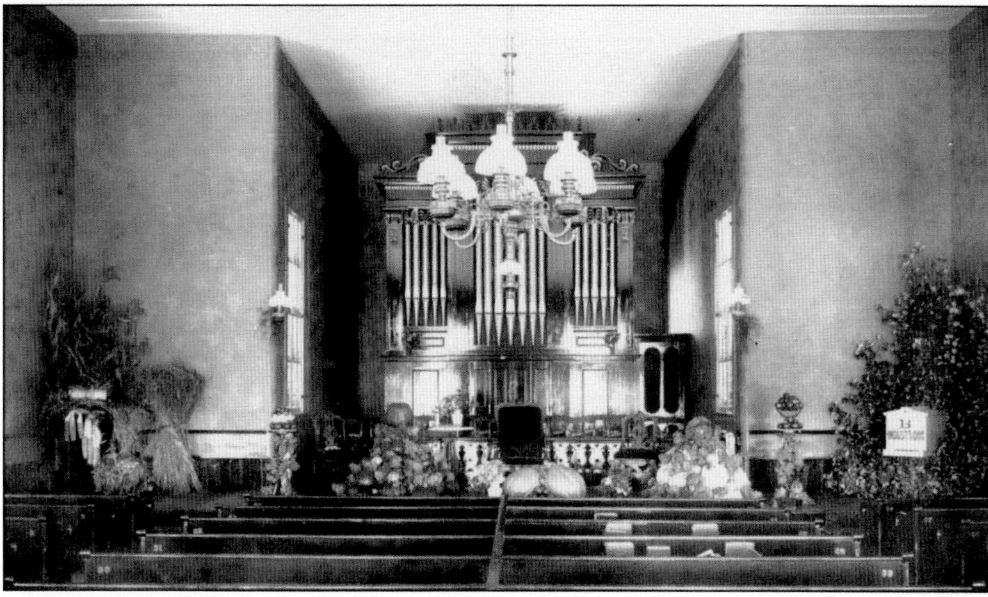

Fred Bailey recalled that Locustville residents came in through the left door of the Hope Valley Baptist Church, while Wyoming residents used the right door; people seated themselves accordingly inside. The oldest part of the church dates back to 1845. Gardner Nichols donated the pipe organ in 1880. This is a Harvest Sunday celebration.

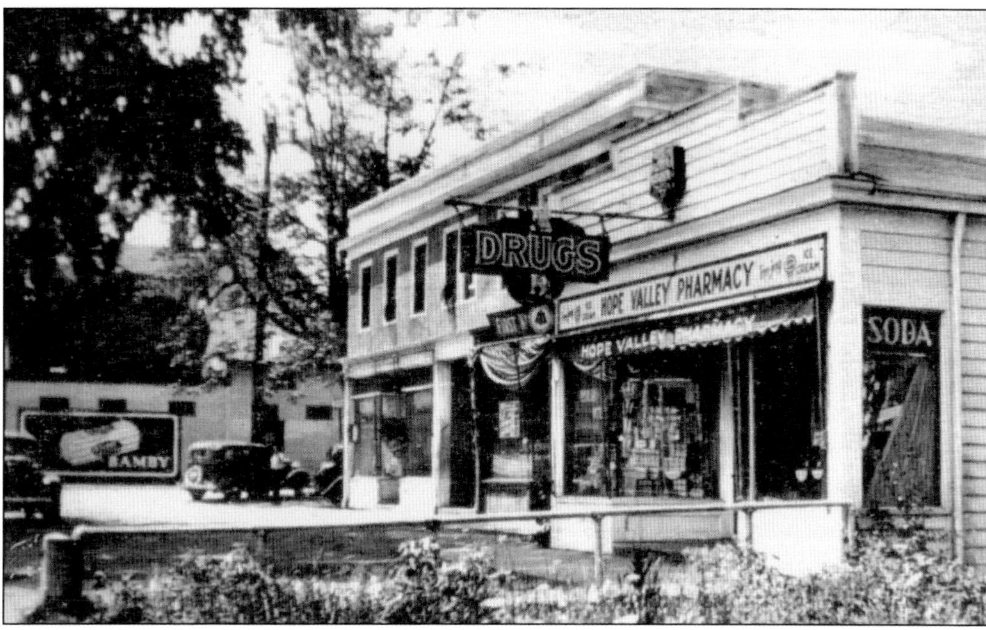

Residents from the 1950s and 1960s—not to mention tired riders of the bus between Westerly and Providence—will recognize the business with the two plate-glass windows on the corner of the two-story building as Cregan's News. Now somewhat altered, it is home to West's Bakery.

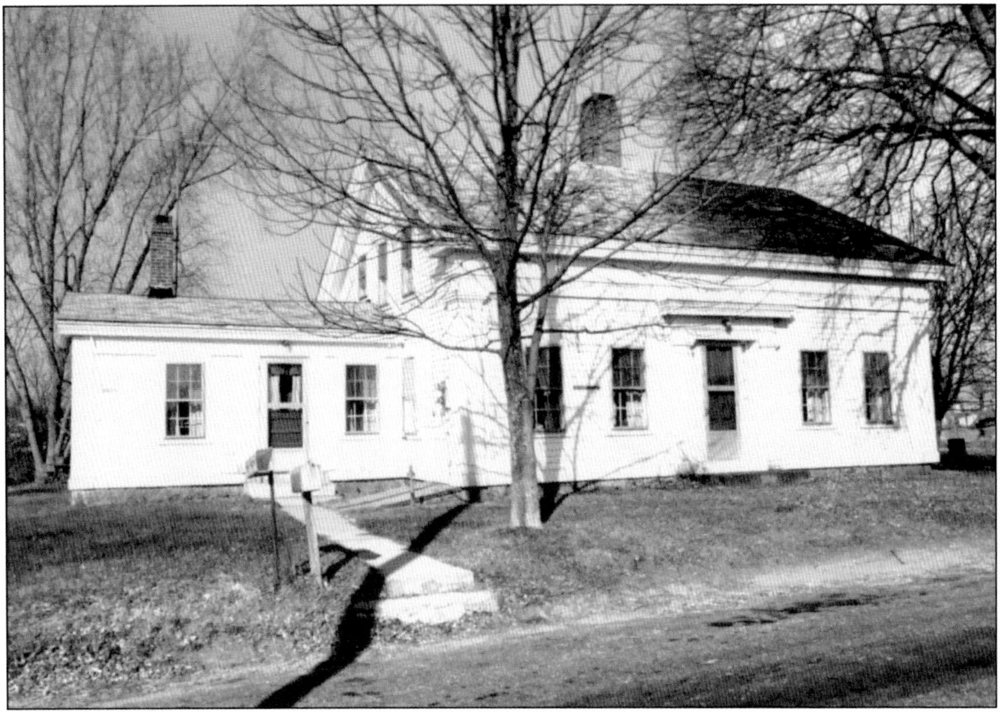

The Federal style inspired many early-19th-century Hopkinton homes, such as this lovely house on Prospect Square in Wyoming.

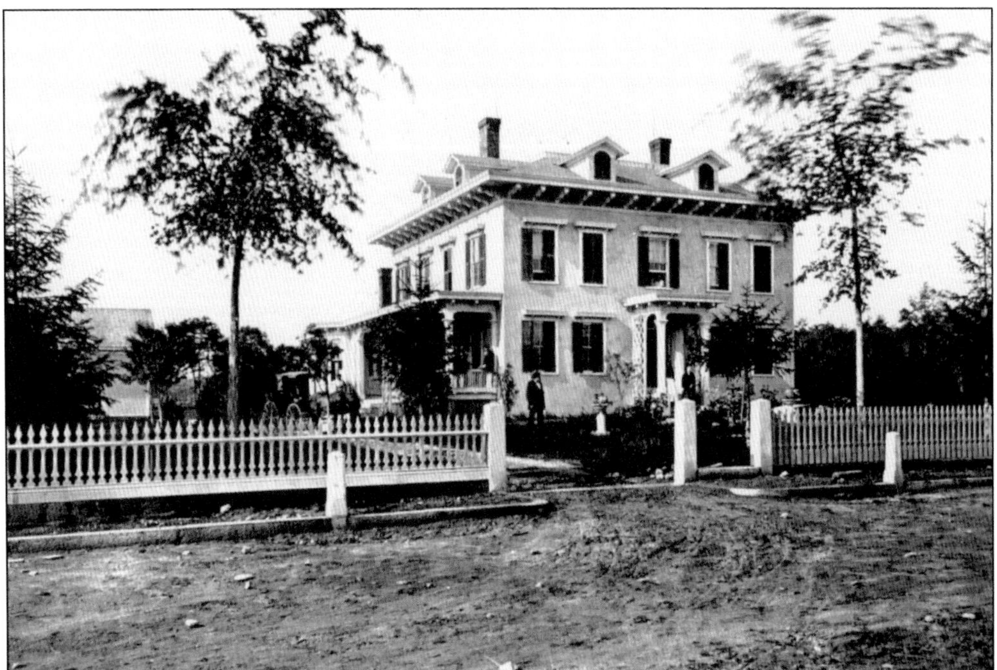

Mill owner David L. Aldrich, who had interests throughout the Wood-Pawcatuck River system, built himself an impressive house *c.* 1860—before income tax!

Four

Mills and Races

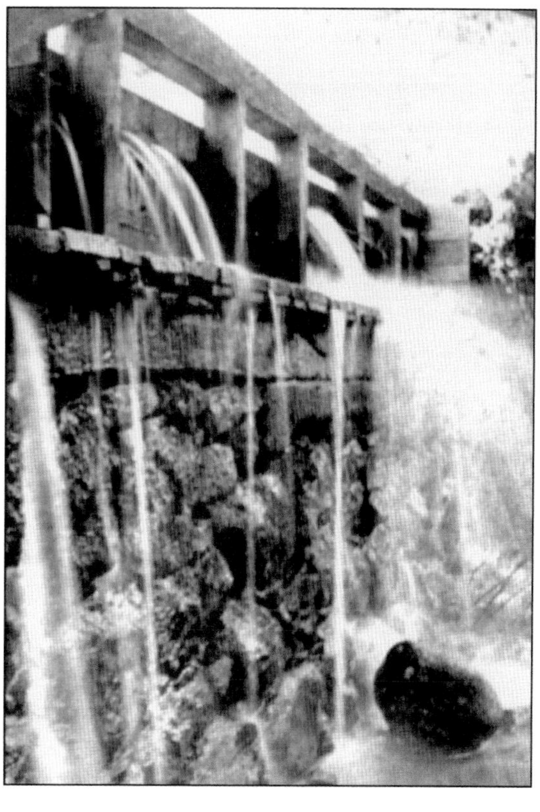

Busy (even frenetic) Yankee settlers leapt upon the streams of Hopkinton, building entire series of dams along each watercourse—just as the beavers had. Rockville Dam, seen here, was among some 30 on Hopkinton streams. Falling water was power begging to be harnessed for sawmills, gristmills, ropewalks, and textile mills. Even tiny Chipman's (or Barber's) Brook in Hope Valley powered tanning, textile, and manufacturing work for a century or more. Early New Englanders' leveraging of waterpower gave birth to America's industrial might. Of course, the mills' wealth was tied inextricably to slave-grown cotton and to "shoddy"—cheap, coarse cloth used for slave clothing. After World War II, the great age of New England mills was gone, and some of the huge stone, wood, or brick structures went with it. Others have been converted, and their dams still control the waters. Beyond rewriting the social and economic history of a nation, they changed the very face of the land.

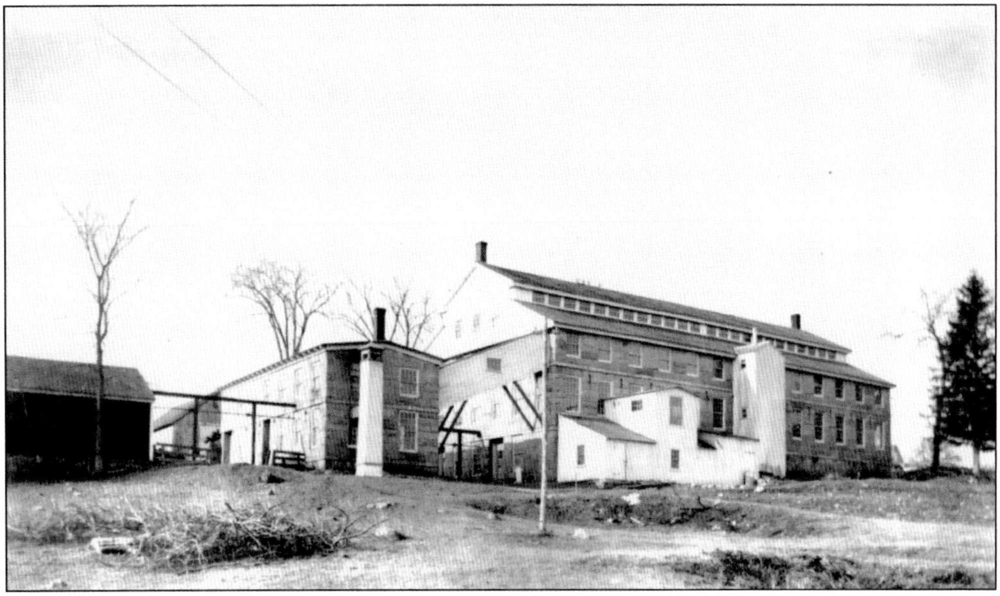

The Rockville Upper Mill, once a spinning operation, is now home to the post office. Notice the ramped "skywalk" connecting the two stone buildings. If typical construction was followed, that square white tower midway along the building on the right provided a privy on each floor. The upper row of windows is a clerestory monitor, admitting light to the attic.

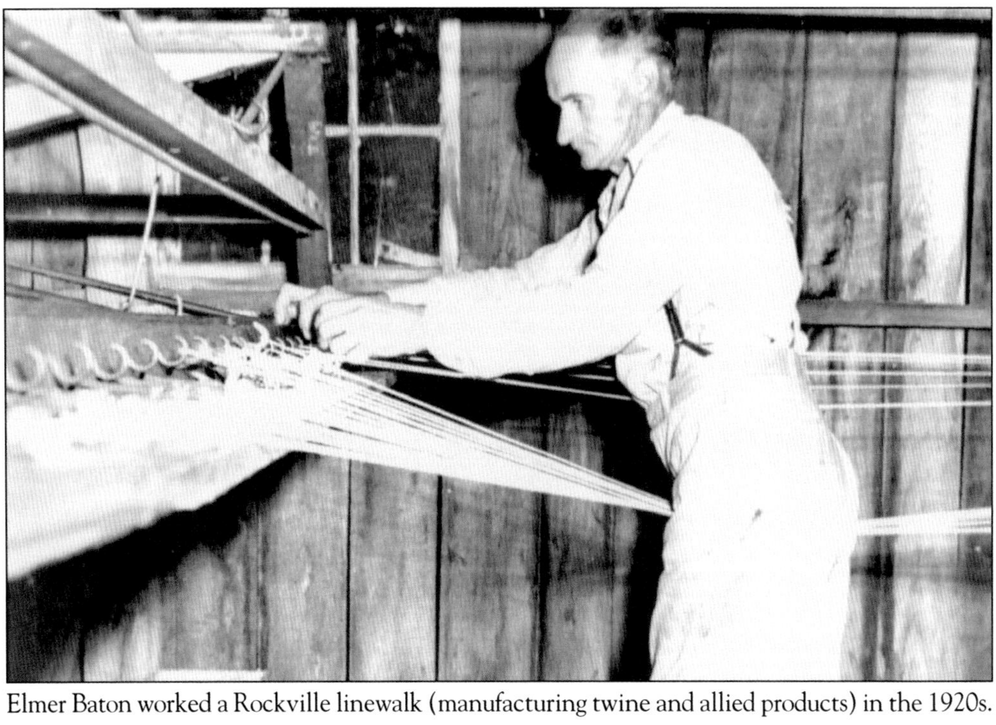

Elmer Baton worked a Rockville linewalk (manufacturing twine and allied products) in the 1920s.

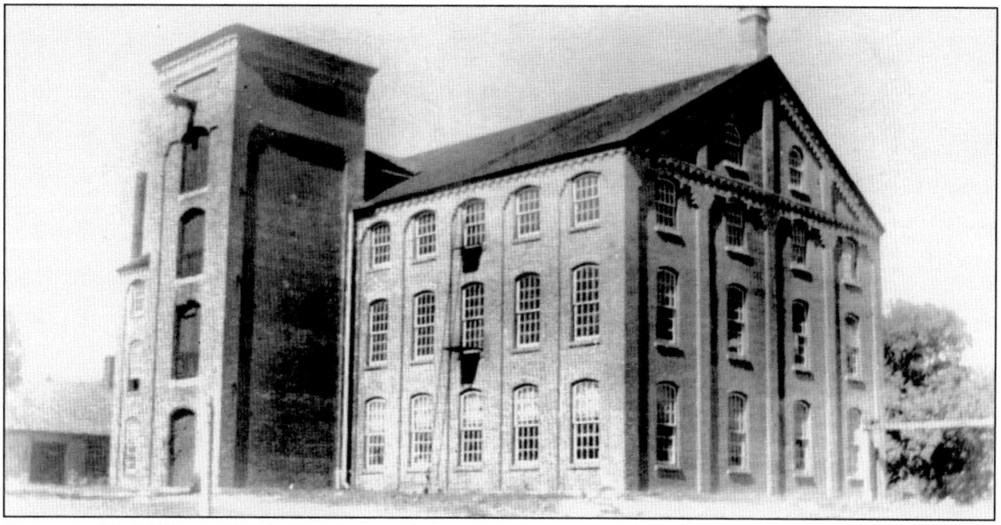

Centerville Mill was built downstream from Rockville *c.* 1865. Just a touch more decorative than the typical factory of the period, at times it ran almost 70 looms. Its bell reportedly once belonged to John Paul Jones, but where the bell came from, and where it went, nobody knows.

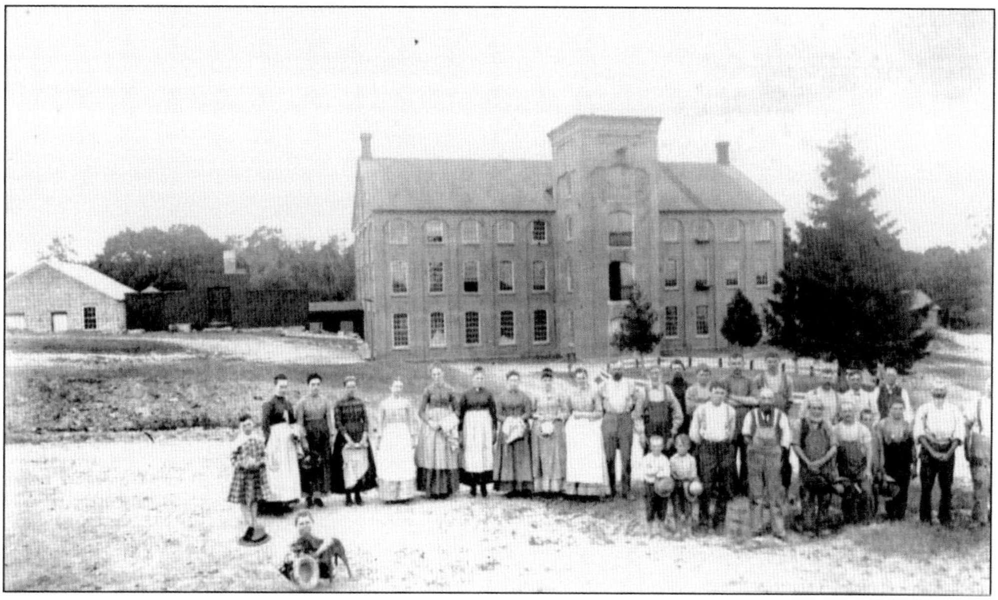

Some of the women employees in this photograph hold their hats; others hold bolts of cloth. Current history rightly makes much of women entering factory work in World War II but often overlooks the fact that they did the same in World War I and for the previous 100 years. While the men are of all ages, the women are mostly young; it was fairly common for New Englander women to work in the mills until their marriage. Notice that children, some of them quite small, are also on staff.

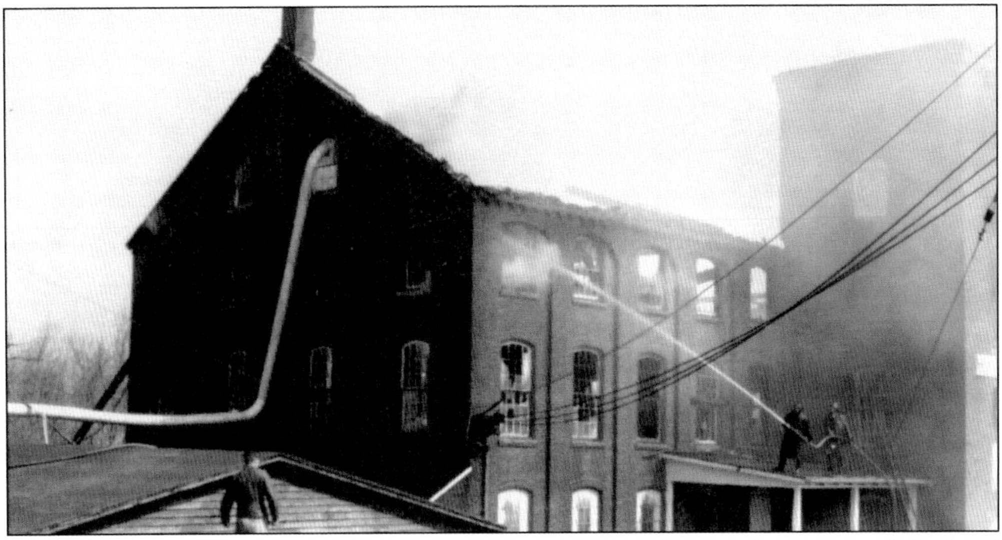

A fire on the morning of April 7, 1947, helped seal the fate of the Wood River Branch Railroad and initiated a slow, sad decline for the Centerville Mill.

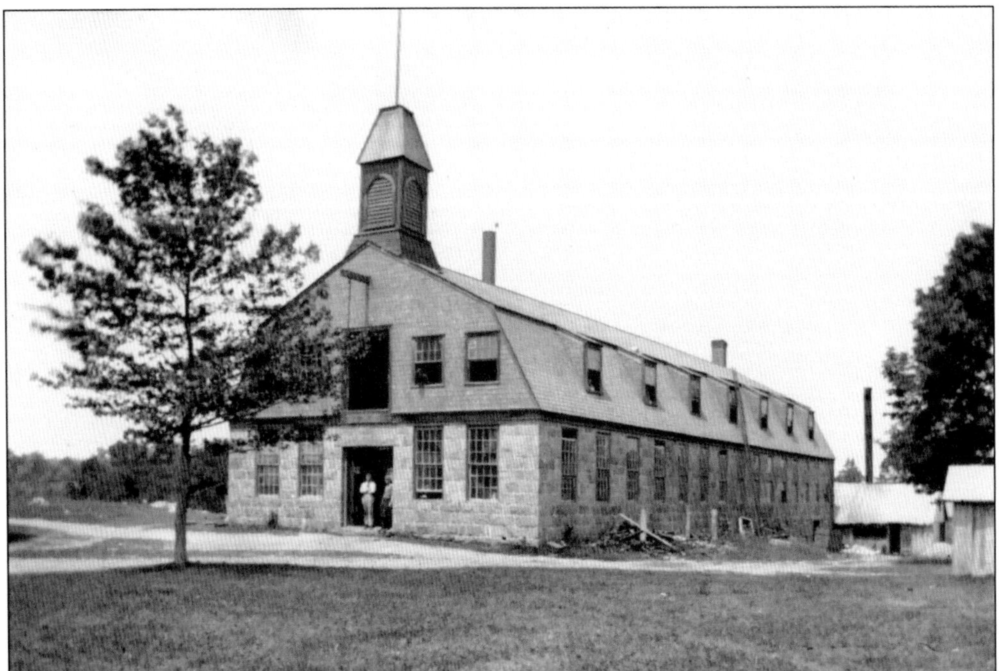

Still farther down Brushy Brook, Moscow Mill was damaged by fire twice in the 1950s; its profile has changed a bit from this earlier photograph. Notice the small boy leaning out of a second-story window. The mill became a rope manufactory after 1960. Swiss-born owner Edward Boeglin, a lovely gentleman, was an energetic early supporter of the Boy Scouts in Rhode Island.

Alva Crandall, who bought the Moscow Mill and the water after an 1870s fire, owned and operated the mill until 1901.

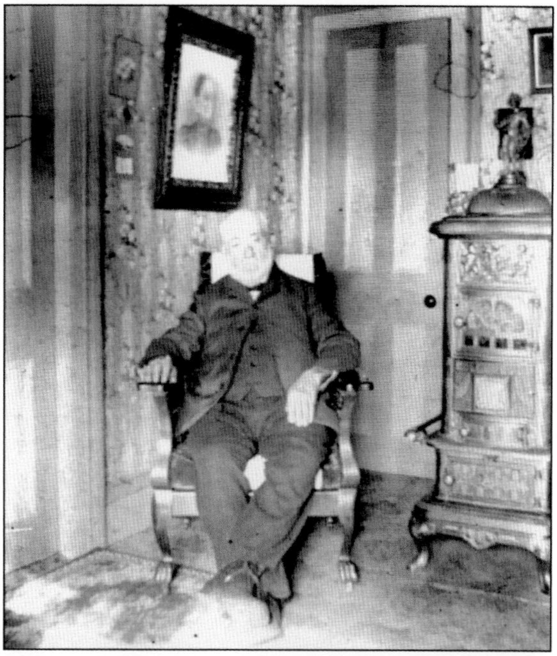

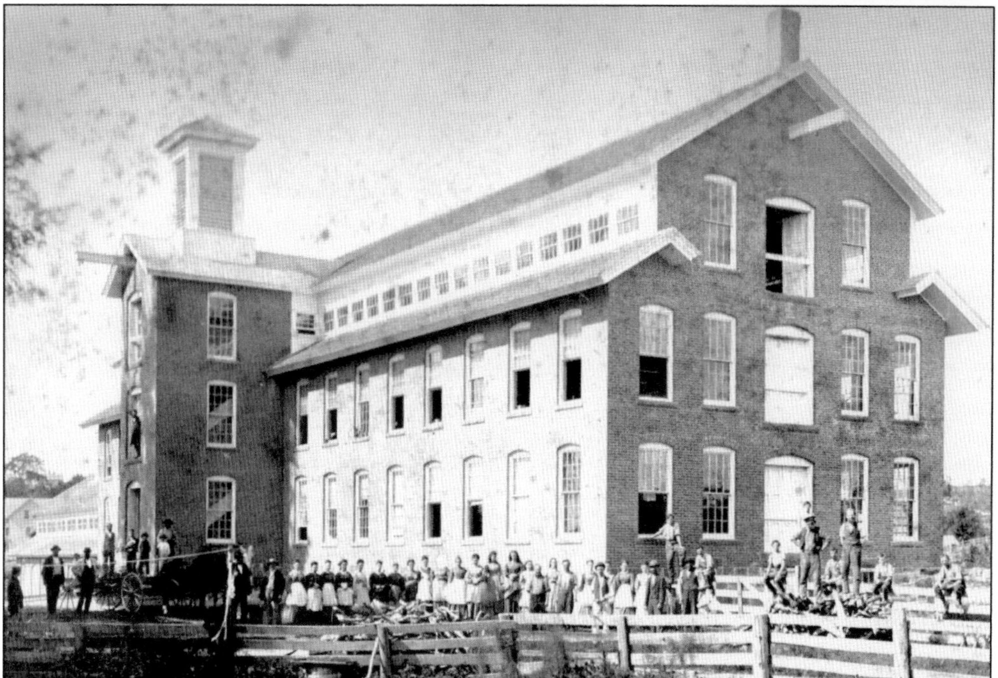

Successive mill owners, who bought more land and water rights, slowly created the current Locustville Pond. They also erected the imposing Locustville Mill, built with local brick, in the 1860s. Notice again the predominance of women workers, plus the horse-drawn dray and the figure on the second stage of the tower. Someone very precisely obliterated the face of the woman under the fourth window back from the front corner. There must have been a story behind that!

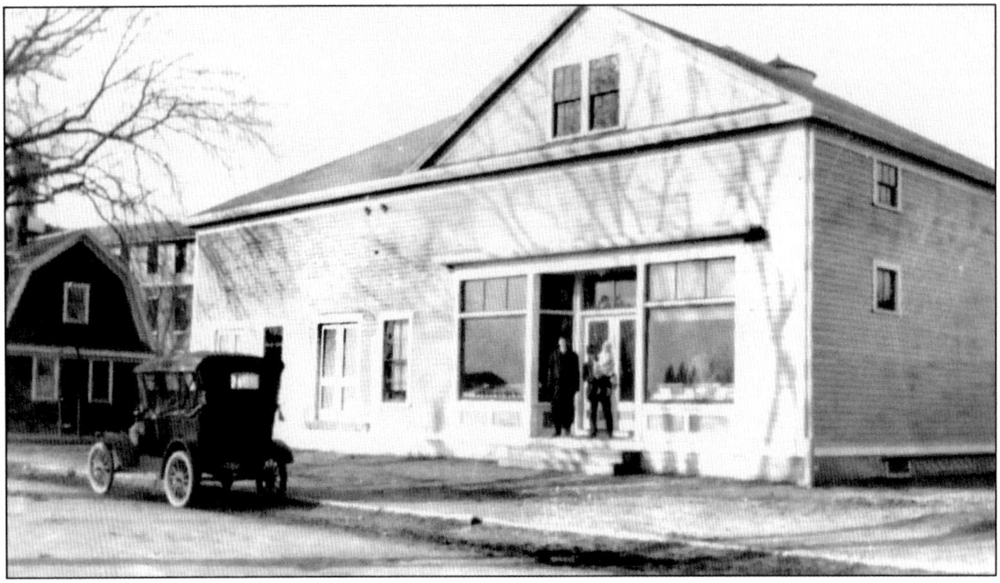

Browning's, at one time the company store for Locustville Mill, stayed in business for 99 years.

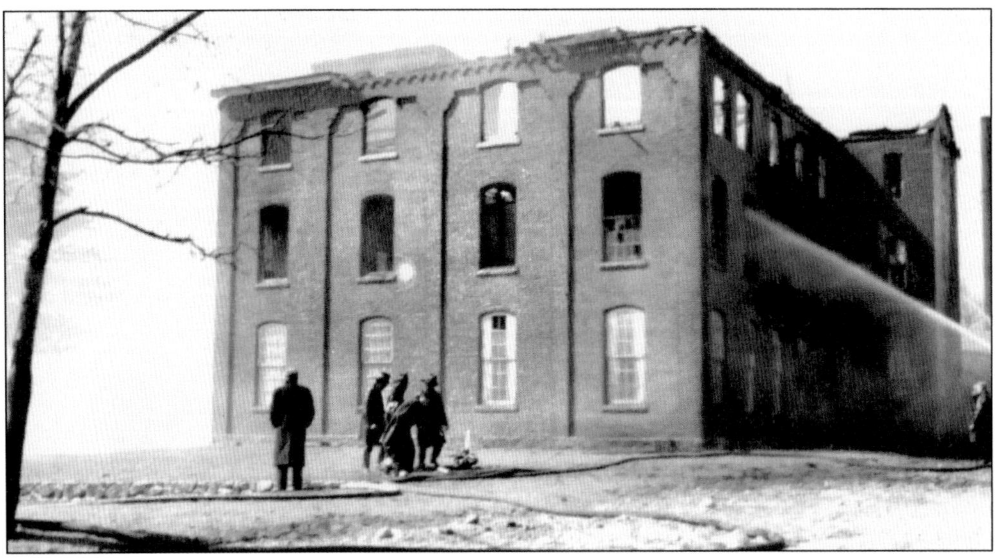

A fire on January 10, 1936, led to the mill being abandoned for a decade. The old Locustville Mill, which has been considerably reduced in size, is now home to Ure Outfitters on Main Street. Some derelict sections remained, hidden from street view, in the 1960s. The author can testify that local youths occasionally explored the roof and interior, generally without troubling to inform their parents.

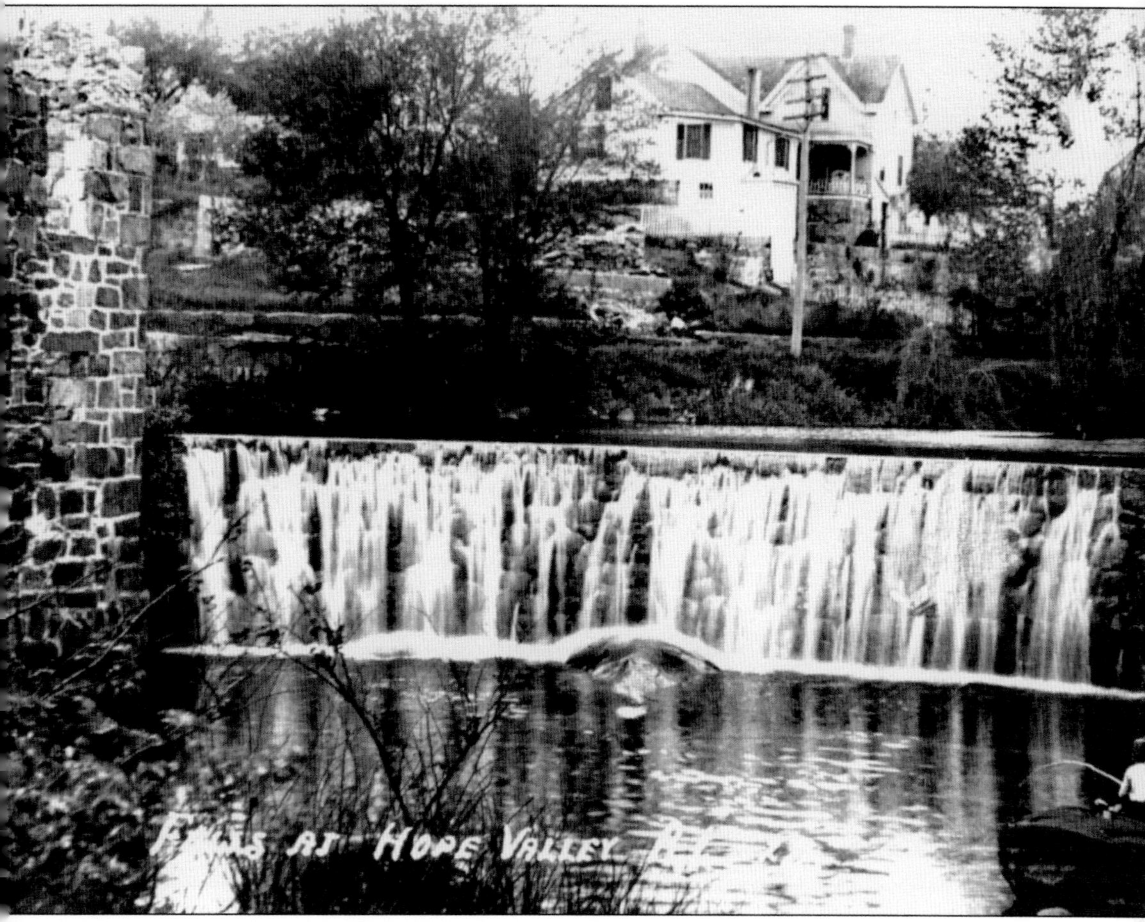

Brushy Brook finally joins Wood River a few yards from Locustville Mill. A short distance downstream, Hezekiah Carpenter dammed the river around the time of the Revolution. Beyond the dam is Mechanic Street and the Wood River Branch Railroad right of way. People still fish the spot, both above the falls and below.

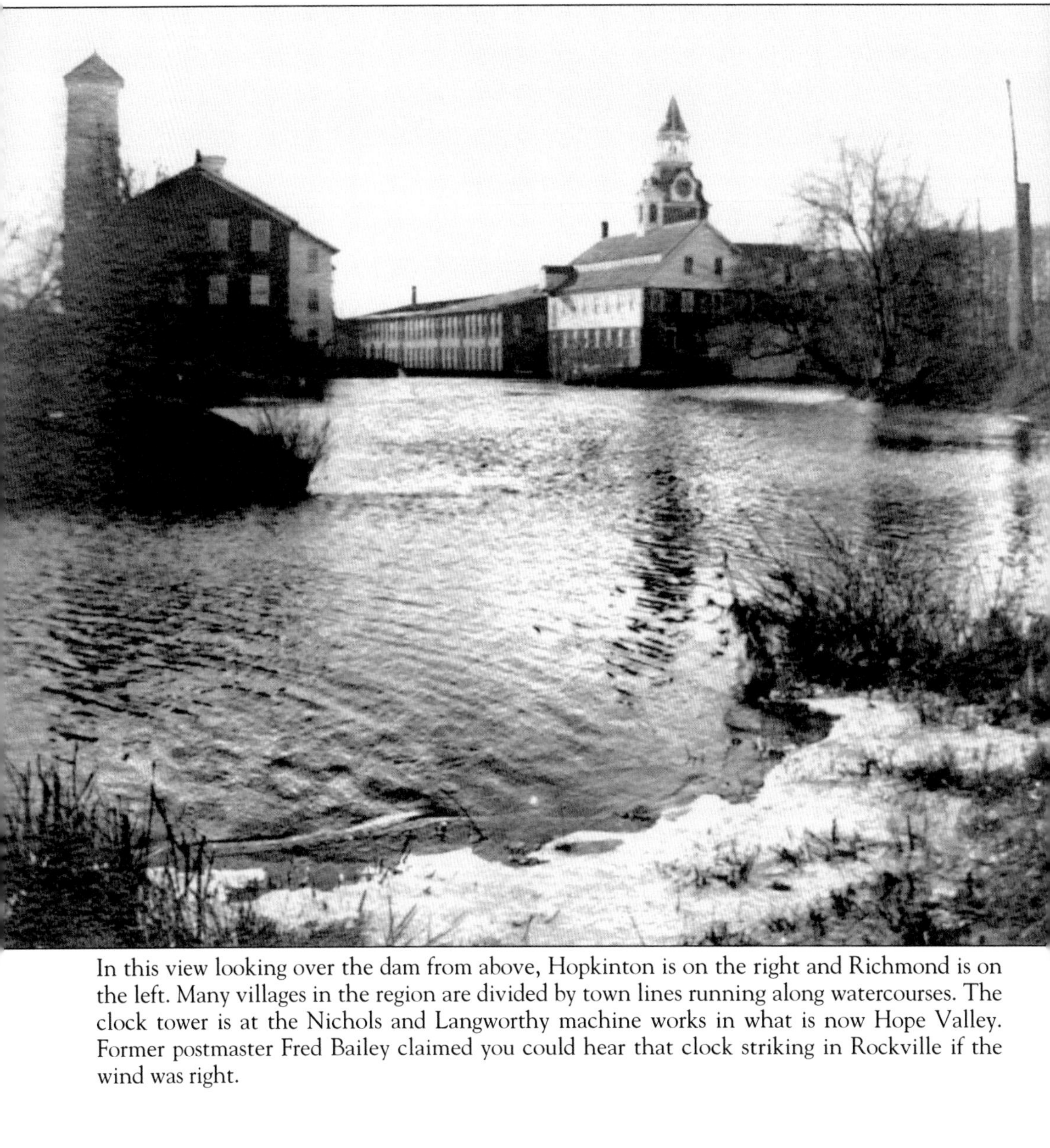

In this view looking over the dam from above, Hopkinton is on the right and Richmond is on the left. Many villages in the region are divided by town lines running along watercourses. The clock tower is at the Nichols and Langworthy machine works in what is now Hope Valley. Former postmaster Fred Bailey claimed you could hear that clock striking in Rockville if the wind was right.

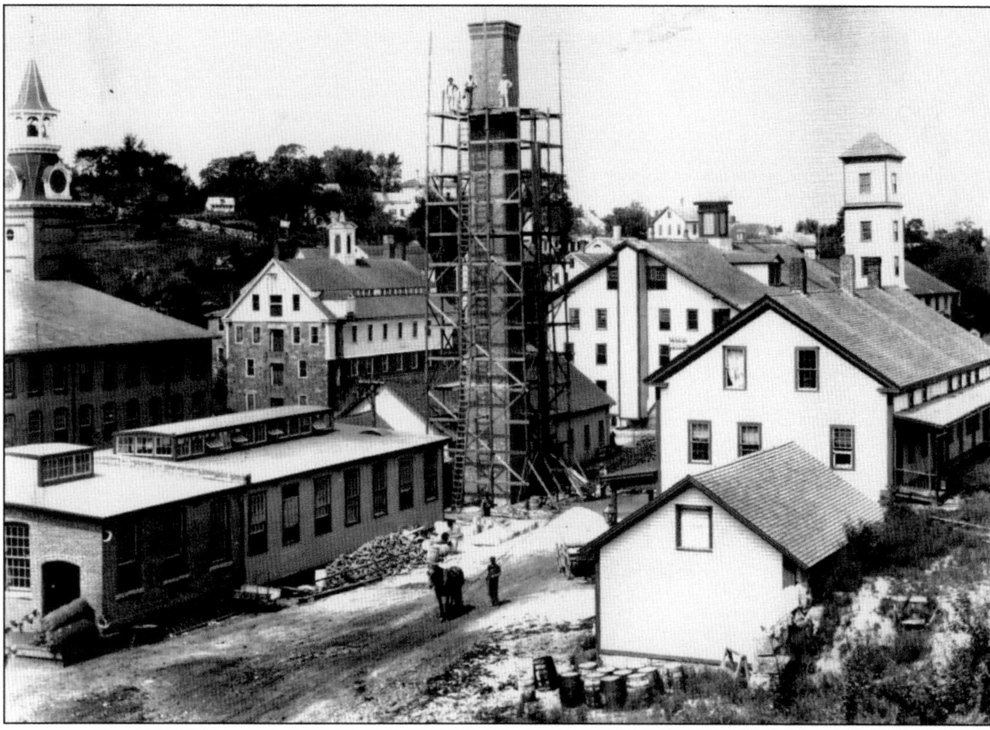

The foreground buildings are in the Richmond portion of Hope Valley; that name originally applied only to the Richmond side of the border. Over the years it crept across the river, swallowing up the Locustville name and a good part of Wyoming. Nichols and Langworthy is on the opposite bank. The building with the long porch at the right was, at various times, a company boardinghouse and the company store.

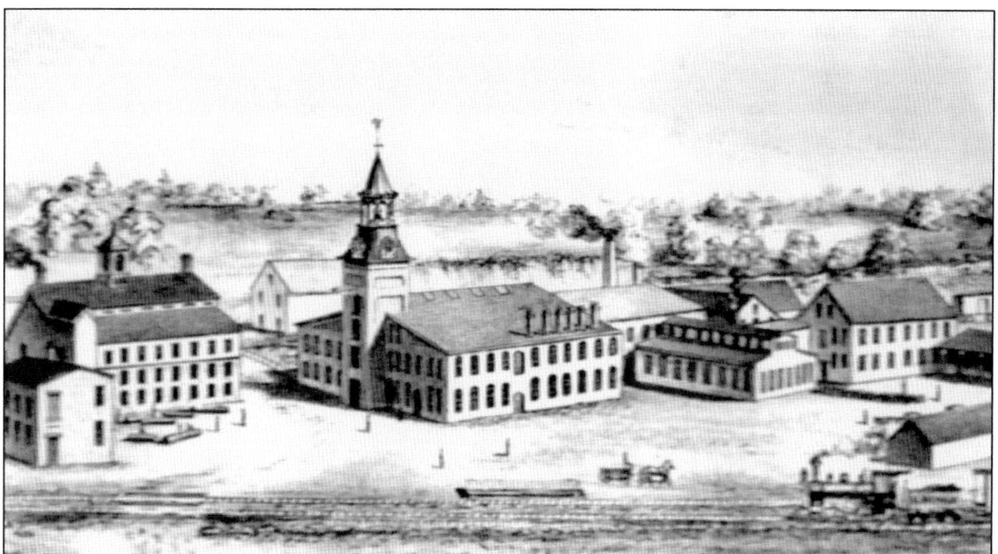

Nichols and Langworthy was a major manufacturer of machinery, printing presses, steam engines, and boilers. Satisfied customers included Thomas Edison.

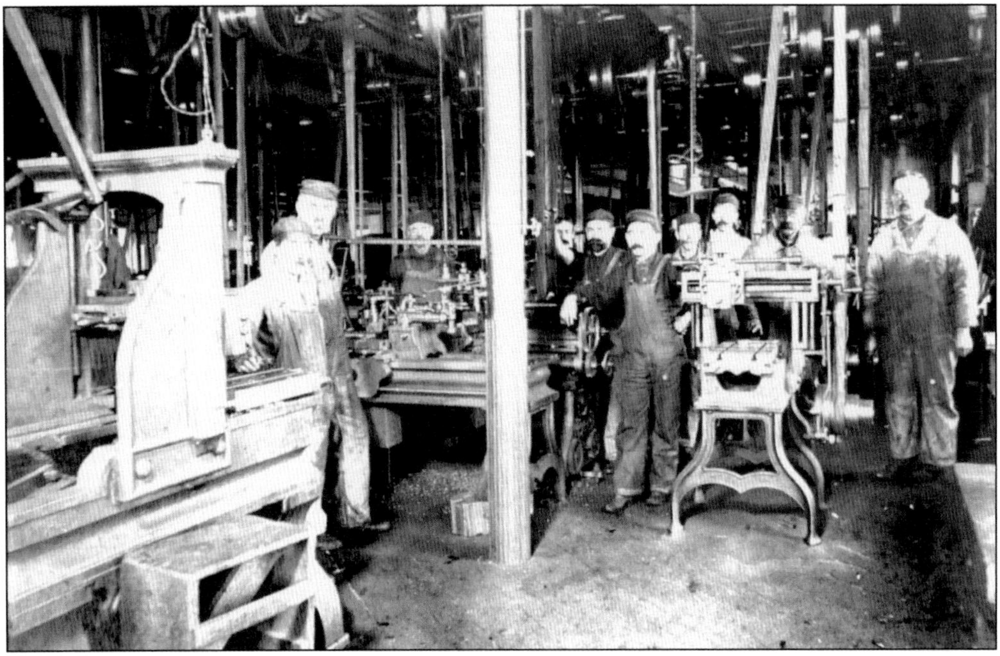

The overhead power trains originally ran with waterpower, an arrangement typical of these noisy mills. By the time of this photograph, though, a few electric cords seem to be snaking through the belts.

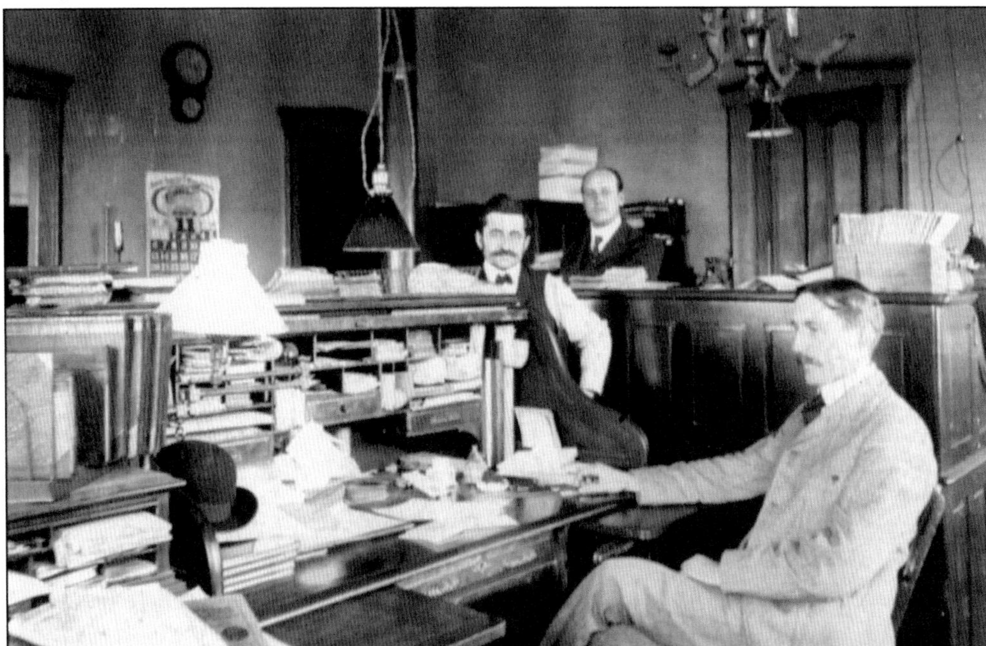

Ernest Crandall, Willis Nichols, and John Arnold, seen here from left to right, were "the Elite" (the Nichols and Langworthy administration office staff) *c.* 1906. Willis Nichols was also one of "the Dudes of Hope Valley" (seen on page 30). At least four electric lamps are visible, one dangling from what appears to be a disused gaslight chandelier.

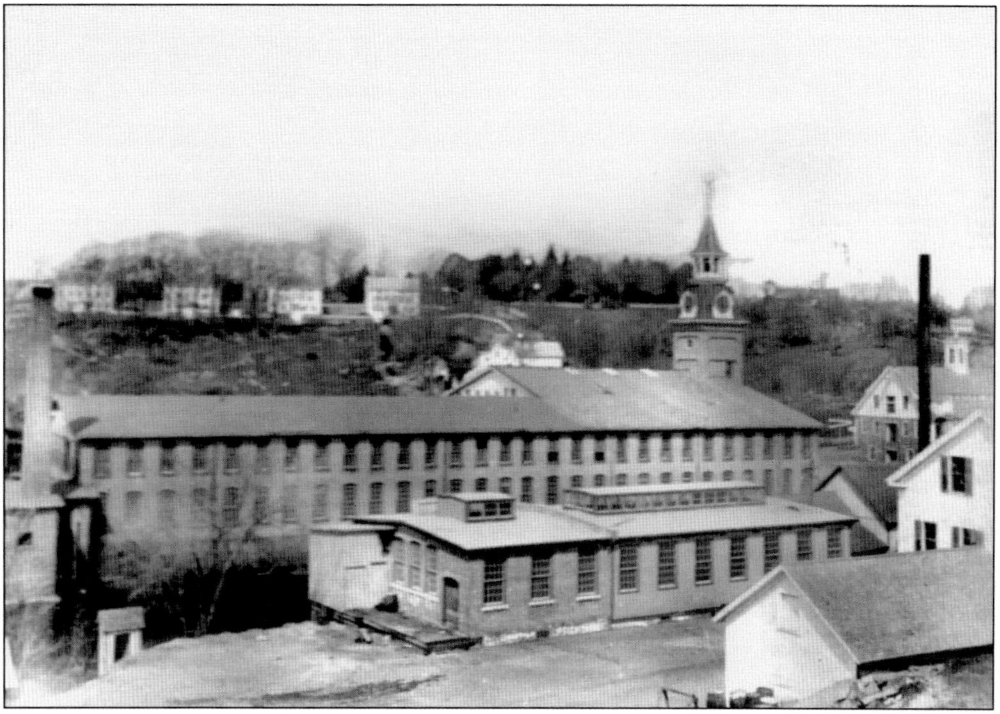

Up on the ridge are mill houses, provided (at a price, but without much choice) by the company—a common arrangement for the time.

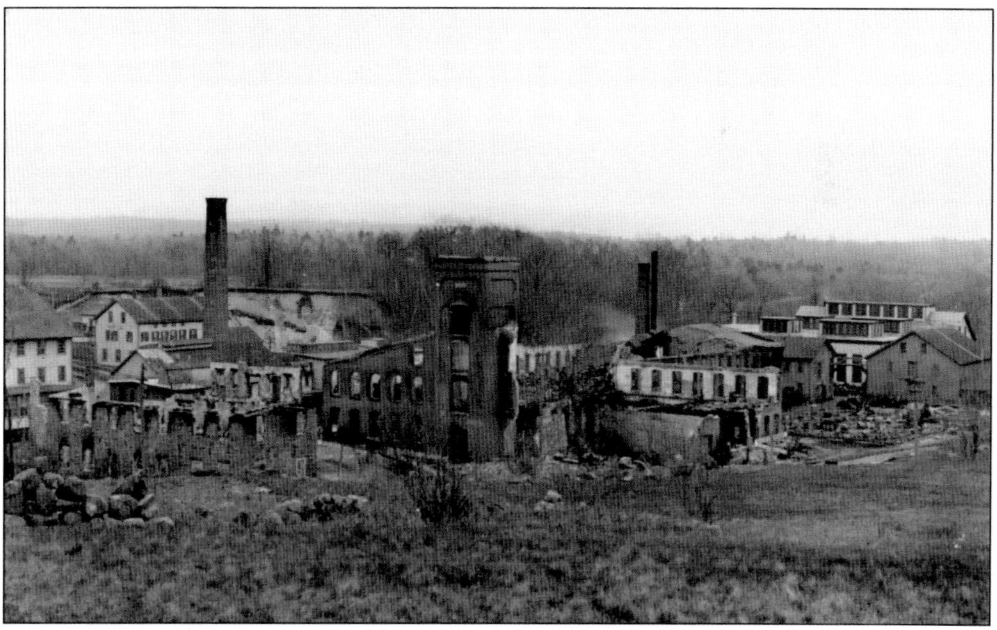

The April 13, 1909, fire at Nichols and Langworthy was truly disastrous. Folks whispered, without any real foundation, that Herman Dock, head of the machine shop, set the fire. Local boys sang, "Hickory Dickory Dock, the fire went up the clock, the clock struck one, and down it come, damned old Herman Dock."

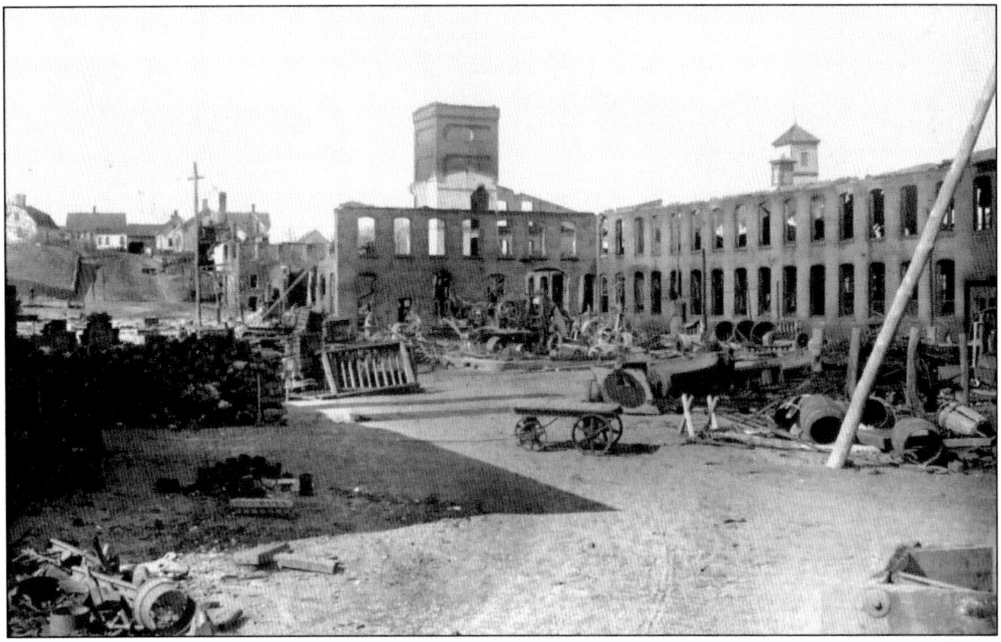

The damage caused by the April 13, 1909, fire at Nichols and Langworthy could have been much worse if it were not for the fact that Mystic Mill across the river had just installed a powerful new pump, which supplied firefighters with water. Residents saved nearby houses with wet carpets and a bucket brigade. Despite the devastation, portions of the building were rebuilt and remain in use today, but the village never recovered its manufacturing prominence.

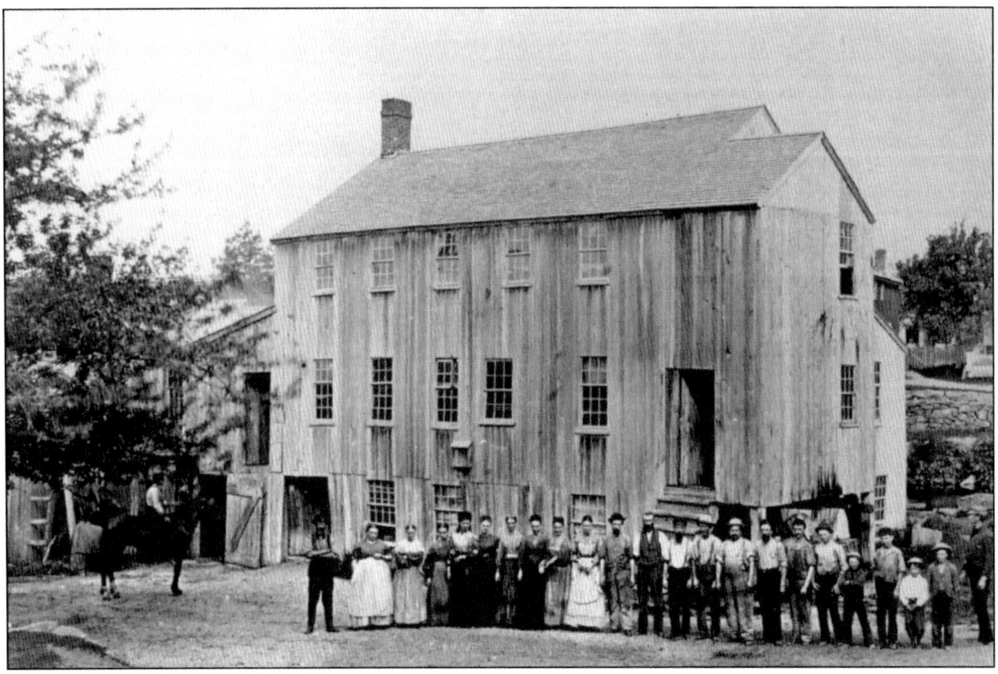

Compare this image of the early Laureldale Mill in what is now Ashaway with the next photograph or with the Rockville Upper Mill (seen on page 82) to see how the science of mill design progressed.

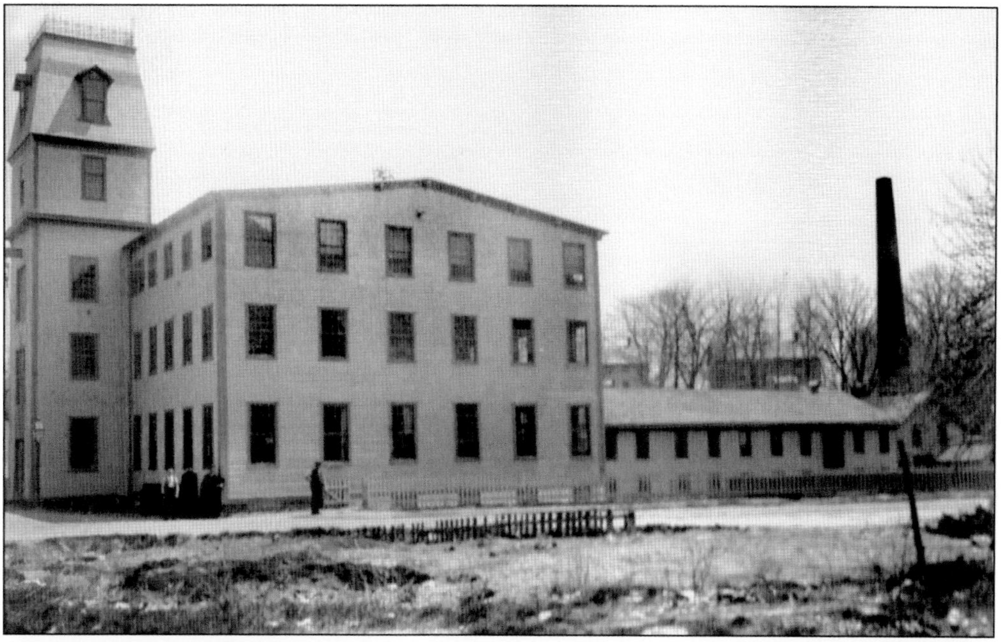

The 1846 Ashaway Woolen mill (later Ashaway Products) at Laurel and Main Streets, while much larger than Laureldale Mill, also seems more permanent and more deliberately thought out. Many mills by this time had towers for stairs and for loading platforms on each level. This saved floor space and reduced the risk of fires spreading.

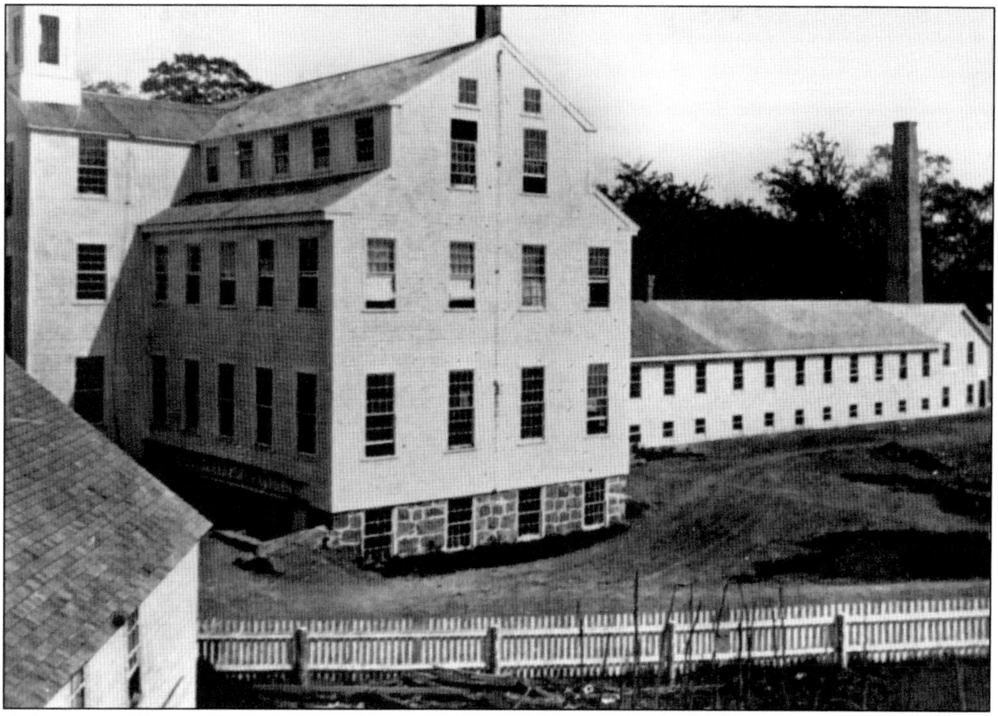

Ashaway Mill, caught here in a stereopticon image, likewise reflects a considerable body of construction and architectural experience going back to the 1700s.

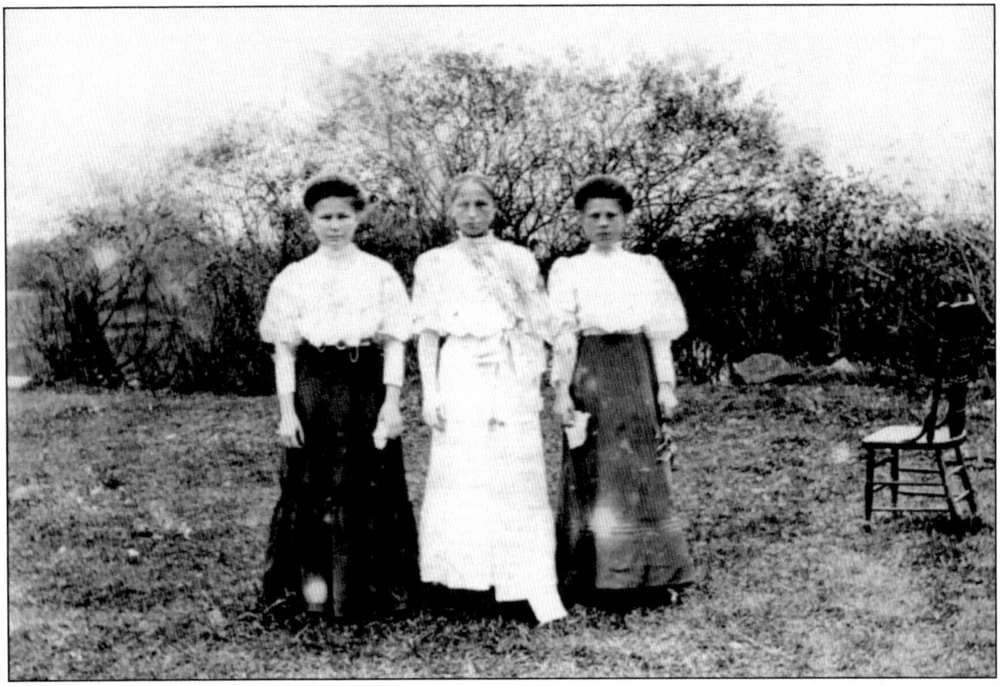

By the turn of the century, Polish families were working the mills. The Richmond section of Hope Valley came to be known as Polish Hill, along with other less complimentary names. These ladies, photographed just before 1900, are identified as Mary Jurcak (wife of Walter Popioliek), Helen Jurcak (wife of Theodore Nadolny), and Katherine Kowalski (Mrs. Czark).

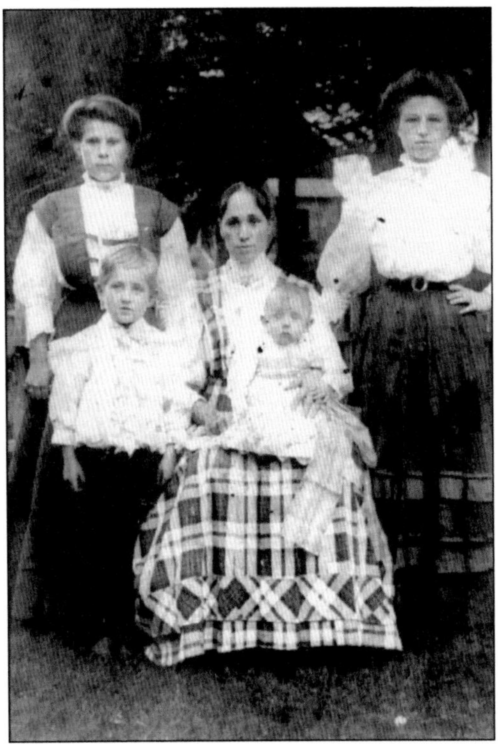

Polish families, such as the group seen here *c.* 1906, left their legacy in the products of their industrious work, their family names, and their exciting cuisine.

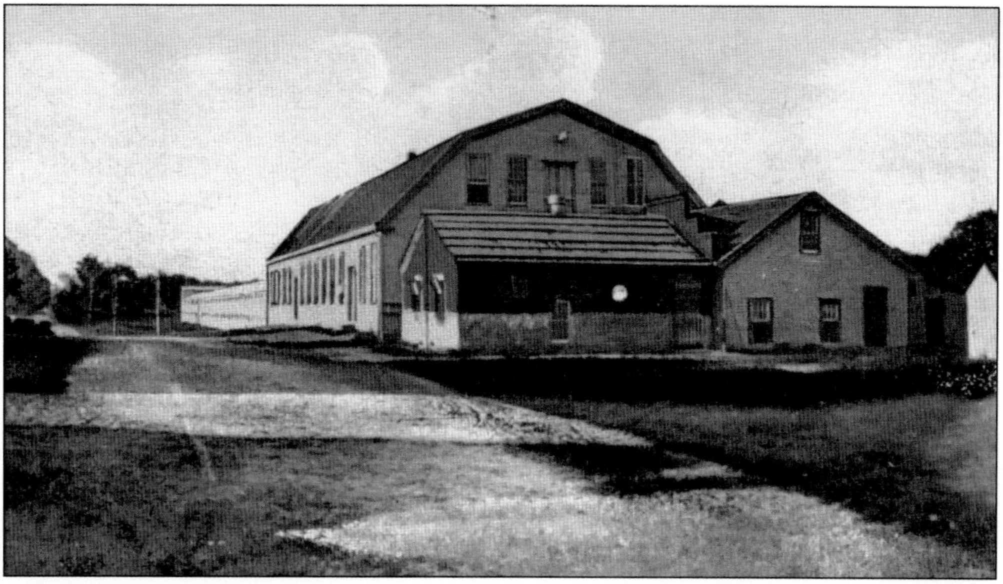

Ashaway Line and Twine is well known to anglers. During World War II, the company provided fishline for navy survival kits, as well as surgical sutures, hammock ropes, glider tow lines, and much more.

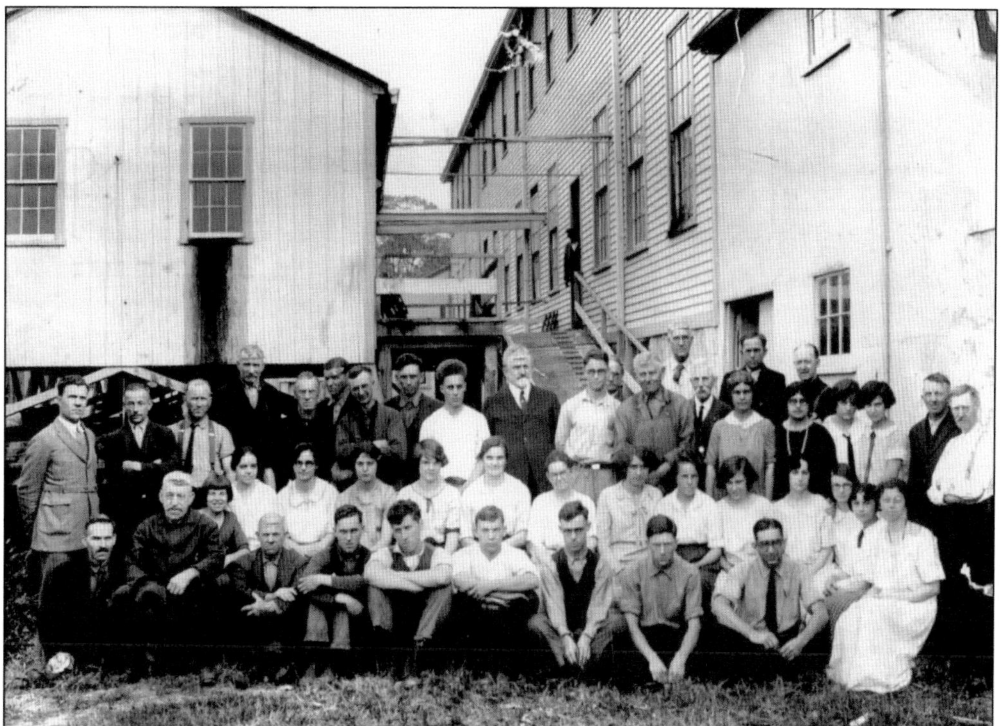

Notice where the lone black (or possibly Narragansett) employee is standing in this 1923 portrait of staff at Ashaway Line and Twine. Despite Prudence Crandall's example, sad to relate, the "color bar" remained wide in the early 20th century.

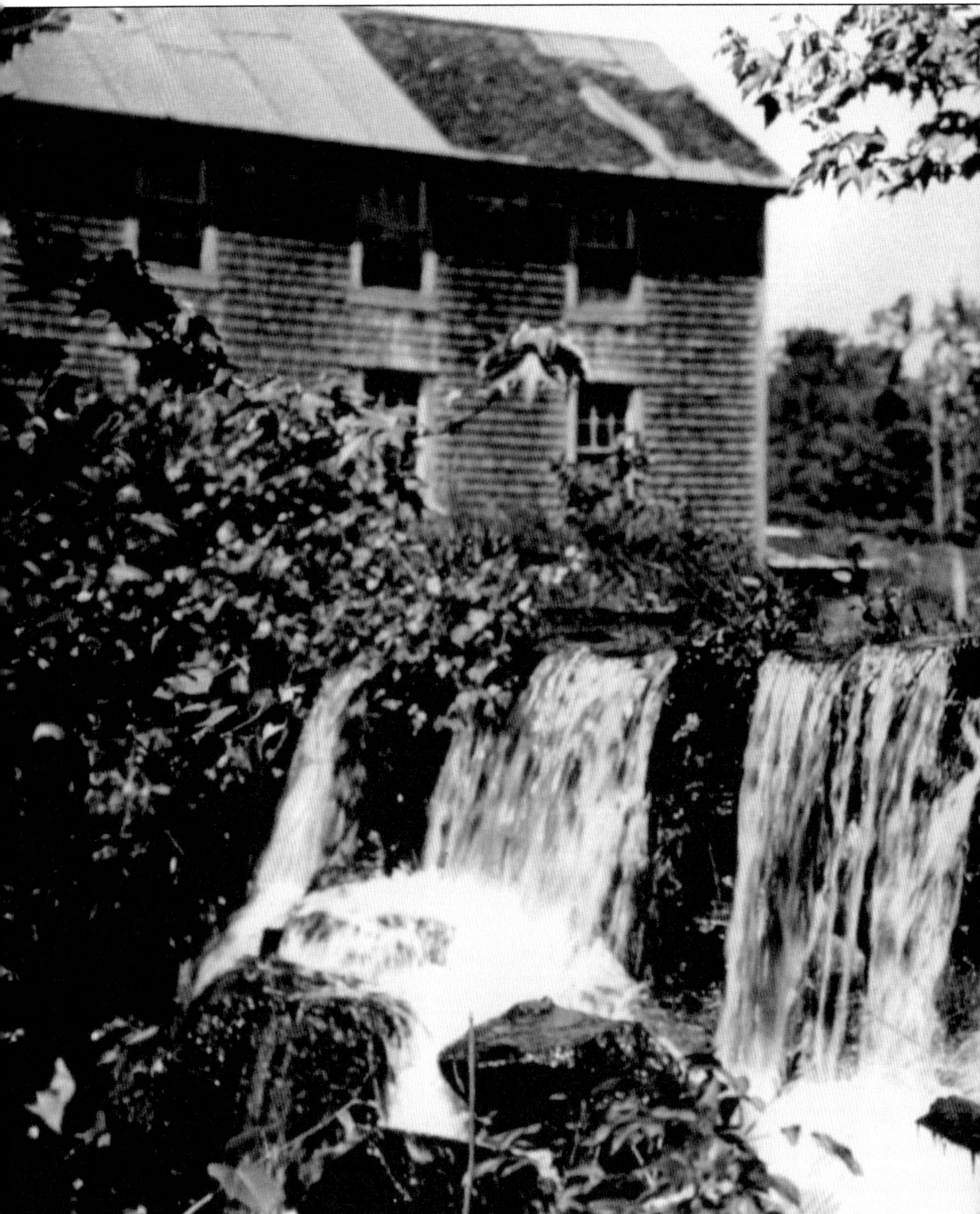

Someone visiting Union Line and Twine at Canonchet in 1940 found beauty where others might have seen only a sad industrial scene. The photographer must have sensed that the

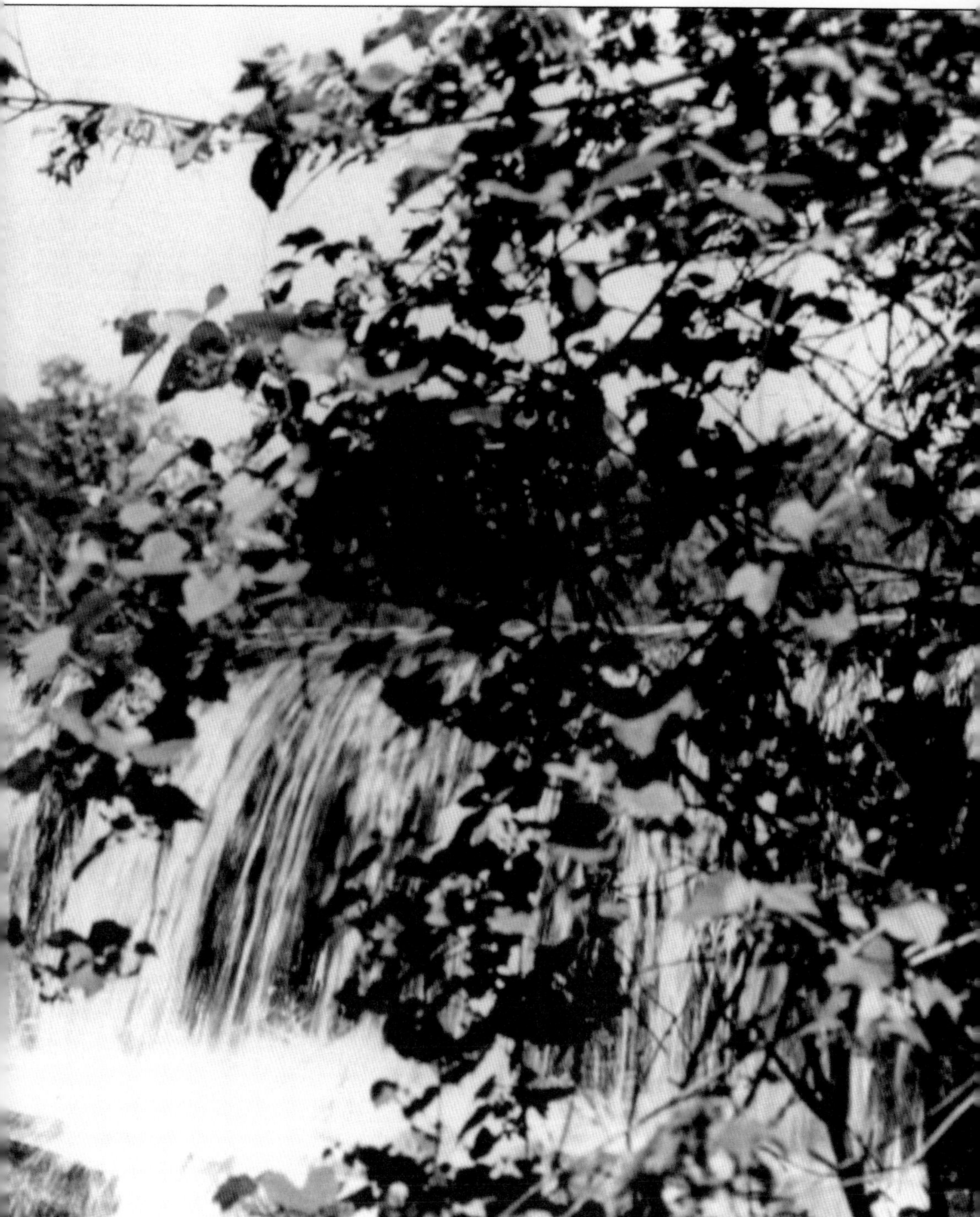

Depression was just about over.

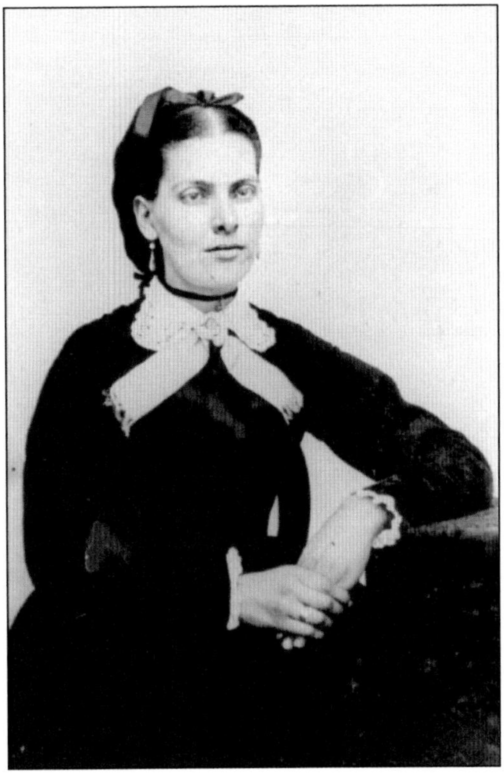

Lovina Palmer, a mill girl at the Locustville Mill, presumably worked until her marriage, but her story took its own singular twist: she married the overseer. James H. Barber and his bride were each born in 1847, before the Mexican War.
Mr. Barber died in 1932. What changes he experienced in his lifetime!

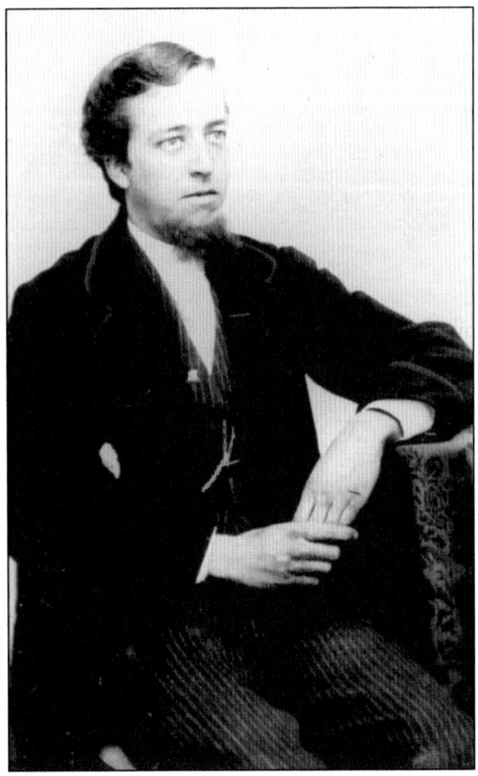

Five

Going Places

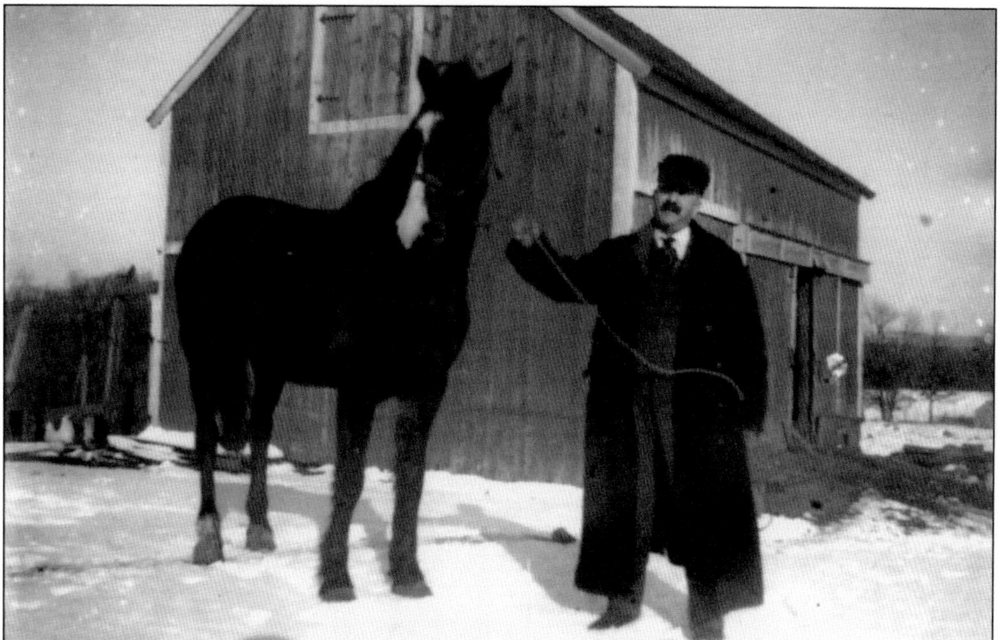

Into the early 20th century, travel on land meant travel by horse. A good steed was an expensive investment that was carefully cared for. Rockville's Byron Kenyon, seen above, was proud enough of his animal to call in a photographer. With Wood River dammed for milling, Hopkinton's main concern was land transportation. The New London Turnpike (now Route 3) ran diagonally through town, just as Interstate 95 does today. Both highways, in their time, were the main road from New York to Boston. Thriving firms in Ashaway and Hopkinton City manufactured carriages. Eventually a railroad joined Woodville, Canonchet, and Hope Valley to the bigger world, while a trolley joined Ashaway to Westerly. By the 1920s, buses chugged Scouts to Camp Yawgoog as the state started paving the roads. Trolleys and horse-drawn vehicles quickly vanished, followed slowly by the trains. Still, to this day it is not unheard of, while strolling down a country lane or village street, to meet a Hopkintonian on horseback.

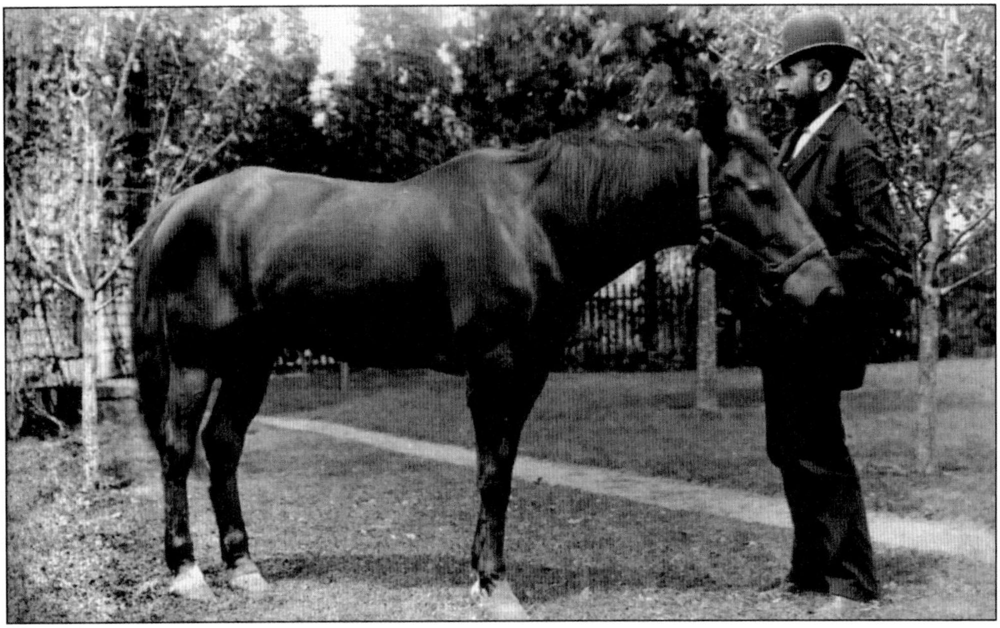

Like Byron Kenyon in Rockville, Amos G. Nichols of Hope Valley must have been quite proud of his horse.

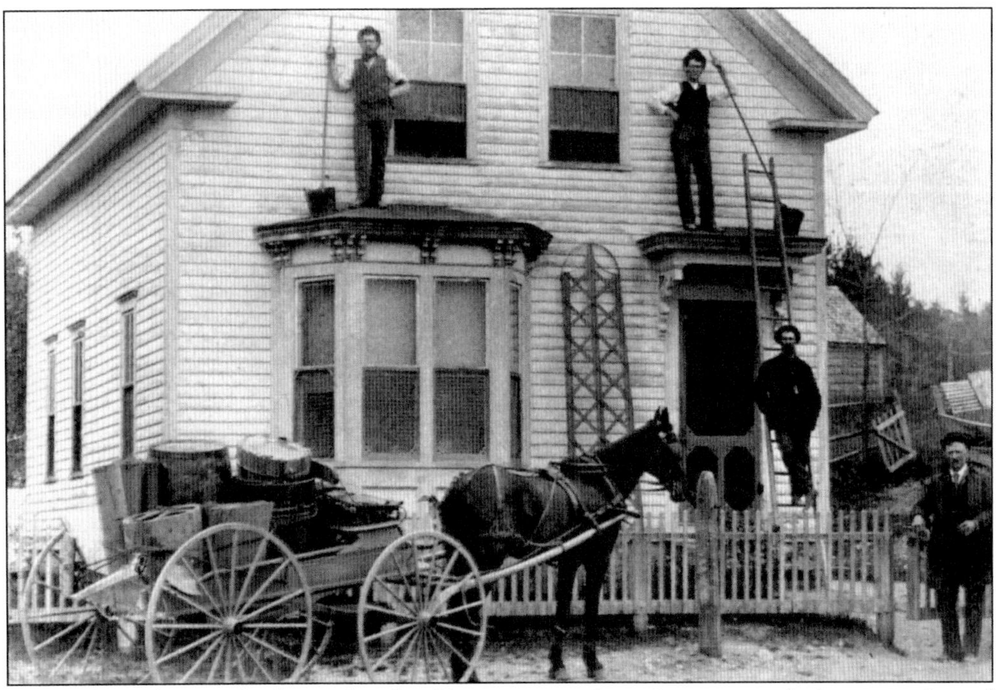

Here is the pickup truck of an earlier day. If you got it in those days, it came by horse—unless, of course, you carried it yourself. David Dutemple, the owner of this Hope Valley home, operated a blacksmith shop on the property.

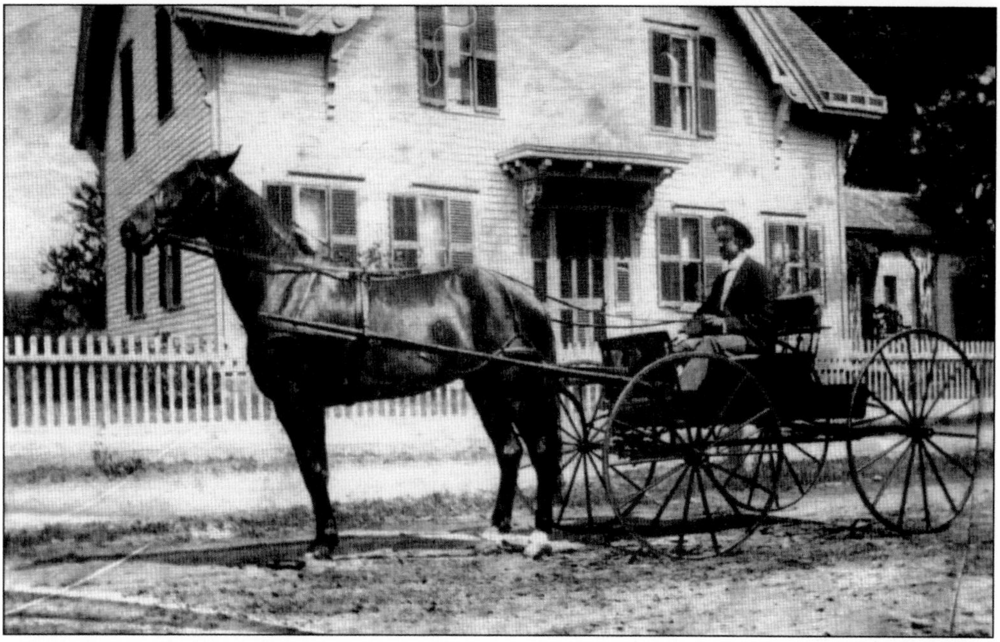

Horse-drawn vehicles served as many purposes and were just as varied as motor vehicles today. This light buckboard is a far cry from the box delivery wagon. This particular image is a lovely, perfectly preserved cyanotype printed on linen.

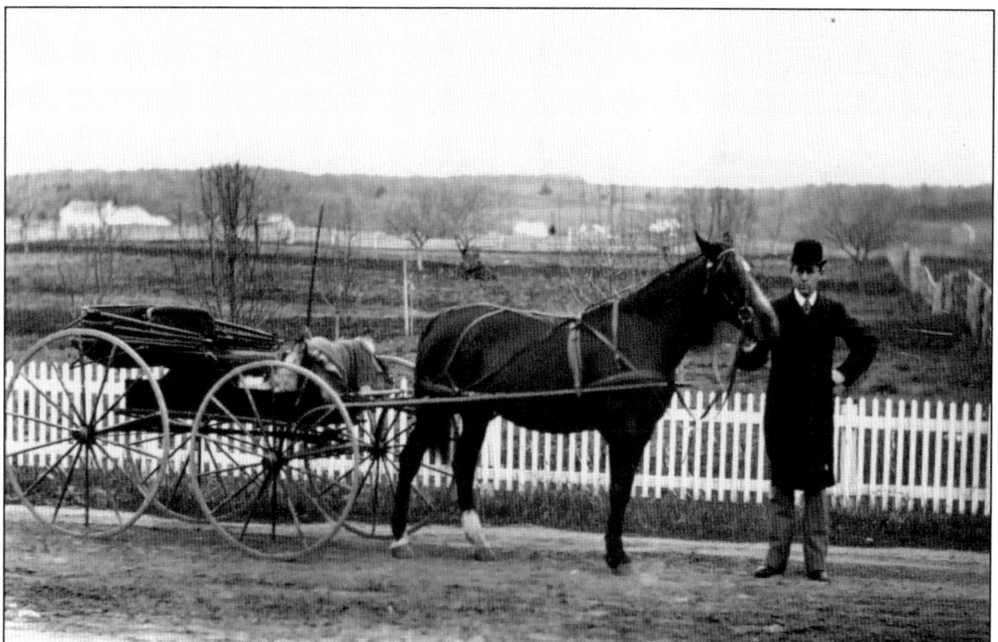

Archivists suspect that this "convertible" buggy may be freshly made at A. L. Wells and Company of Hopkinton City, in its time the largest carriage manufacturer in Rhode Island. There were at least two other makers in Hopkinton City, where Spicer's Tavern kept a stable of 40 or 50 horses as fresh teams for the 10 or 12 stagecoaches that stopped there daily.

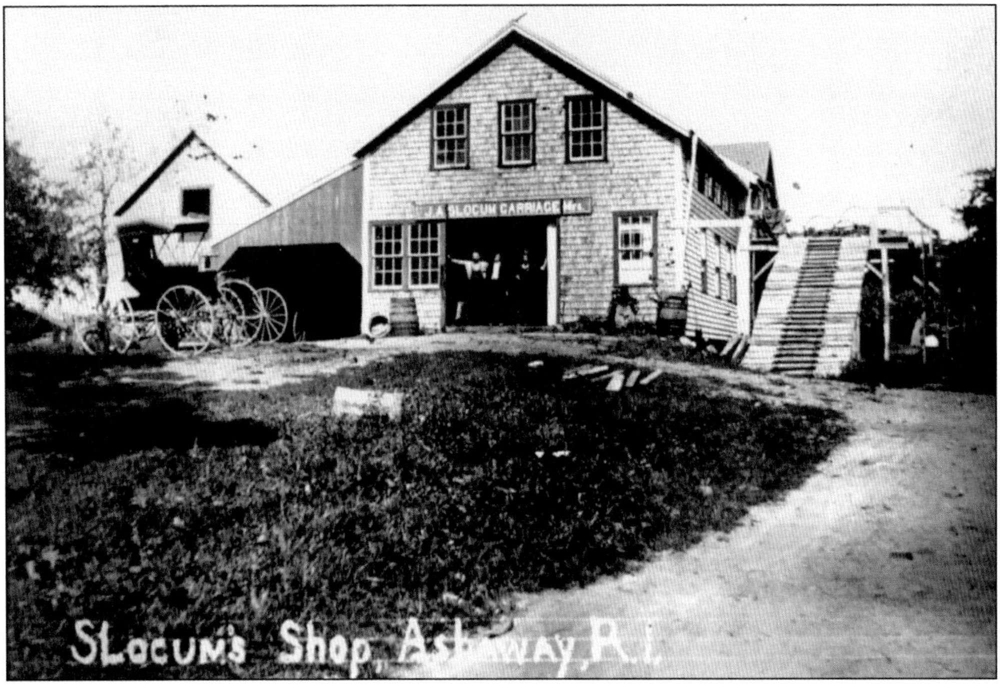

Notice the wheels on the platform at the right.

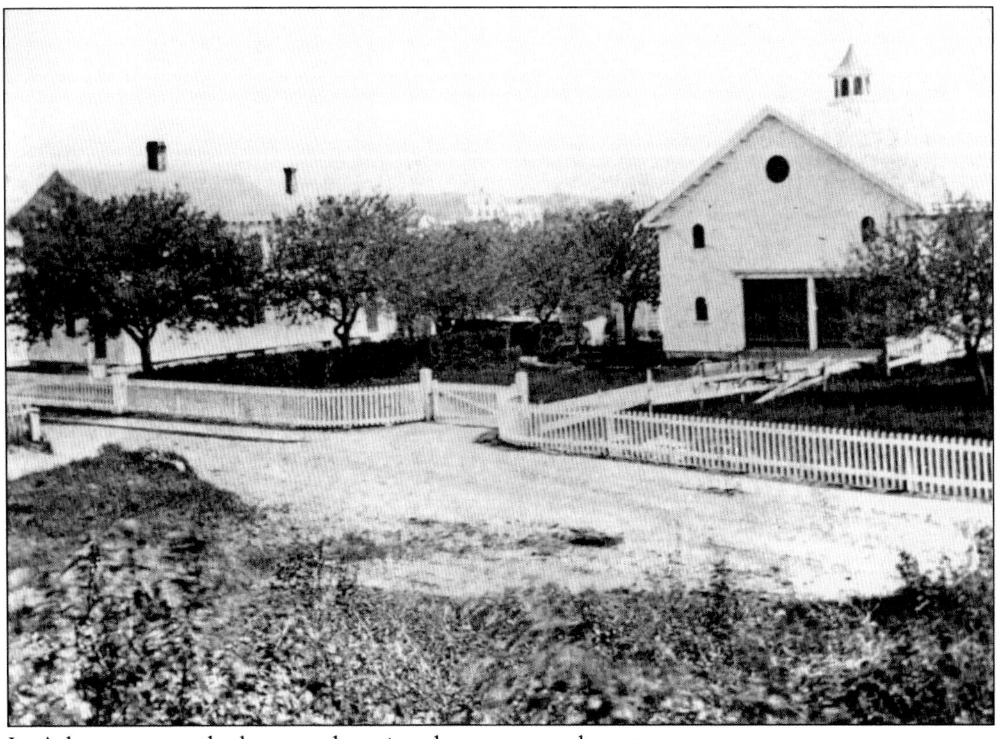
In Ashaway, even the barns and carriage houses were elegant.

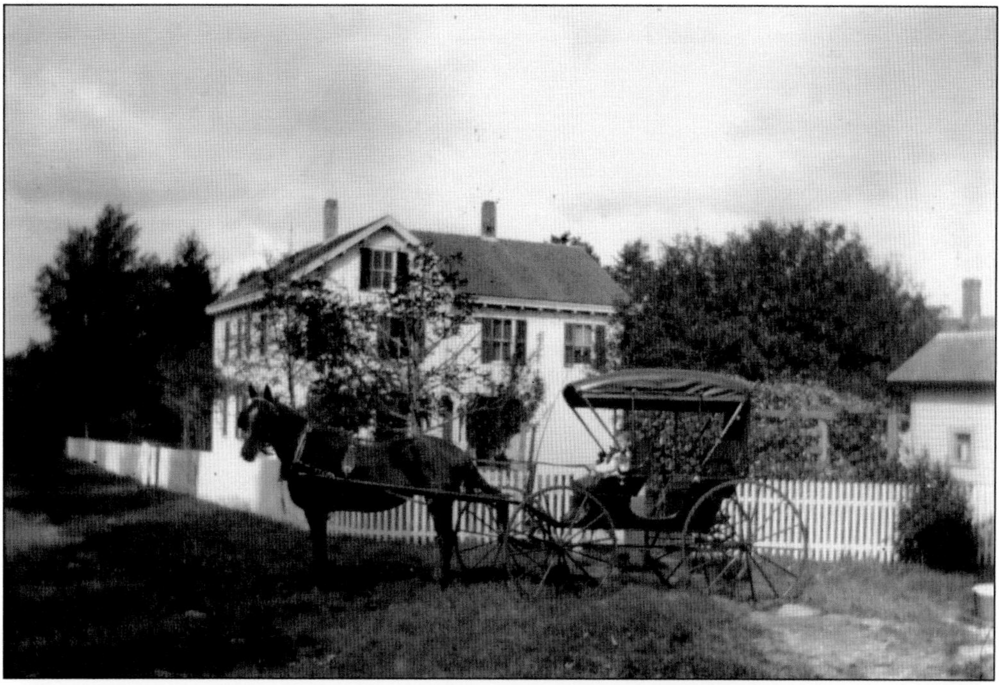

Perhaps this boy in Rockville has been told to wait in the buggy while his elders do something important inside. If so, he seems to be thinking of making a break for it.

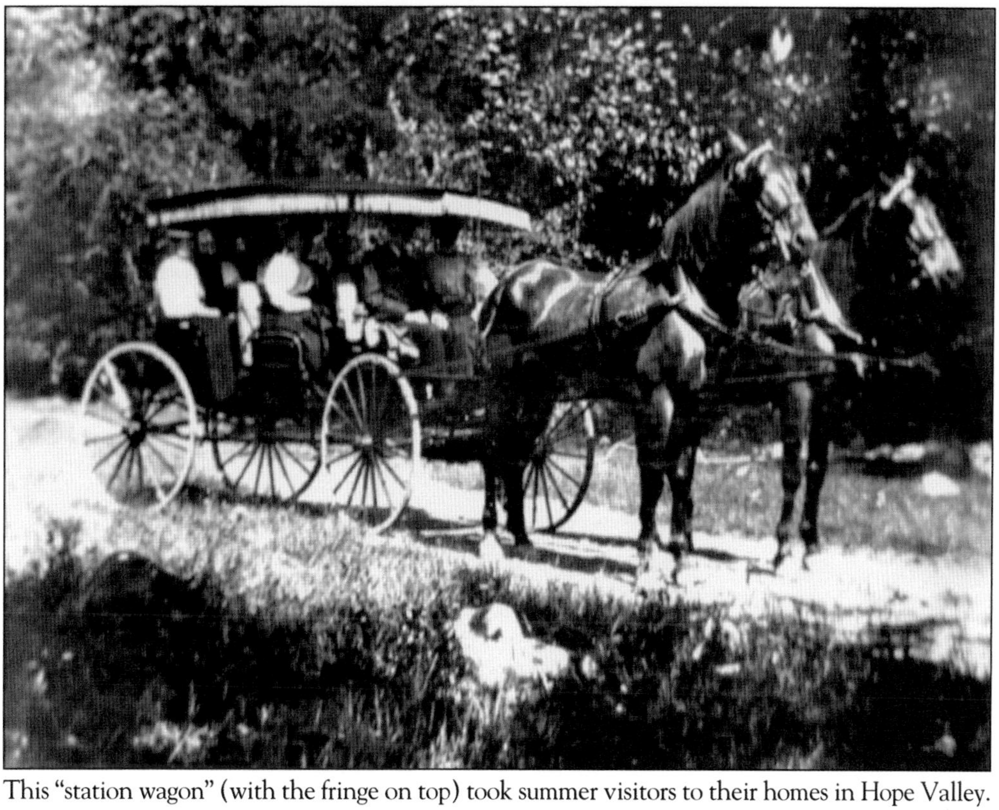

This "station wagon" (with the fringe on top) took summer visitors to their homes in Hope Valley.

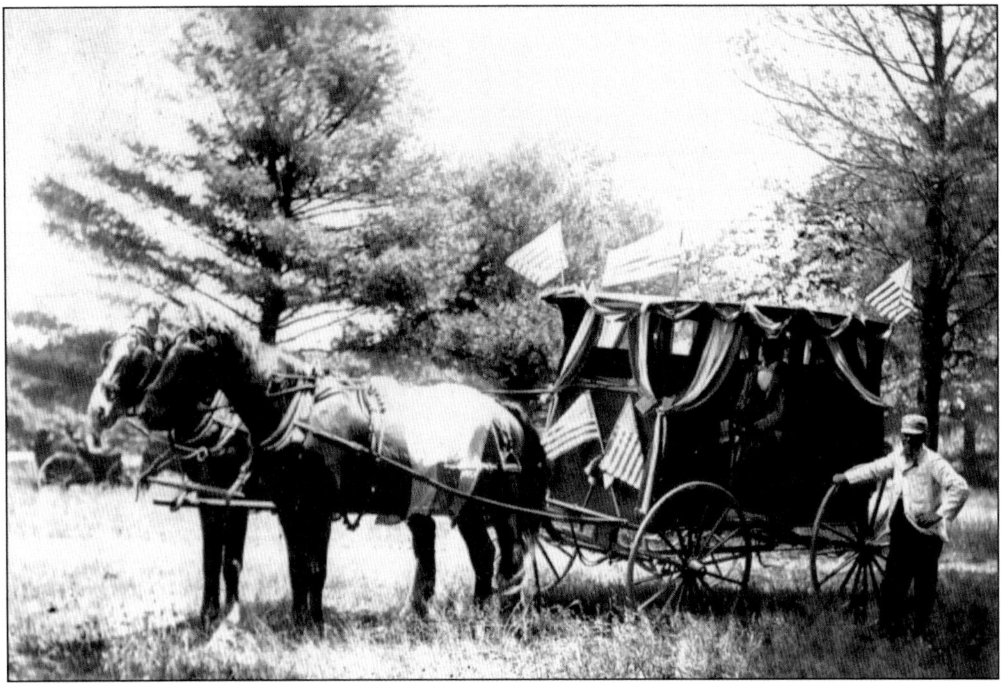

In a day when most folks did not even have a horse, groceries came to you. The Nichols Bakery wagon was not always this decorative. Presumably it is the Fourth of July.

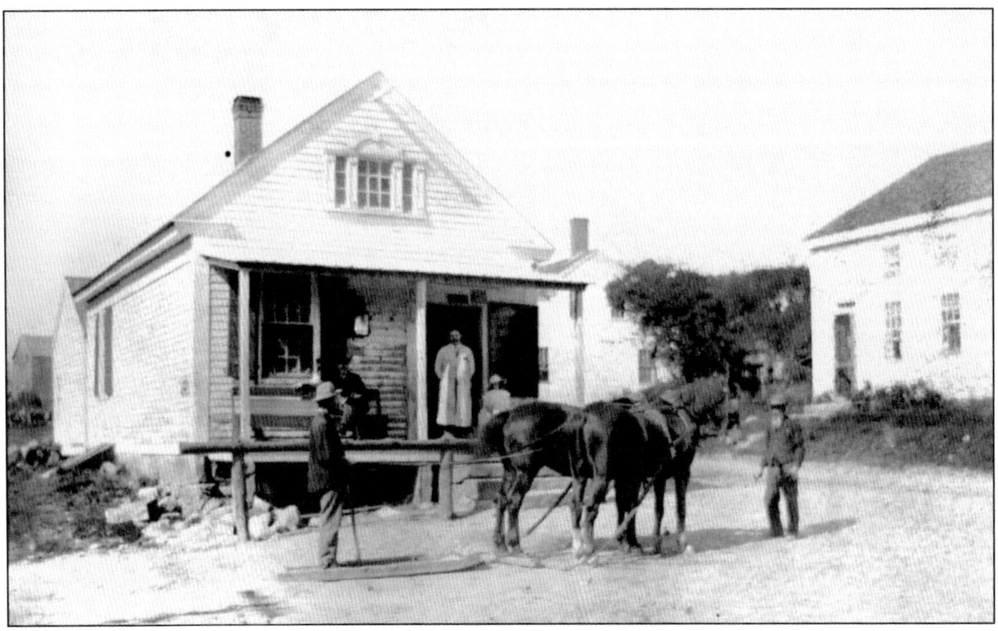

Stones and other heavy weights were moved by sledge. This building still stands; Rockville's post office remained here almost to the end of the 20th century. Postmaster Albert Jordan kept a little shop there in the 1950s and 1960s. Homemakers could pick up milk or bread, while kids at play piled in for soda and licorice.

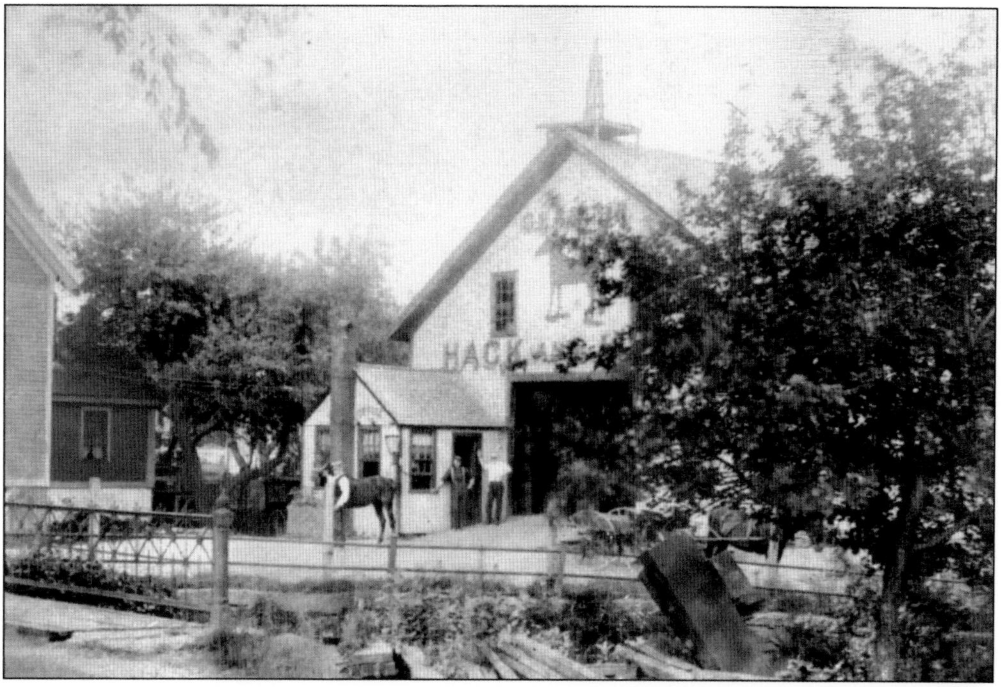

Rather than owning horses or rigs, many people rented them for short-term needs. Hope Valley's Hack and Livery was on Main Street, handy to the depot. Horse rentals being down, Doug and Peggy Yattaw now run it as a gift shop.

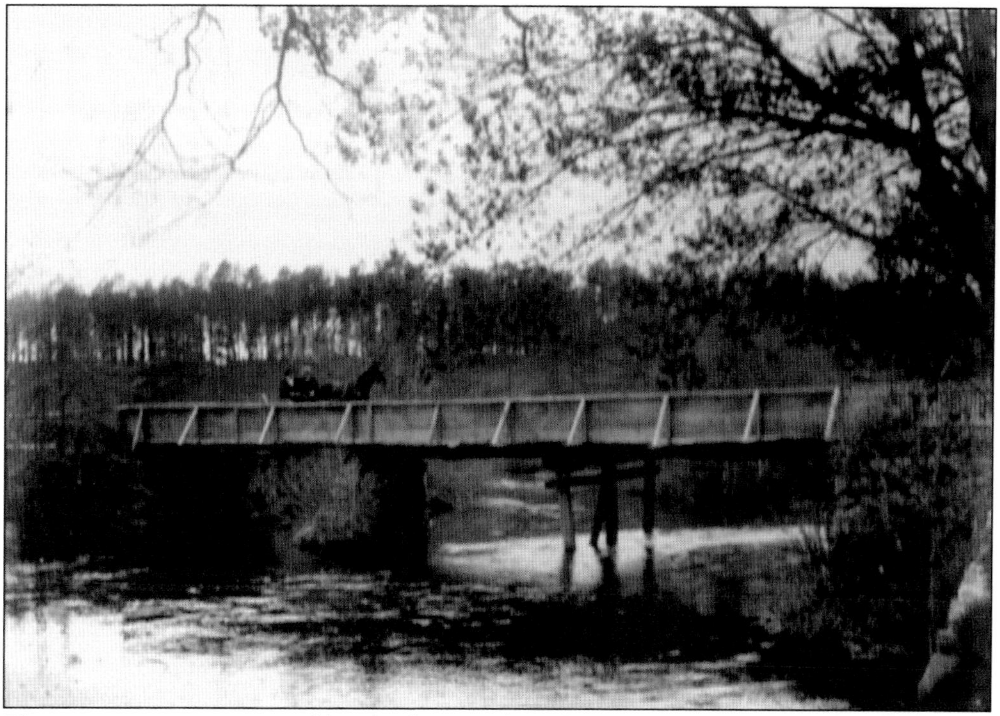

The many rivers, streams, and brooks that run through Hopkinton made bridges a vital part of town life. Wyoming Bridge links Hopkinton and Richmond across Wood River.

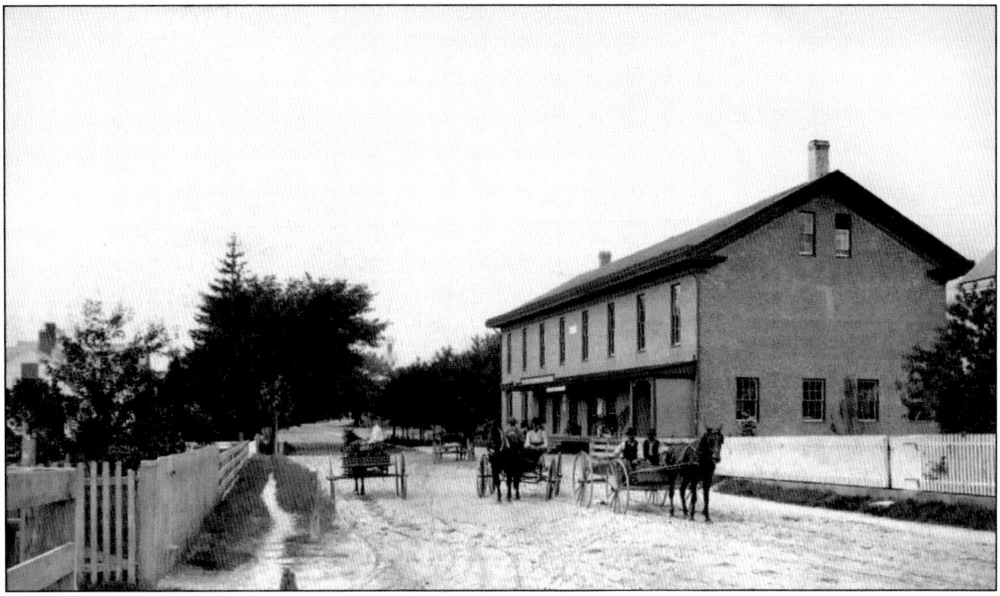

Drag racing is not unknown on Hopkinton streets, but presumably these folks have different plans. The brick building is Barber's Hall, the old Washington Trust on Main Street in Hope Valley.

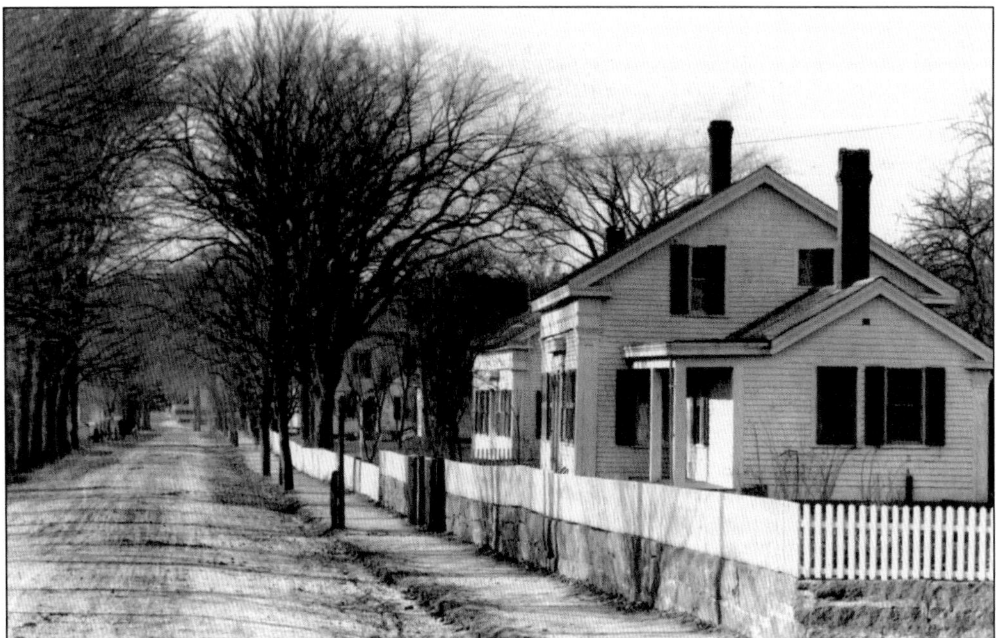

It is hard to believe, but until the 1950s this was the main road between New York and Boston. It had been paved in the interim, though.

At a time of narrow wheels and unpaved roads, mud was the bane of horse-drawn conveyances. Road crews, rather than removing ice and snow, packed it hard so it would last as long as possible, facilitating travel on runnered vehicles. This stereoscopic view shows Dr. Joseph Kenyon's house near Ashaway. He must have dreaded late-night calls in a wet spring.

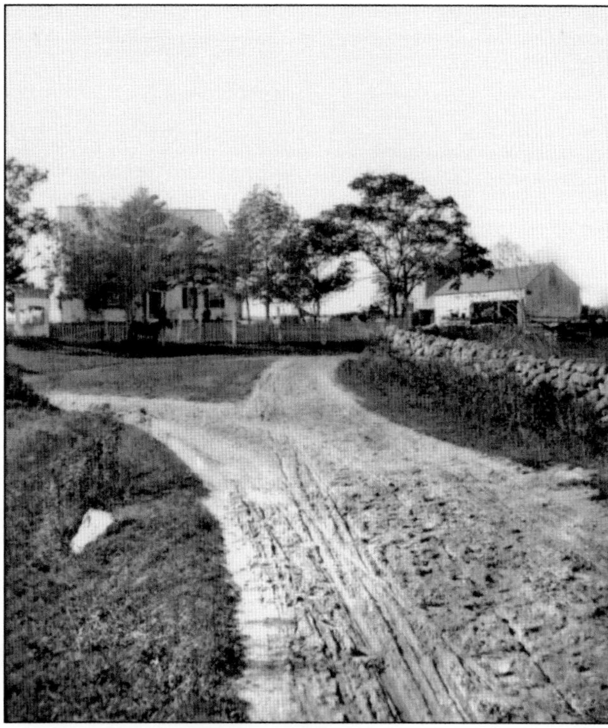

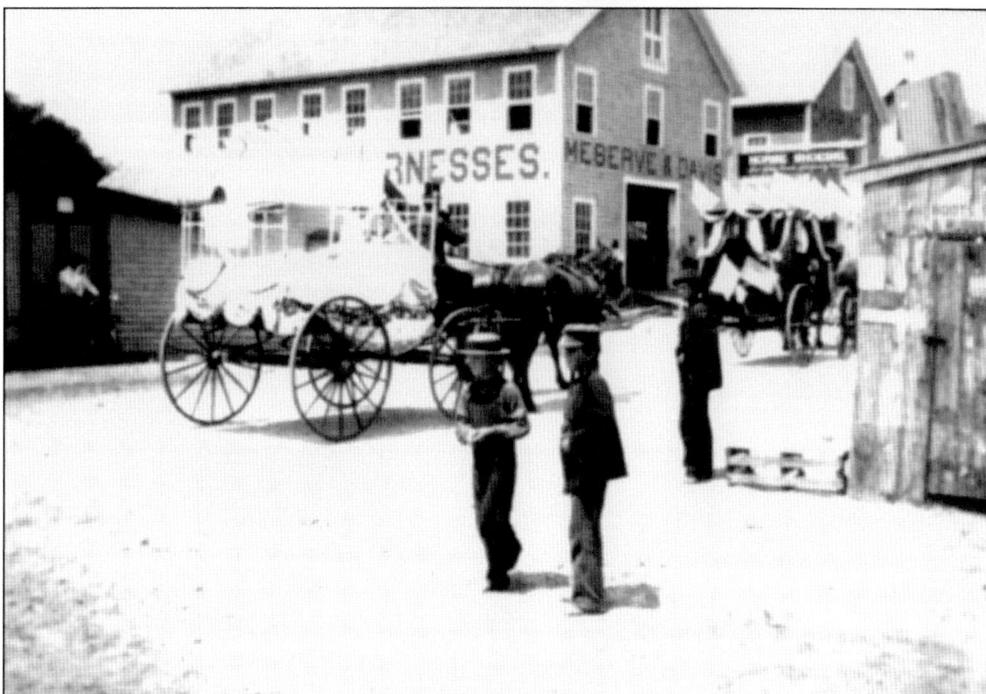

All those horses required a gigantic support industry (just as automobiles do today), including the manufacture, sale, and repair of harnesses. Is that the Nichols Bakery wagon (see page 102) on the right?

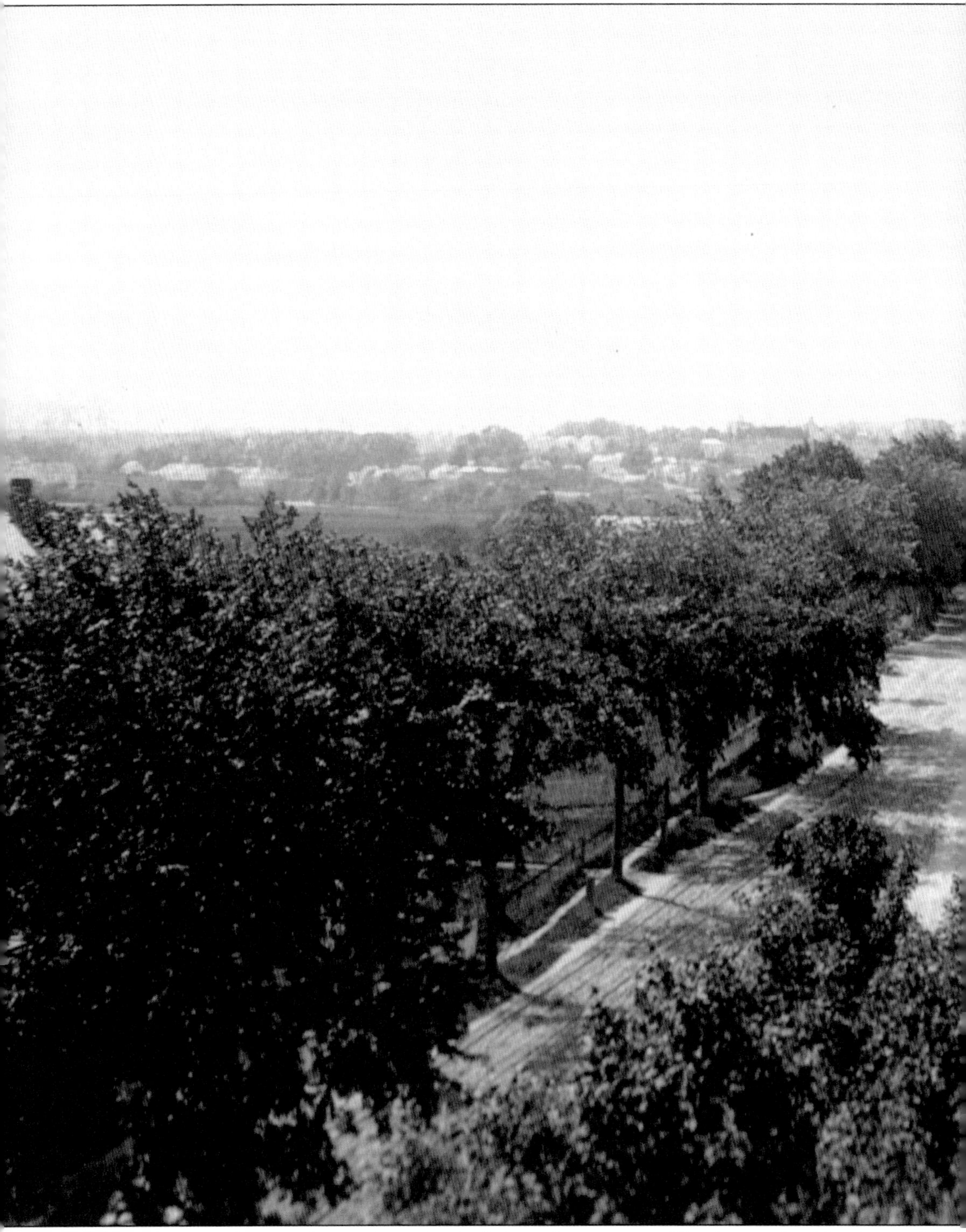

Not so long ago, locusts, elms, and maples shaded our sleepy streets. The devastating Hurricane of 1938 coincided with campaigns to widen the roads; blight finished off most of the giant trees that

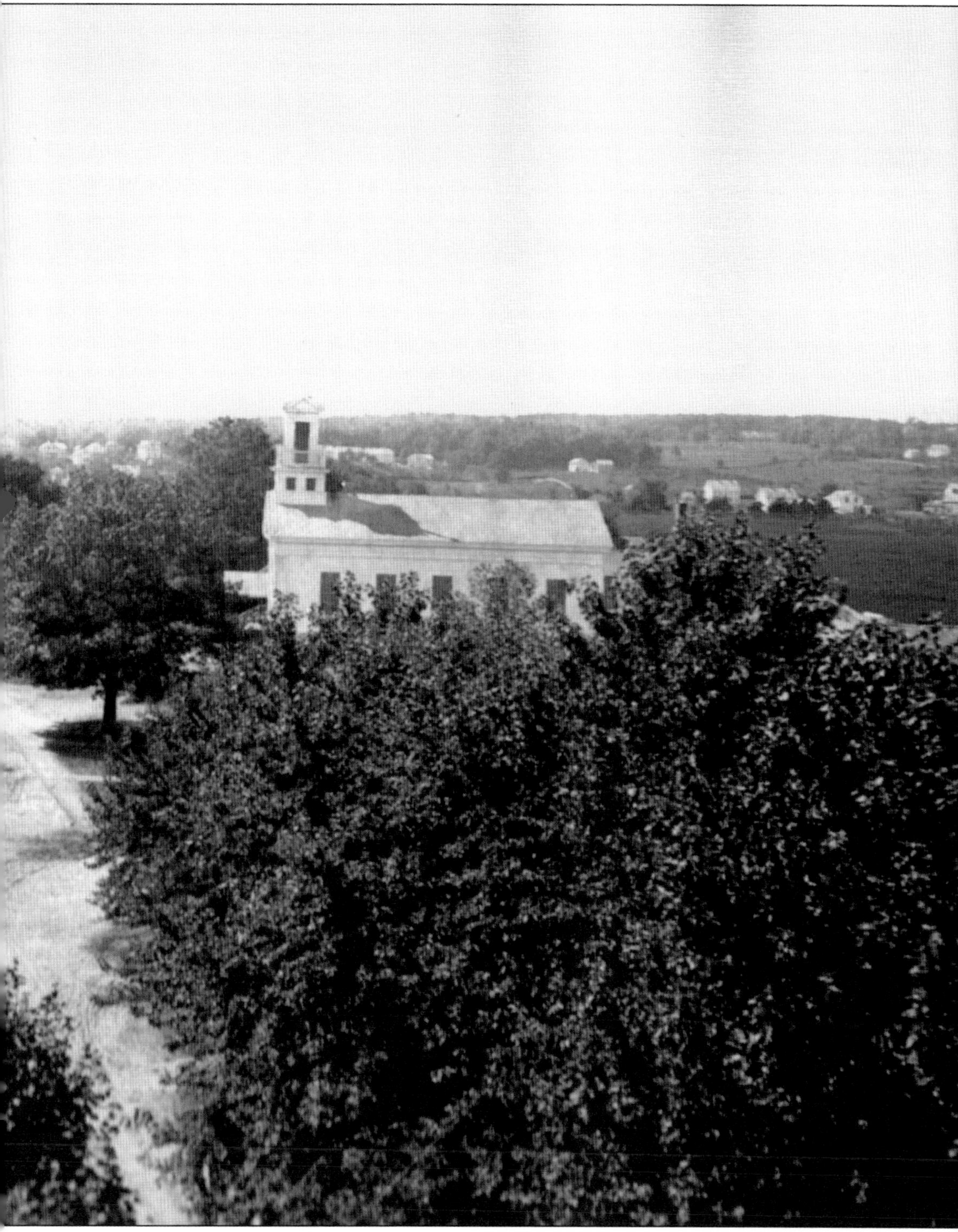

remained. Those who remembered the early years of the 20th century often said that the motorcar changed life more than any other invention. Our world would never be so quiet again.

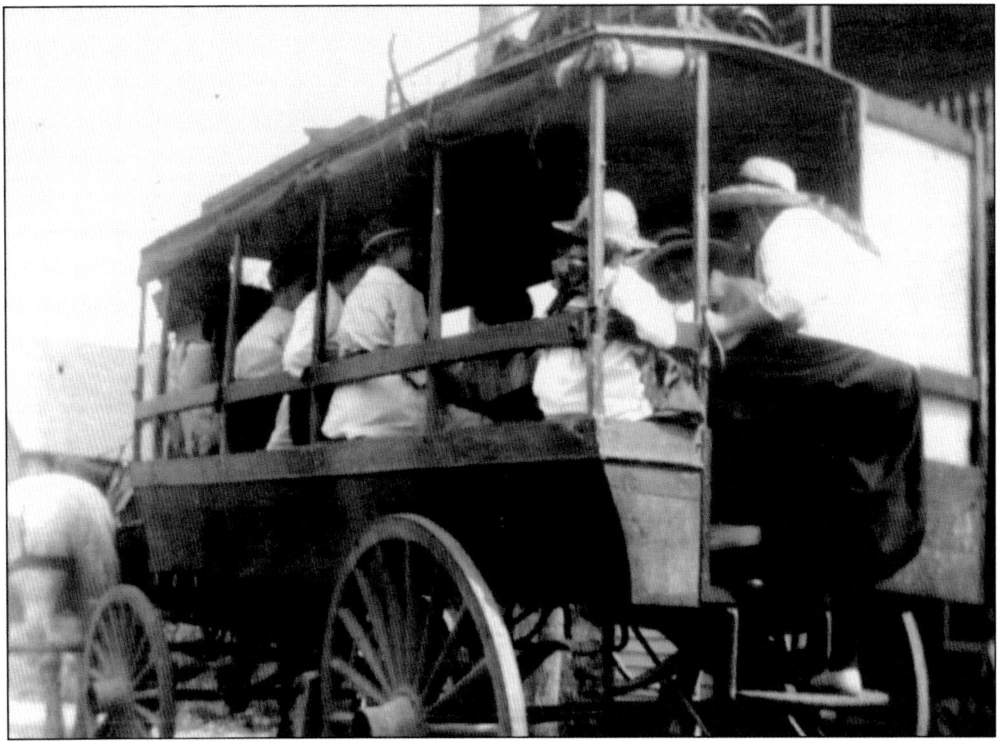

Even as late as 1915, Gladys Segar took her Camp Fire girls to Camp Yawgoog by horse and wagon. Frances Gangawere-Lanphere is just boarding at the foot of Spring Street in Hope Valley. Those of a certain age will recall the building at the right (now gone) as the old A & P.

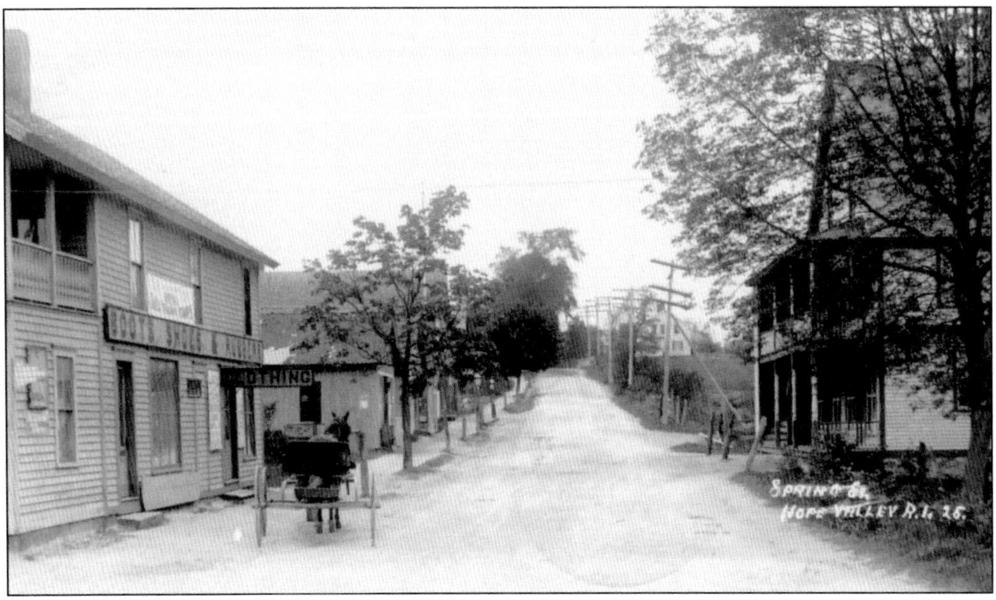

Slopes meant considerable trouble in the days of the horse and even in the early days of the automobile. The hilly terrain inhibited movement in a town like Hopkinton. The house on the rise is the Eva Sheldon Wright home. The library, two homes, and several businesses were later built below it.

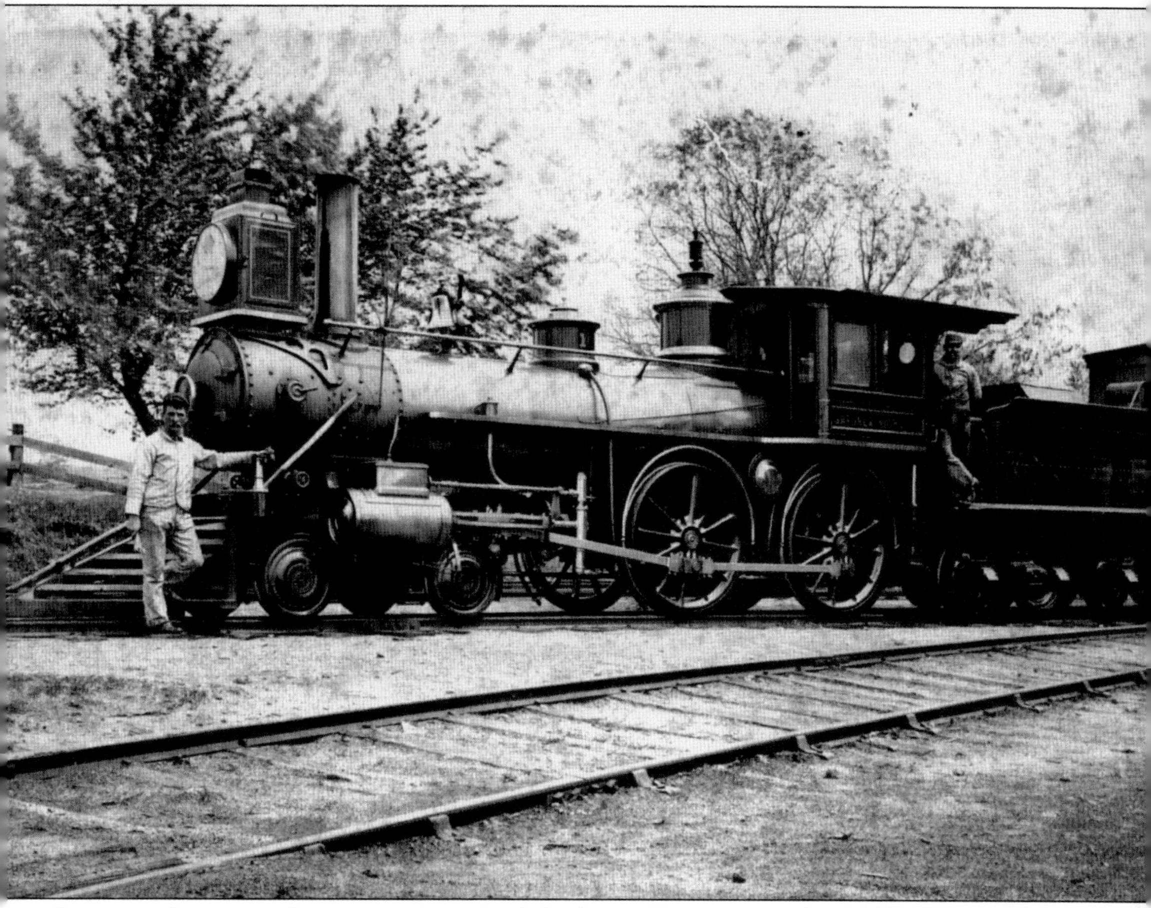

In time, other types of transportation joined the horse. Beginning in the 1870s, the six-mile, one-track short line Wood River Branch Railroad linked the New Haven line at Wood River Junction with Hope Valley (which prevailed in desperate struggle with Wyoming for the honor). The railroad's first engine was the 20-ton *Gardner Nichols*, with fireman Charles Roy Nichols and engineer Henry F. True.

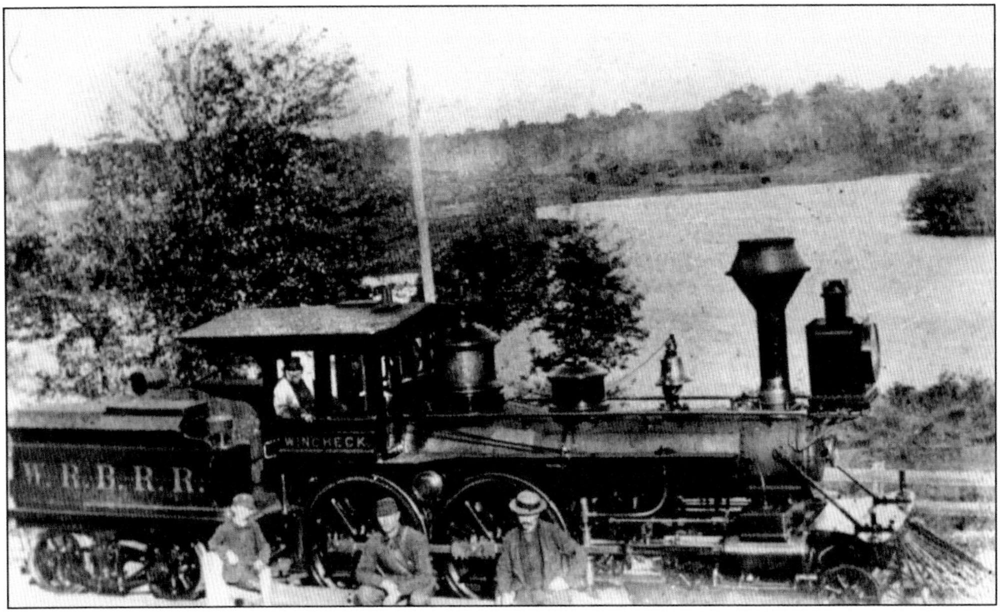

The 18-ton *Wincheck* came secondhand.

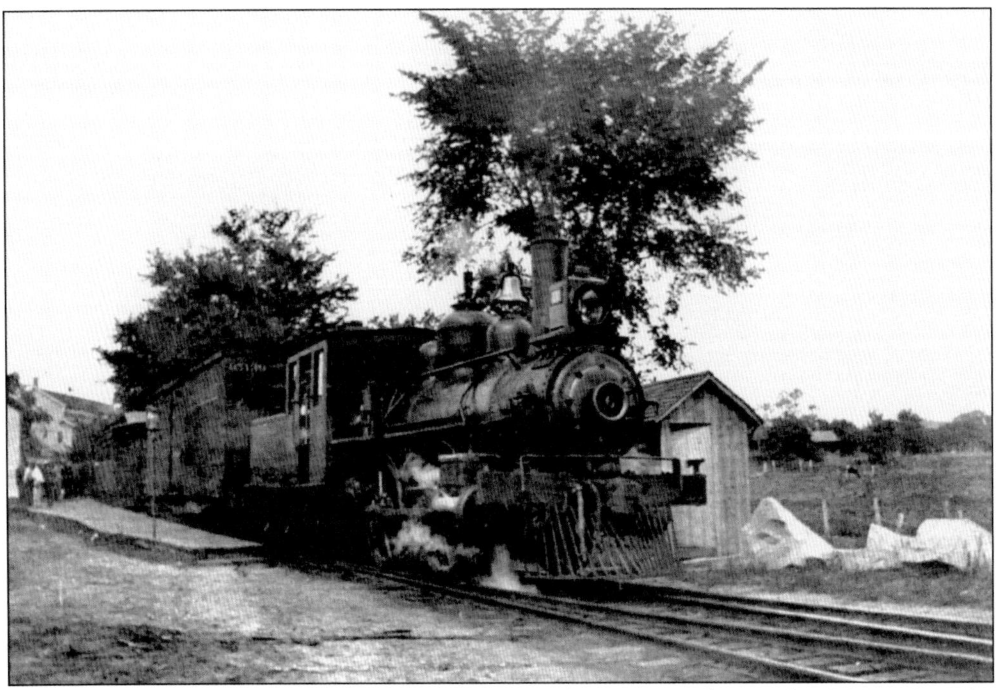

Five daily trains carried almost 20,000 passengers in the centennial year of 1876. In 1884, the fare increased from 25¢ to 30¢.

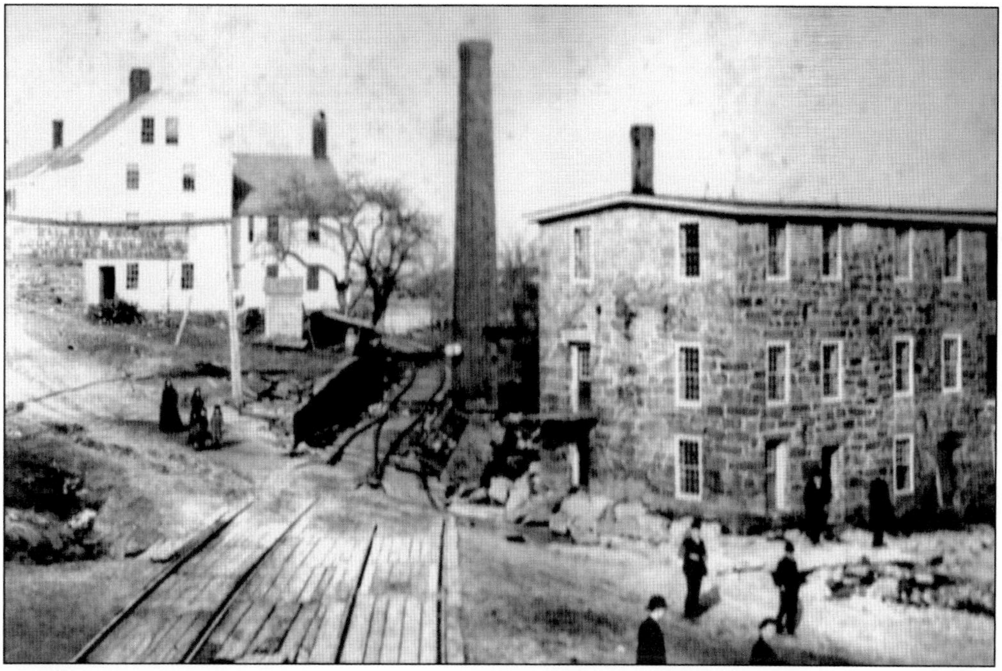

Flooding in 1886 not only damaged mills such as Nichols and Langworthy but also wrecked portions of the Wood River Branch. The sign at left reads, "Railroad Crossing. Look out for the engine while the bell rings."

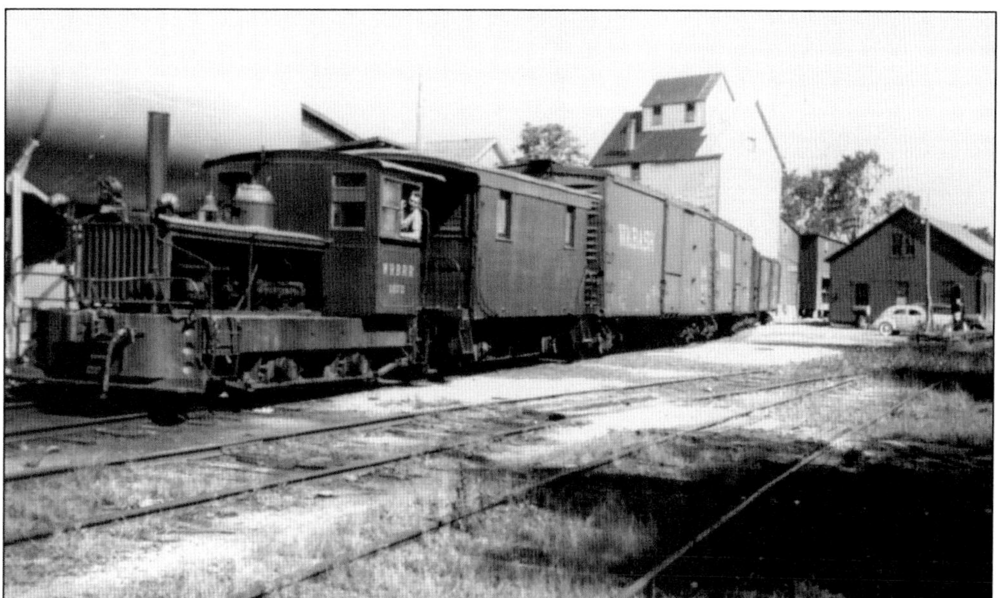

A 1927 flood almost forced abandonment of the line. But Roy Rawlings, who operated the largest grain elevator in Rhode Island (seen at the rear) at the Hope Valley terminal, helped engineer a takeover by the New Haven line. By the time this internal-combustion locomotive pulled out in 1938, Rawlings had bought the line himself.

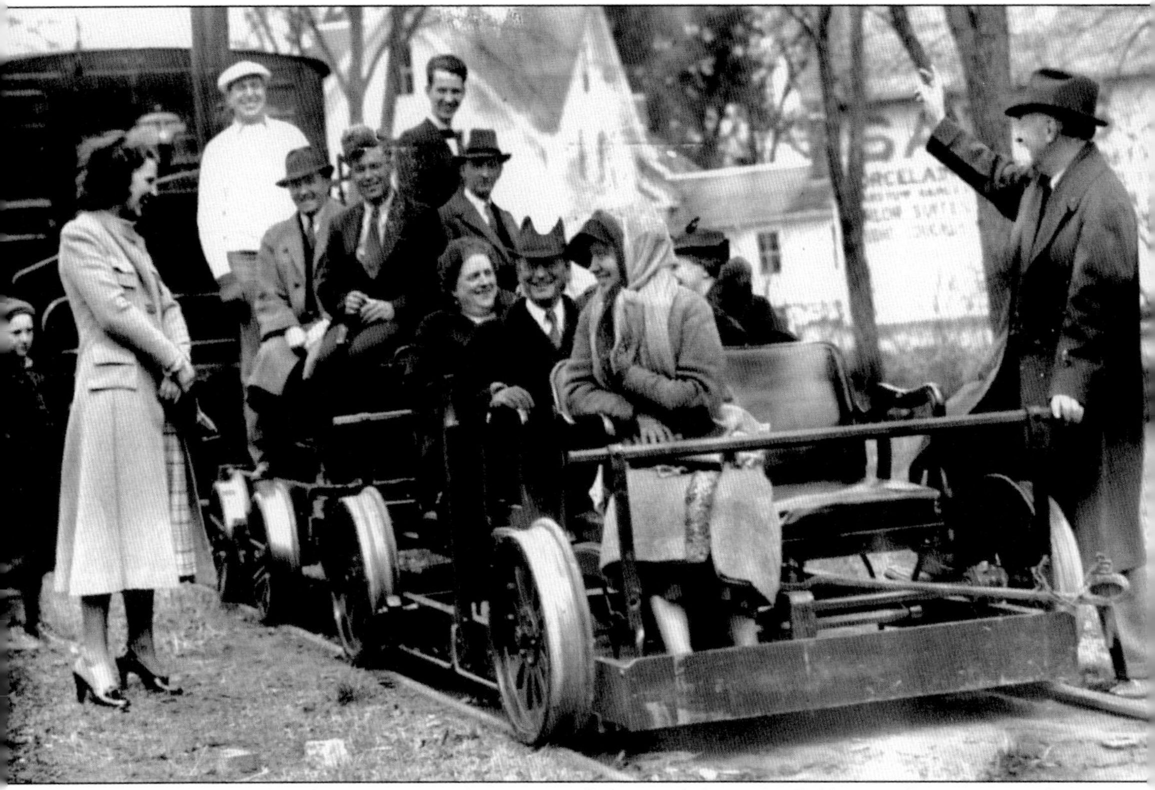

Roy Rawling's daughter Lucy Rawlings Tootell (second from the left), seen here on April 12, 1938, was reportedly the only woman railroad vice president in America. The Rawlings' business generated about 85 percent of the line's traffic.

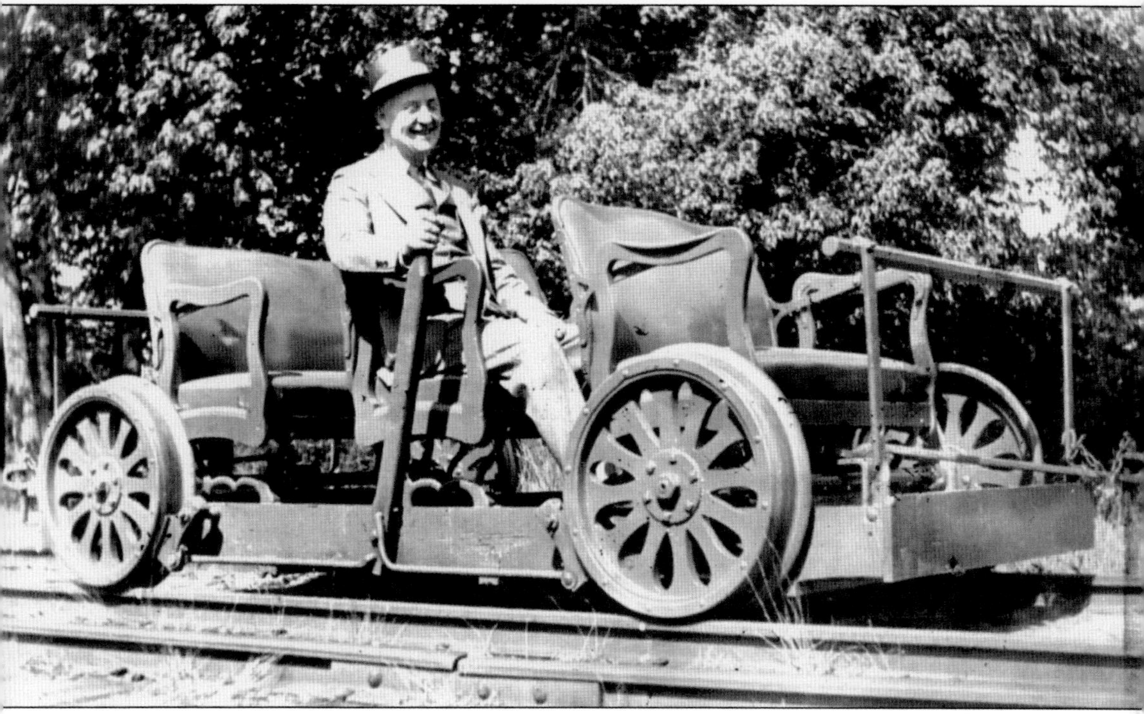

Roy Rawlings had once been speaker of the house in the Rhode Island General Assembly. His son Rob Roy Rawlings later held a state senate seat; he represented Charlestown, Richmond, Hopkinton, and other towns from the Connecticut line to the middle of Narragansett Bay.

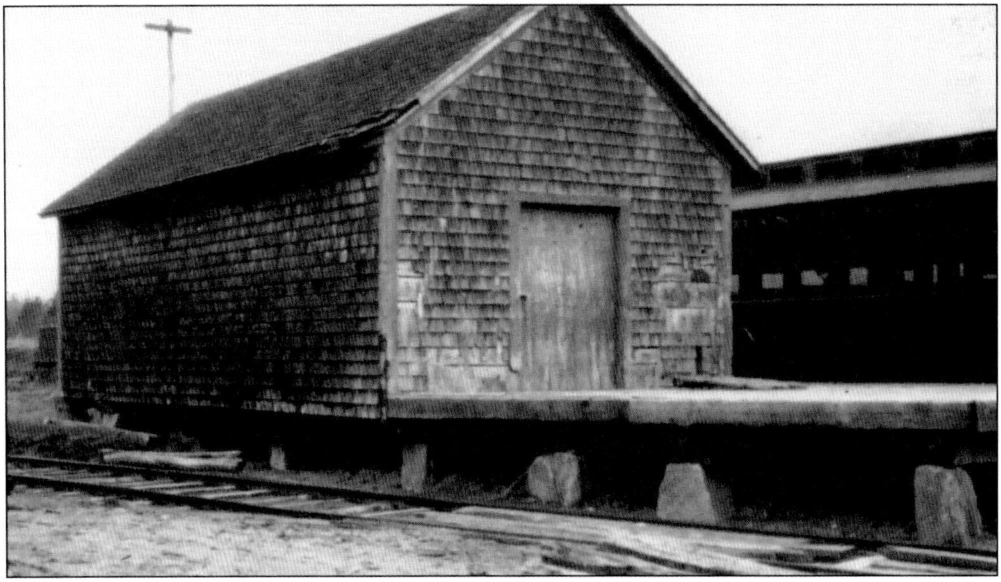

Passenger stations at Canonchet, Hope Valley, and Woodville were originally painted yellow, prompting the nicknames of "Yellow Dog Houses" and the "Yellow Dog Line." By the waning years of the Great Depression, decoratively painting Canonchet station was not much of a priority. Even so, the passenger cars still made their stops.

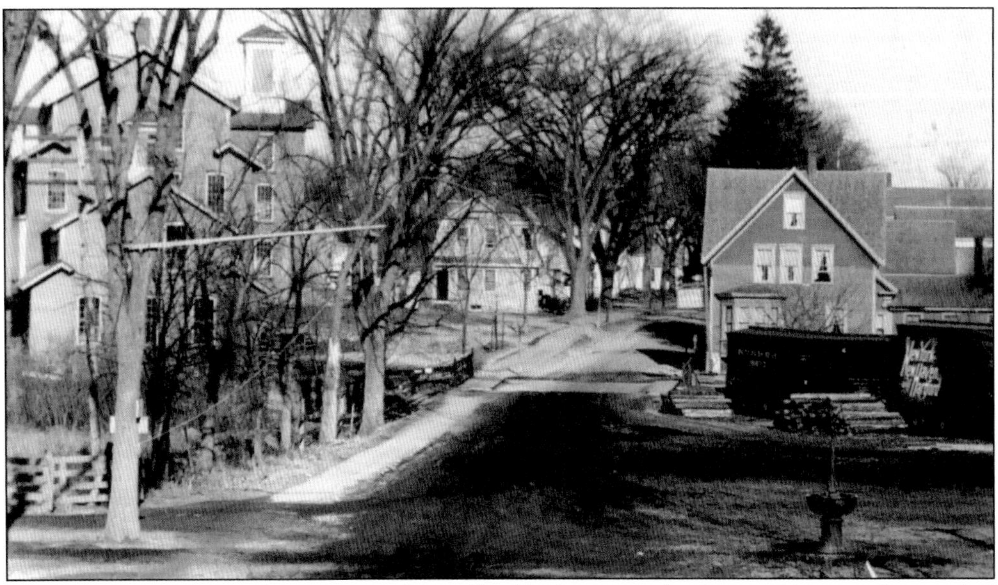

The depot is long gone, but Hope Valley still calls this area "the Square." Notice the stacked railroad ties; ties were big business in Hopkinton, especially at the Hope Valley end of town. The brick building at the left is Locustville Mill; now somewhat smaller, it currently houses Ure Outfitters. At the front right is a circular watering trough for horses.

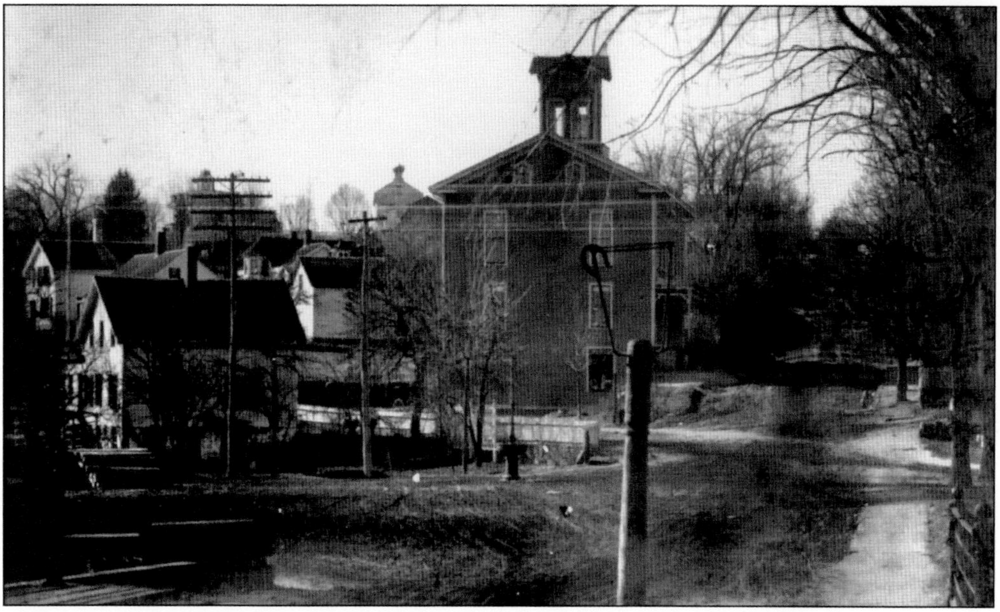

This view, looking in the opposite direction from the previous photograph, shows the Odd Fellows Hall (now Woodmansee Oil), which stood in the fork of Main and Mechanic Streets. The cupola blew off in the Hurricane of 1938. Directly in front is the pole and bracket for a street lamp. Each lamp had to be individually lighted.

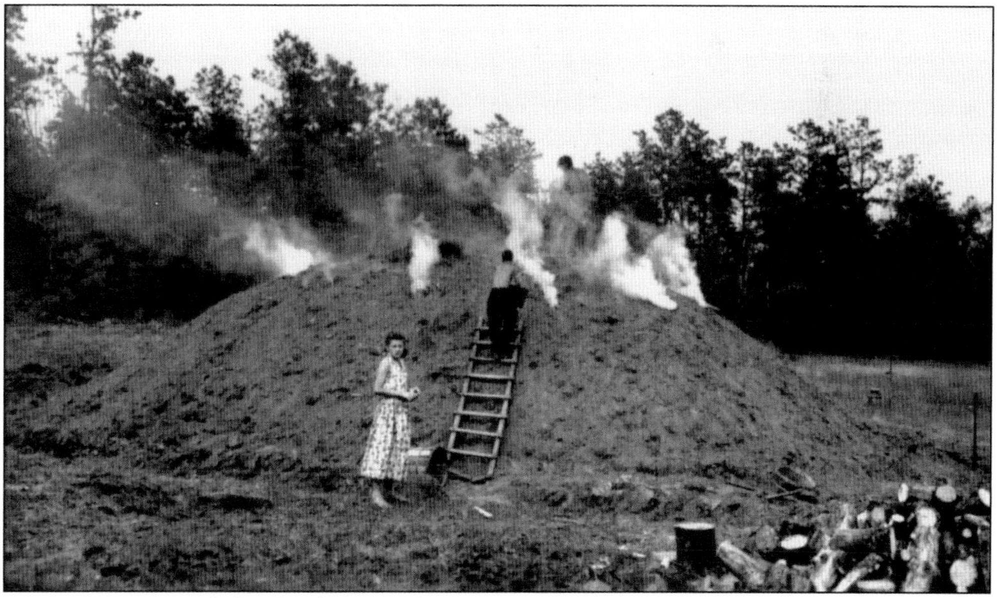

A counterpoint to all that lumbering and sawing was charcoal burning, which continued at least until 1941, as this photograph shows, on Spring Street in Hope Valley.

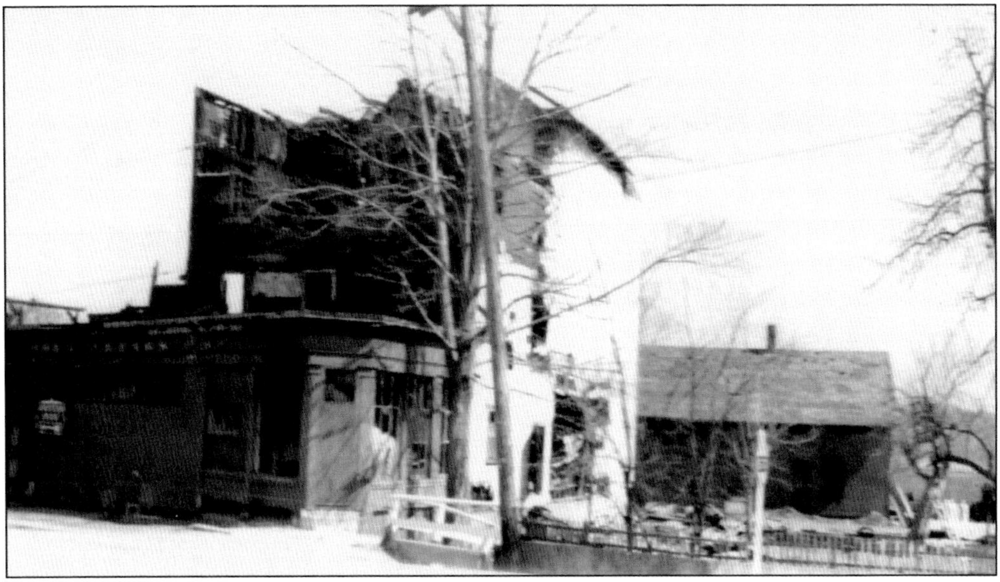

The grain elevator burned on March 14, 1947, followed by the woolen mill in Centerville and the box shop in Wyoming. With no further need for it, Roy Rawlings finally closed the Wood River Branch.

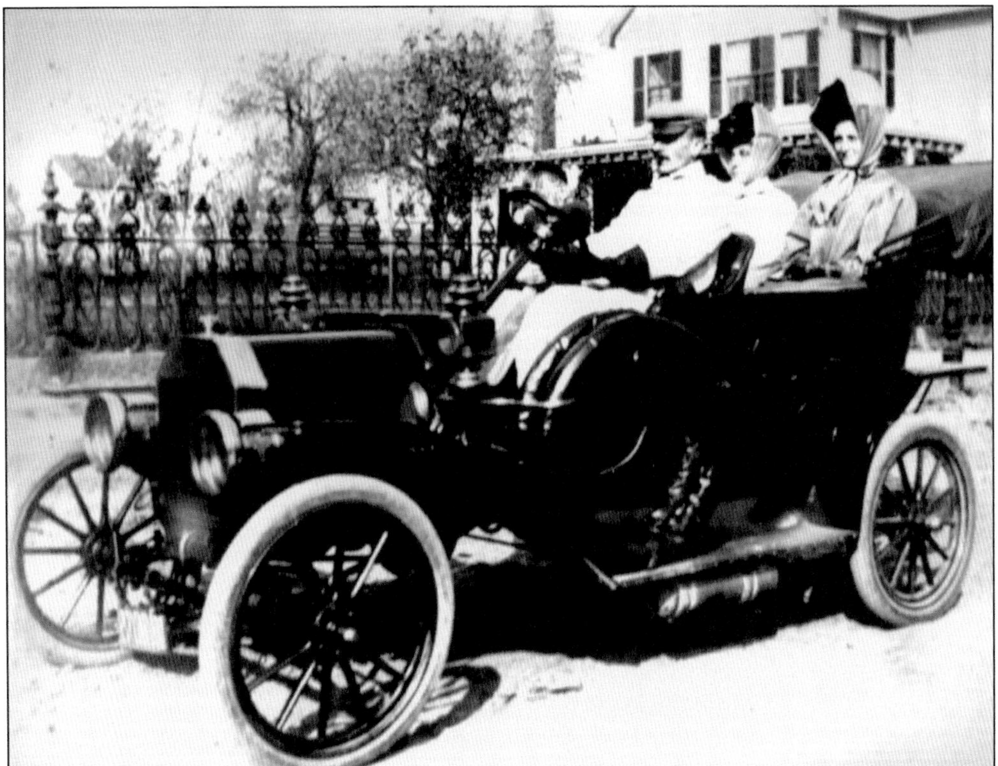

Long before the railroad closed, of course, trucks and automobiles were taking over. Many years earlier, Mrs. Thomas B. Segar enjoyed a ride with Mr. and Mrs. Christopher. Young Master Christopher (see page 42) is obscured by the steering wheel.

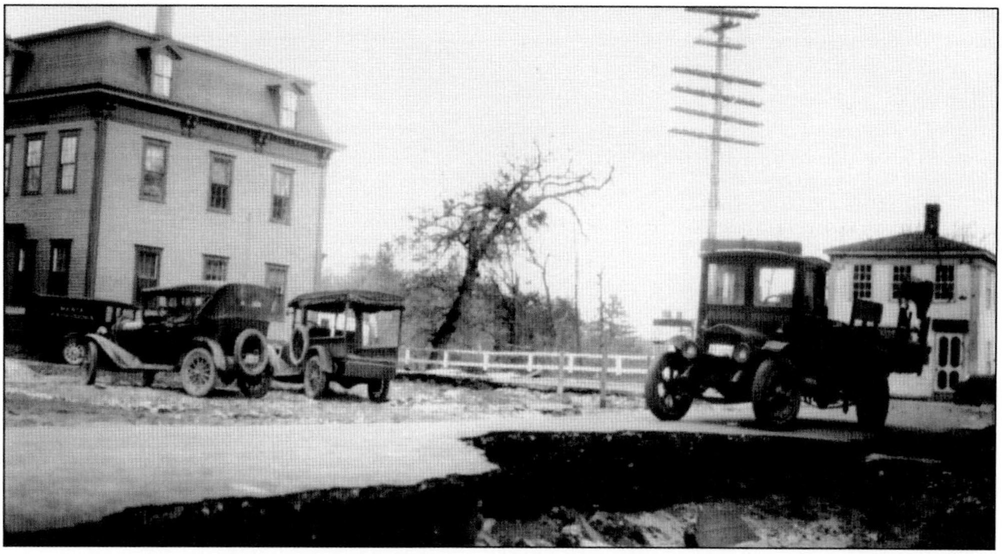

The cab of the "Sudden Service" truck is oddly high and blocky; perhaps this is a local customization, possibly of a Ford Model TT. Notice that this truck has wide tires and heavy wheels as compared to the other vehicles. It even has double rear wheels, making it well suited to respond to such emergencies as this destructive flood in Ashaway.

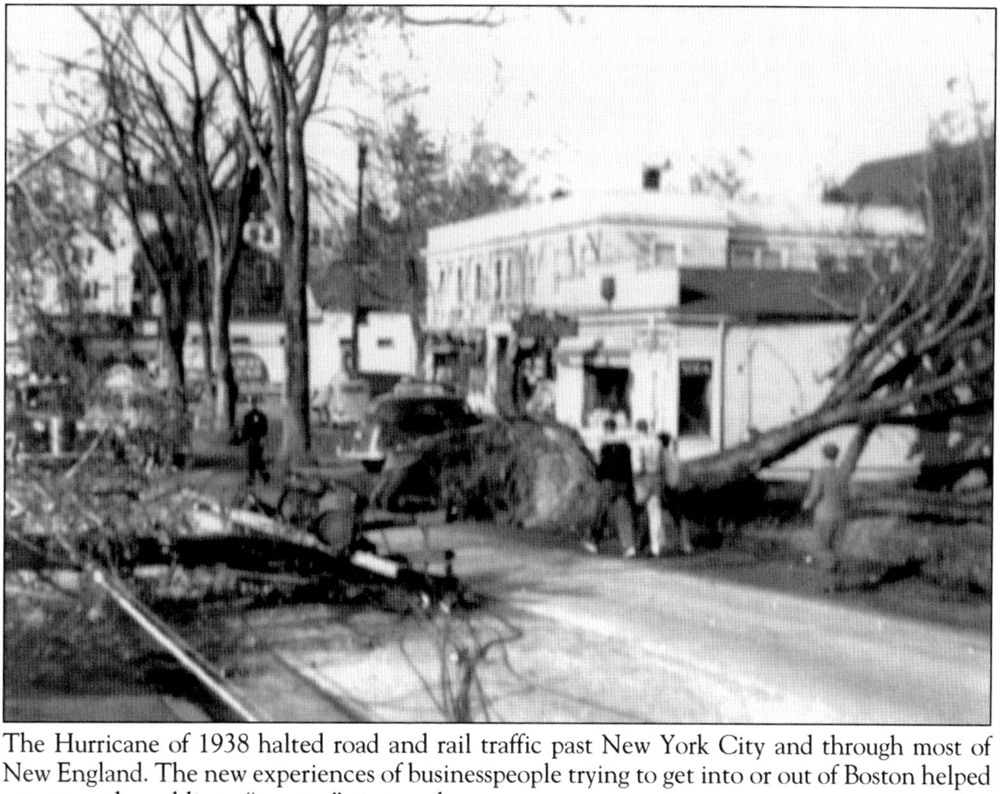

The Hurricane of 1938 halted road and rail traffic past New York City and through most of New England. The new experiences of businesspeople trying to get into or out of Boston helped accustom the public to "routine" air travel.

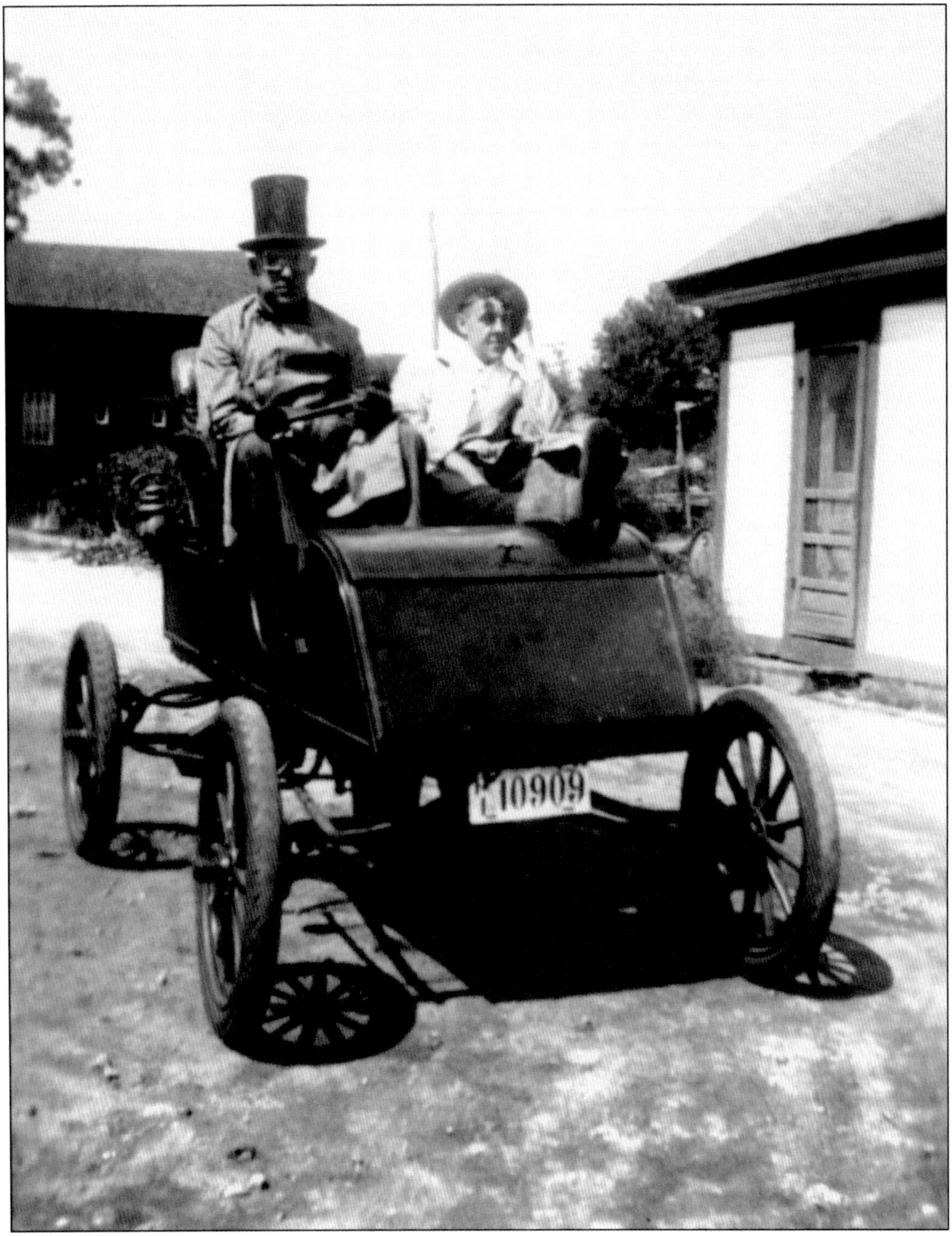

By 1935, when Roy Sherman and Kendall Knerr rode in the Legion Parade, automobiles that were snazzy 20 years before had become quaint and amusing. Hopkinton, like the rest of America, had fallen in love with the car.

Six

Enduring Graces

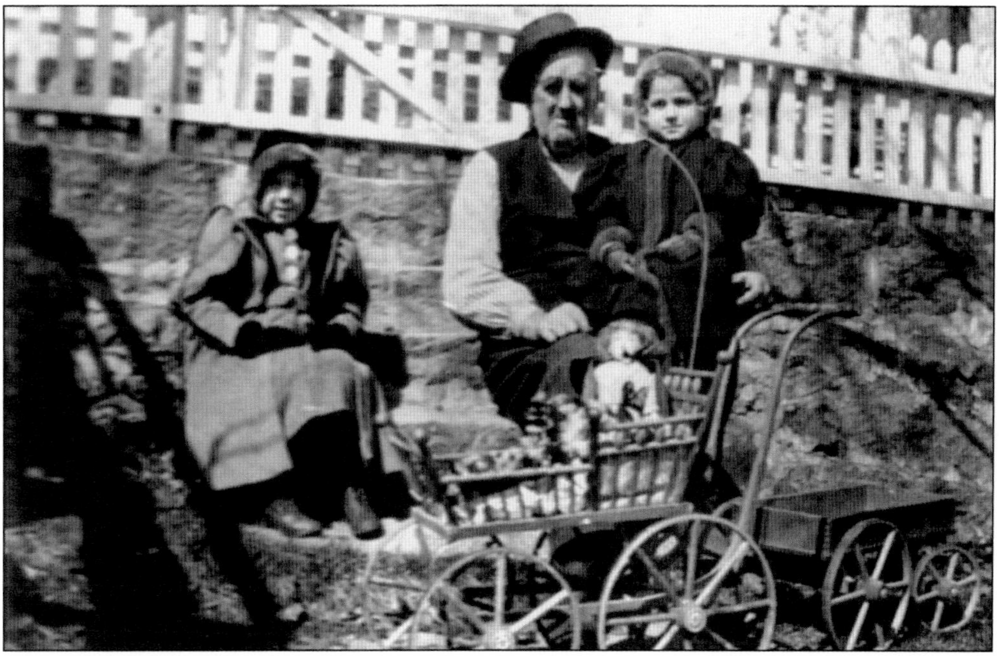

Gladys and Wilfred Segar enjoyed having Uncle Christopher Lillibridge over for Christmas in 1897. Gladys, at six years old, presumably did not imagine the remarkable career that would leave her memory honored in two states. As a librarian, she squeezed $1.01 out of every book-purchase dollar. Her own reading embodied a popular library slogan, "History, Mystery, and Info to Go," which tickled her tremendously. As a historian and author, she delved into the pasts of her homes in New Jersey and Rhode Island. She saw to it that many of her historical collections—and her extensive memories—became community treasures. Gladys Segar was a trailblazer, one of the first "new women" of the 20th century. If librarianship might seem today like stereotypical "women's work," she made it a highly professional career. She made her own way, traveling America, riding the Grand Canyon on a mule in the 1920s, and climbing the Rocky Mountains in the 1940s. She inspired generations of both women and men.

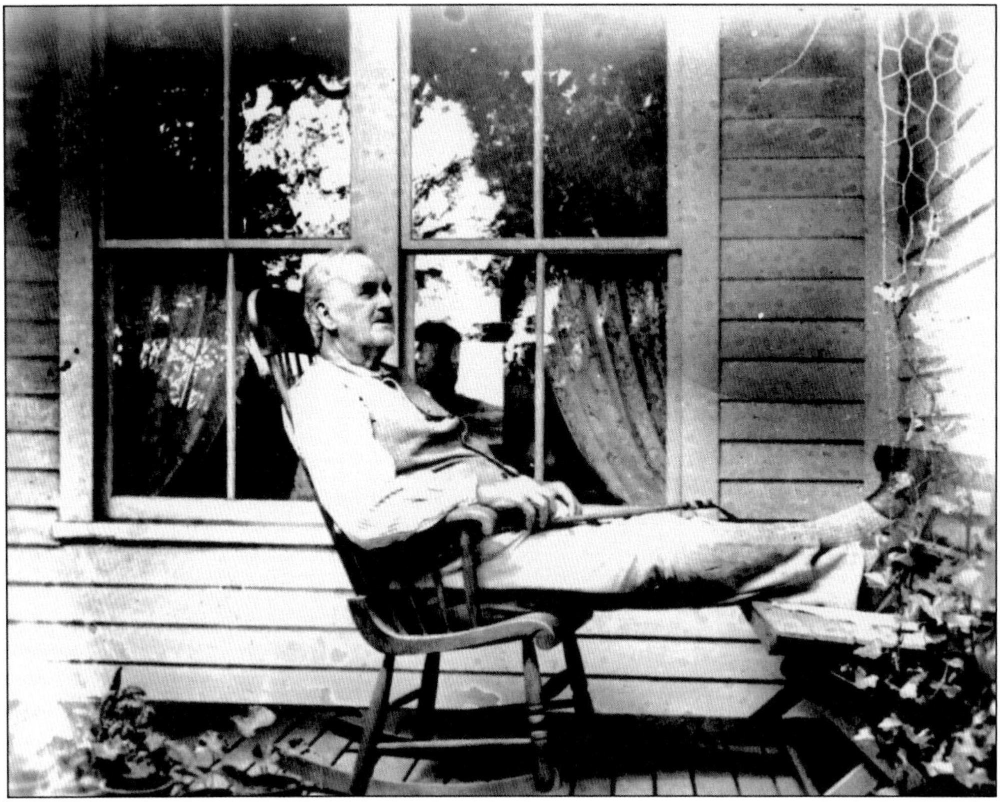

"Uncle Kit" seems to have maintained his own agenda through life.

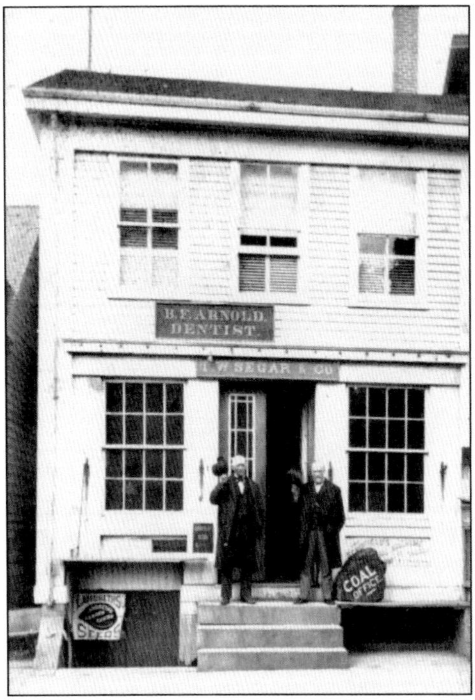

The Segar clan was involved in several businesses, mostly in Wyoming. Thomas Wanton Segar had himself photographed with a visiting friend from Chicago.

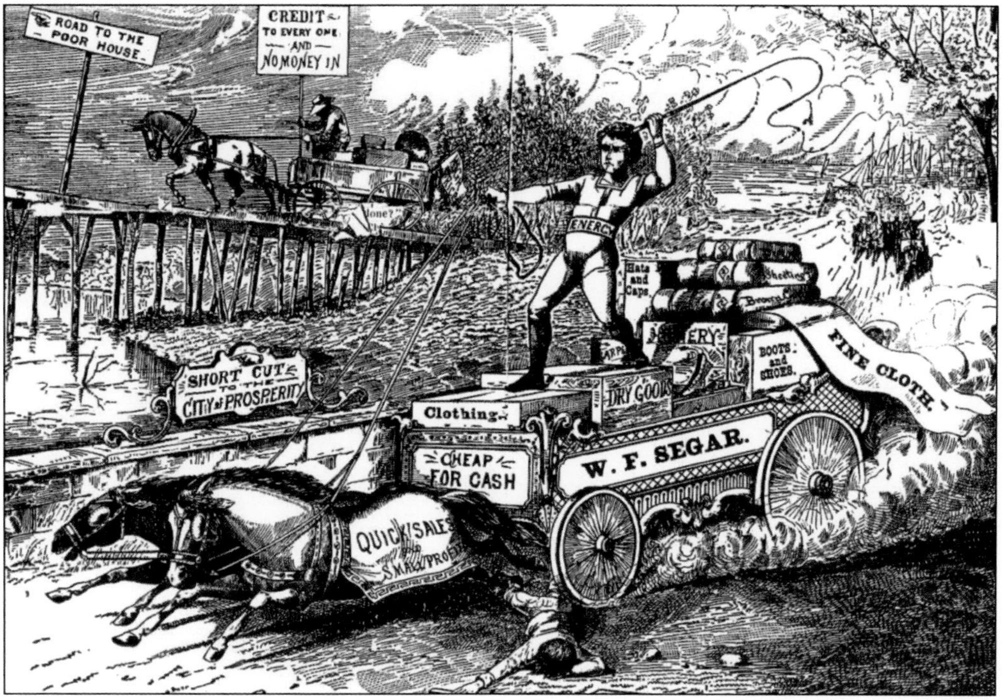

If giving credit was the road to the poorhouse, W. F. Segar was not taking it!

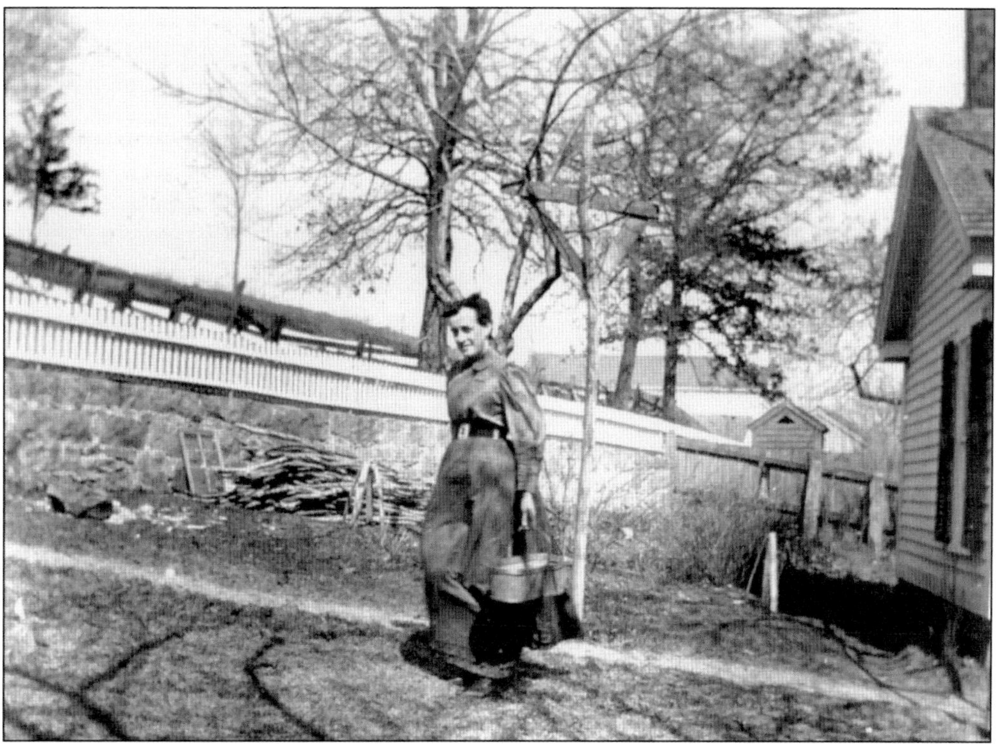
The Segars may have been middle class, but even in comfortable homes, life required a good deal of hard labor.

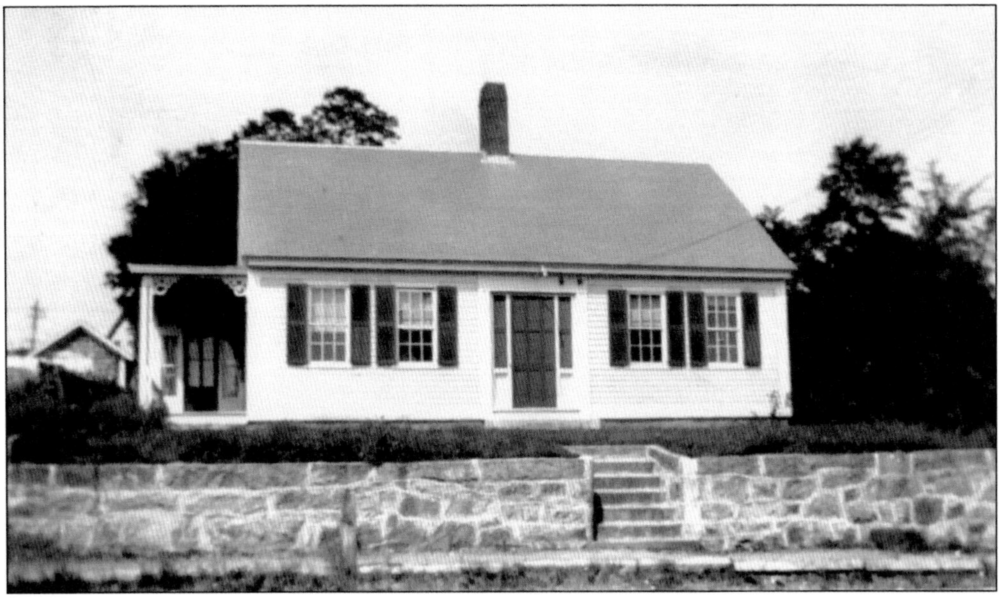

In 1910, the teenaged Gladys Segar was, as she recalled, "pushed into" the job no one else wanted—running the Langworthy Public Library, then in the Chipman House on Mechanic Street. She got $75 a year for opening up two evenings and two afternoons a week. She also chopped the wood and kept the fire going.

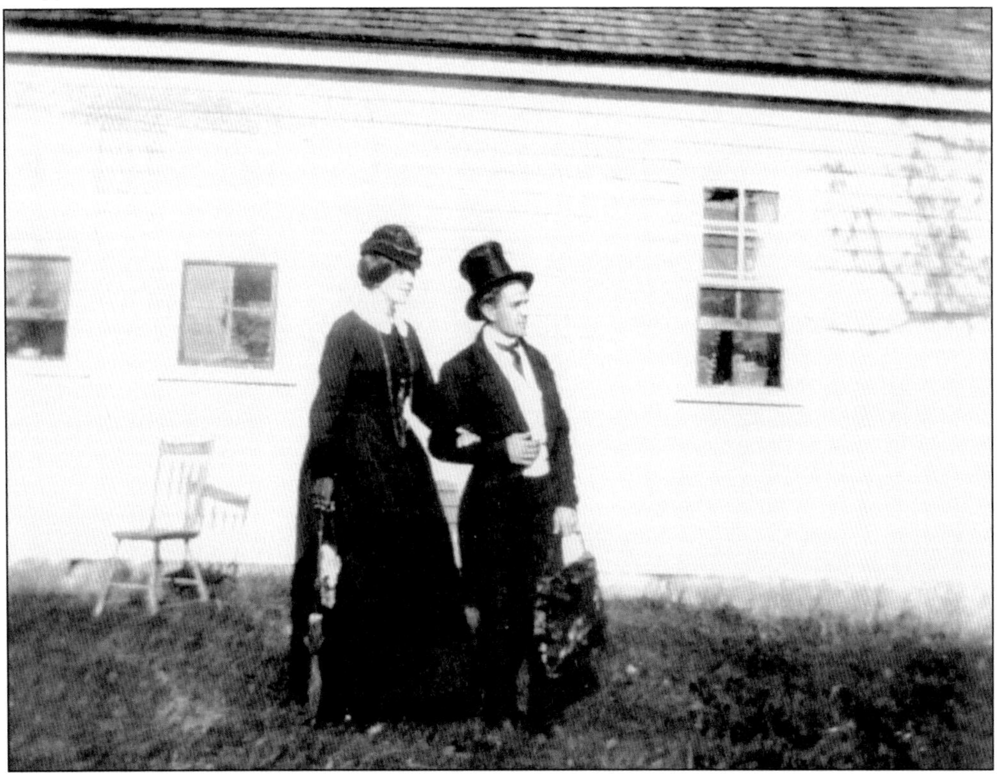

Gladys Segar, seen here with an unidentified person who may be her brother Wilfred, gets ready for the "Old Folks Concert" on May 19, 1914.

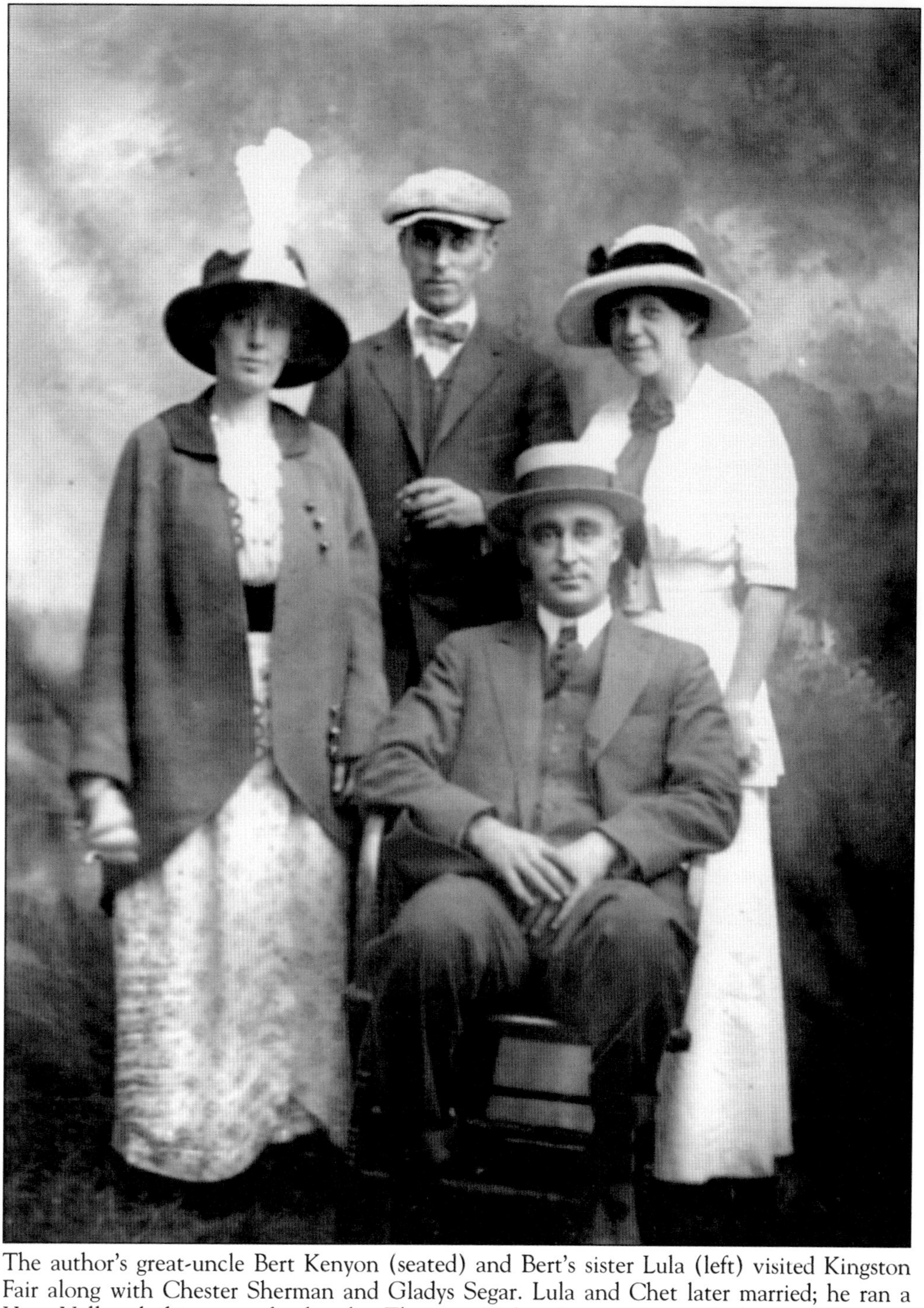

The author's great-uncle Bert Kenyon (seated) and Bert's sister Lula (left) visited Kingston Fair along with Chester Sherman and Gladys Segar. Lula and Chet later married; he ran a Hope Valley clothing store for decades. Their son Nelson later took over the business. The two couples formed a familiar foursome around town.

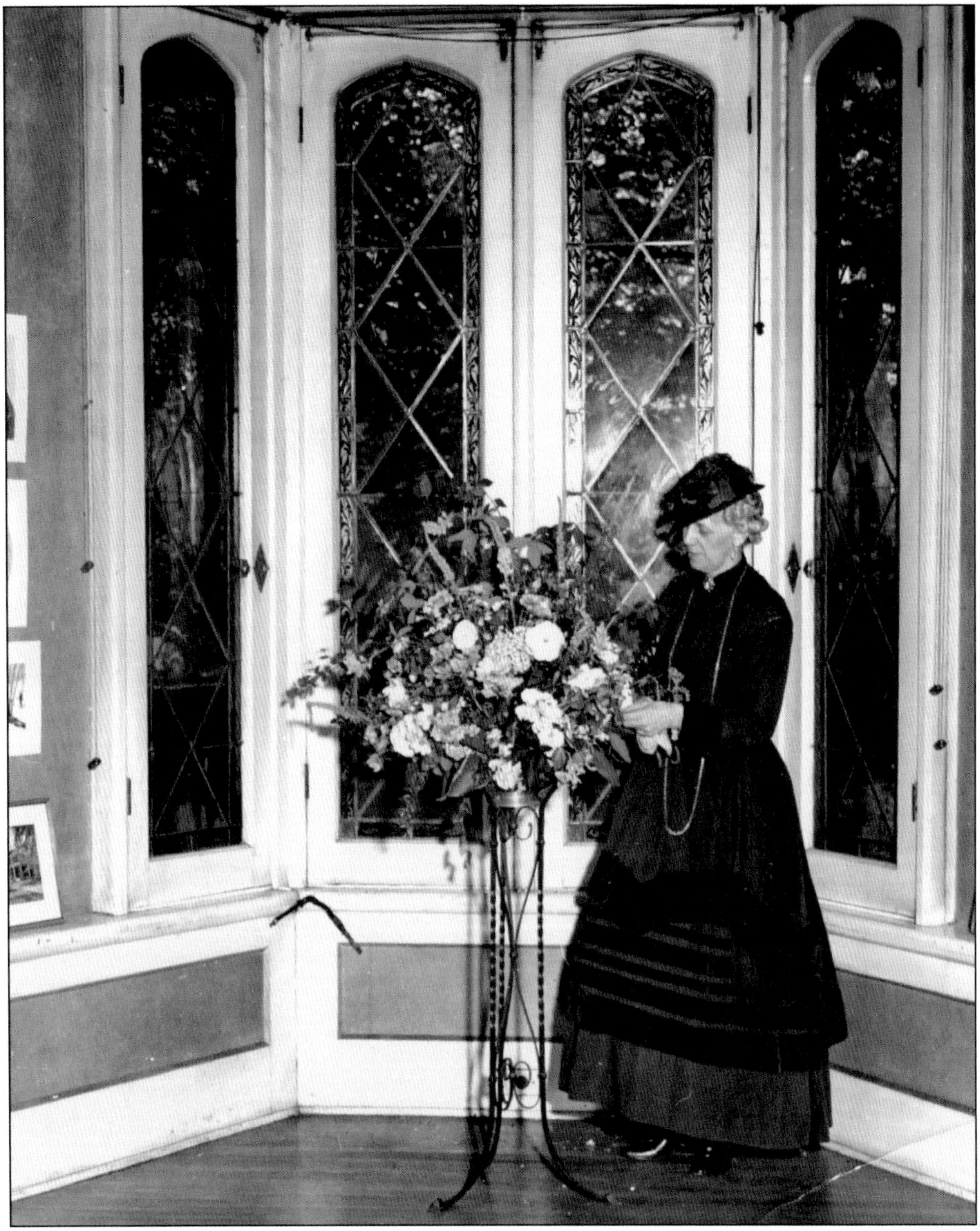

After a stint at Westerly Library, Gladys Segar studied at the New York Public Library, then worked for many years as a reference librarian and readers' advisor in Montclair, New Jersey, where she is still honored as a leading historian of the region. That is the same dress she wore for the Old Folks Concert in 1914.

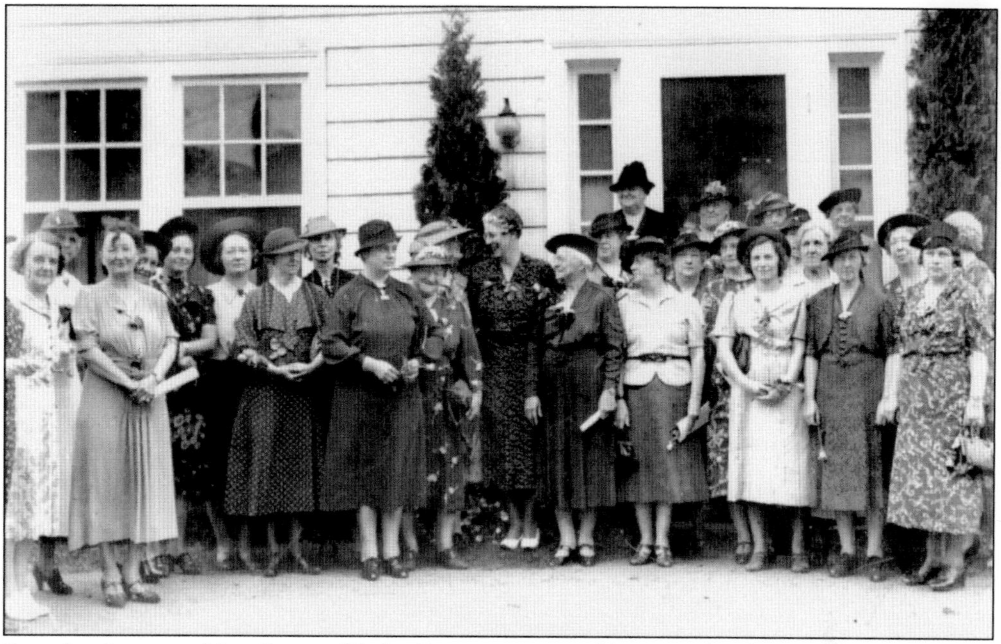

From her home in New Jersey, Gladys Segar maintained her membership in the Hope Valley Women's Club. Growing from informal literary societies, the women's club supported Scouting for boys and girls, worked at servicemen's relief during World War I, and assisted women in their careers. Around 1920, the group once payed $1 to buy a young woman's ticket to Providence, where she could take a professional certification exam.

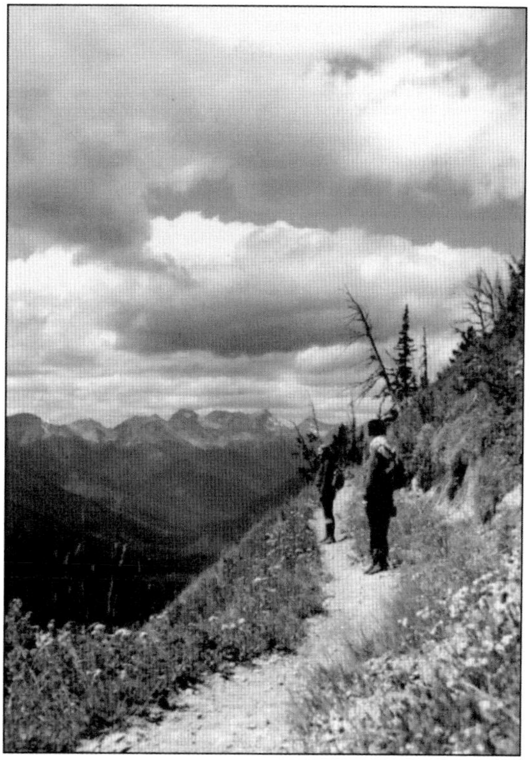

Miss Segar's independent lifestyle opened endless opportunities. She enjoyed climbing the Rockies on what she described as "a windy day."

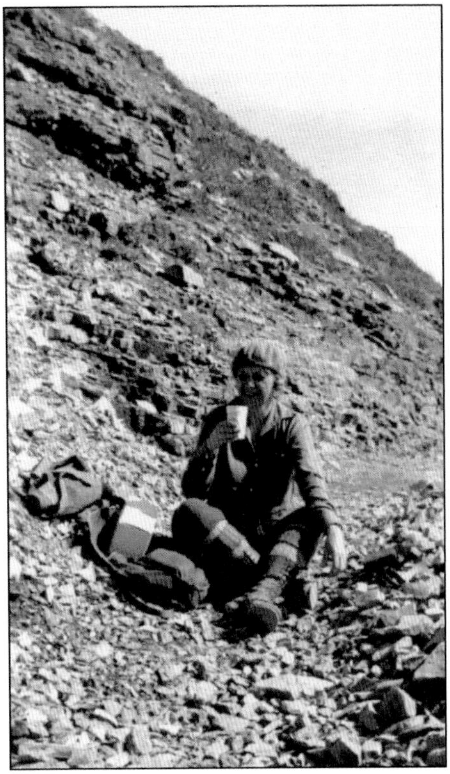

Gladys Segar used this photograph of herself taking a break on the "Garden Wall" for her 1941 Christmas card, writing on one of them, "I just didn't know what to do about coming home." She was 50 years old at the time.

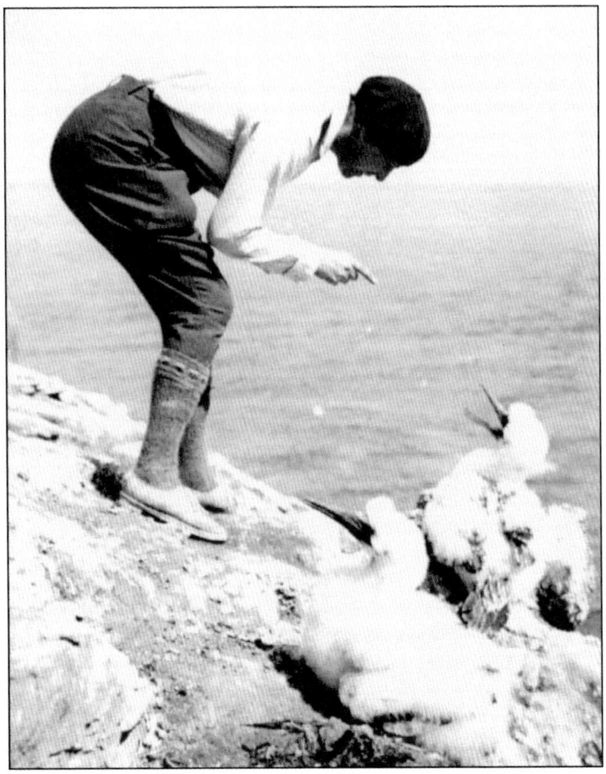

Years later, Miss Segar told the author's sister, "I guess I just never wanted to get married."

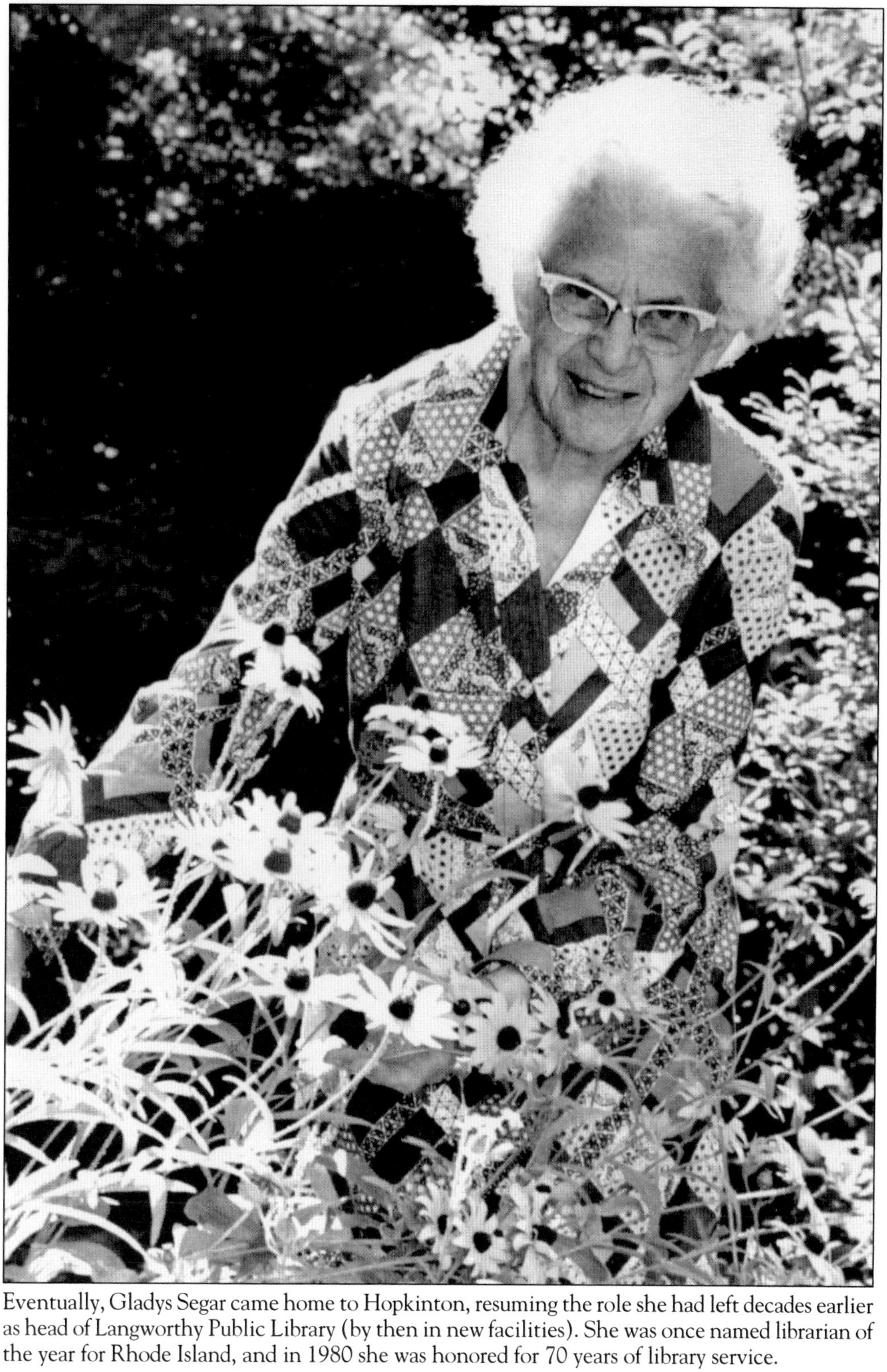

Eventually, Gladys Segar came home to Hopkinton, resuming the role she had left decades earlier as head of Langworthy Public Library (by then in new facilities). She was once named librarian of the year for Rhode Island, and in 1980 she was honored for 70 years of library service.

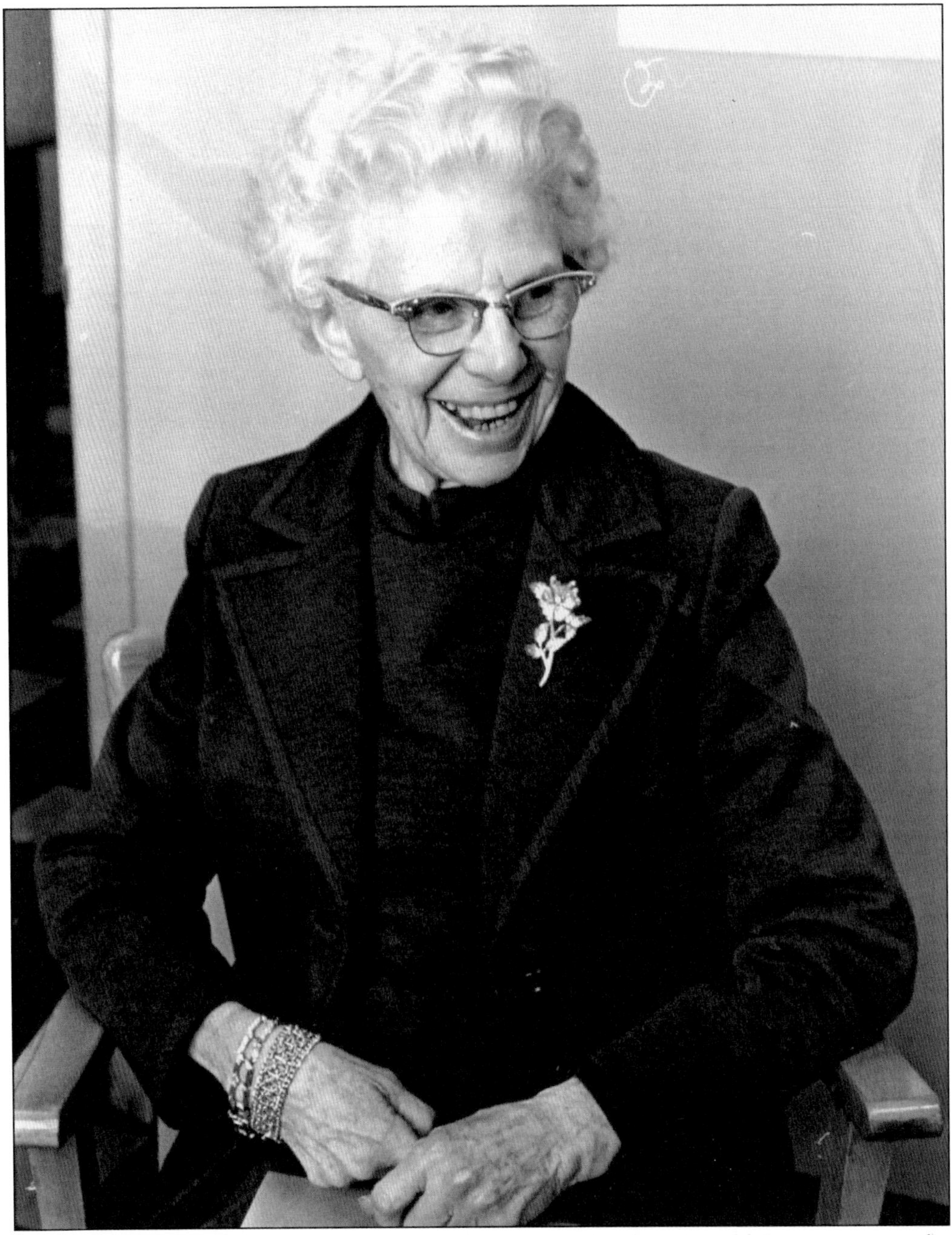

Gladys Segar died just short of her 93rd birthday in 1984, when Ronald Reagan was in the White House. Her life overlapped that of Mercy Burdick (seen on page 40), who was born when George Washington was president. Miss Segar had enjoyed 40 percent of Hopkinton's incorporated life up to that point—and her town was better because she had been there.